WALKING
TALL

For Marian

'You and me, we can light up the sky. If you stay by my side,
we can rule the world.'

<small>TAKE THAT, 'RULE THE WORLD'</small>

WALKING
TALL

The Autobiography of a
World Champion and
Olympic Medallist

ROB HEFFERNAN

with Gerard Cromwell

The Collins Press

First published in 2016 by
The Collins Press
West Link Park
Doughcloyne
Wilton
Cork
T12 N5EF
Ireland

A CIP record for this book is available from the British Library.

Paperback ISBN: 978-1-84889-288-0

PDF eBook ISBN: 978-1-84889-599-7

EPUB eBook ISBN: 978-1-84889-600-0

Kindle ISBN: 978-1-84889-601-7

Typesetting by Patricia Hope
Typeset in Bembo
Silhouette artwork courtesy Bright Idea

Printed in Malta by Gutenberg Press Limited

CONTENTS

Prologue

I didn't really know what to expect when I first put my toe to the start line of an athletics race. Eight years of age and half the size of the rest of the lads assembled on the freshly cut grass of Ballyphehane Park at the back of my housing estate, I had never raced before and was only there because it was close to home and my friends had all gone.

With one leg in front of the other in a crouched position, I watched as some of the others shuffled forward to gain whatever advantage they could before the starter said 'Go'. When he did, I copied the rest of them and just ran as fast as I could. The race was maybe only 100m long but when you're eight years old and running as fast as you possibly can, that's long enough.

As parents, friends and onlookers cheered us on, I just aimed myself for the rope being held across the opposite end of the green and ran. By halfway, my chest was pounding, my breathing was the only sound I could hear and my legs were beginning to hurt. Still, I ran. As others, kids who had got a better start than me, began to run out of steam, I passed them and just kept running. I kept running until there were only two fellas in front of me. I tried to catch them but the line came too quickly and I finished third.

Nowadays, probably everybody who started that race would get a medal. Kids get medals for participation these days and I know twelve-year-olds who've probably already won more medals than I've won in a seventeen-year career. While it is great to encourage any child to keep going in sport, medals were much harder to come by in my day. To get a medal when I was a kid, you had to finish in the top three. Third place got you a small round disc of bronze, second got silver and only winners got gold.

On that summer's day in Ballyphehane Park, Cork, a bronze medal was draped around my neck and I was so proud of it that it stayed there for most of the following week. At night, I slept with that medal under my pillow. During the day, I inspected it for scratches, bits of dirt or lint and I polished it whenever I deemed it necessary – which was pretty often. Any time I walked past a mirror I stopped disbelievingly to check that it was still around my neck and that it was me who had actually won it. I've been obsessed with medals ever since.

My uncle John made me a wooden plaque with little brass hooks on it to hang that first medal on and that plaque was displayed centre stage in our house for everyone to see. Over time I added county medals, Munster medals and even All-Ireland medals and the thrill of winning them seemed to increase each time one was draped around my neck. If you'd asked me at the age of eighteen how many medals I had accumulated, I would have been able to tell you the exact amount, what colour they were and when and how I won them.

For the past seventeen years I've chased medals around the world and have been privileged enough to do so at European Championships, World Championships and the Olympic Games. If medals were hard to come by as a kid, though, they have been ten times as hard to attain as an adult.

After weeks, months and years of training and sacrifice, sometimes the stress of wanting a medal too much crippled me in major competitions and for a long time I could only manage a top ten, or a top five at best. My first international medal as an athlete didn't come until 2013, almost two decades after I first represented Ireland at my chosen sport of race walking. But when it did, its colour was gold. To stand on the podium in the centre of the Russian track that day was one of the proudest moments of my life and it took a long time to realise I was actually the world champion.

For a while, winning that medal was a bit like buying a brand new car. You've worked so hard for it that for a long time after you bring it home, you have to keep checking if it's still there. First thing in the morning, last thing at night and for the first few days, weeks even, you're afraid something is going to happen to it.

Within a few months, I had another international medal to gaze upon. I was in the gym in Fota Island Resort with Marian one day in early 2014 when my training partner Alex Wright texted to tell me the news that I had been upgraded to bronze for the 20km walk at the 2010 European Championships in Barcelona after original race winner Russian Stanislav Emelyanov had been retrospectively banned for doping. After checking it out and finding he was right, I couldn't sleep that night and simply lay there in the darkness with a smile on my face for the whole night. I had waited for what seemed like an eternity for one international medal and then suddenly I had two. It was a lovely feeling.

For any athlete, though, the biggest and best medal you can add to your collection is an Olympic medal. The Olympics, to me, are the pinnacle of sport. Coming as they do, just every four years, if you want to be one of the lucky ones who can call themselves an Olympian then you have to spend that entire four-year cycle building towards one day.

Years of dedication, self-sacrifice and hard work might get you qualification for the Games, but even after that you still have to time everything right to be in the best form of your life on that one day that counts, the day of your race. For most people, simply getting to represent their country at the Olympics is the pinnacle of their career. For the select few, though, there are medals to be won.

Ever since I saw Michael Carruth jump around the boxing ring after he became Olympic champion at the Barcelona Games in 1992 and watched Jimmy McDonald finish sixth in the 20km walk, I wanted to win an Olympic medal. Some people drift off at night wondering what it would be like to win the lottery but, for me, standing on a podium in my Ireland kit and having an Olympic medal hung around my neck has always been my biggest dream. I have competed in five Olympics now, a record for any Irish athlete, and came closest to fulfilling that dream when I finished fourth in the 50km walk in London 2012.

Ahead of me were Sergey Kirdyapkin of Russia, Australian Jared Tallent and Si Tianfeng of China. While I drowned my sorrows with friends and family in a nearby bar afterwards, those three were the ones who stood on the podium and got the gold, silver and bronze medals draped around their necks. Although I suspected the Russian winner had been fuelled by performance-enhancing drugs that day, it would take four years and a wide-ranging investigation into Russian state-sponsored doping before the International Association of Athletics Federations (IAAF), the International Olympic Committee (IOC) and the Court of Arbitration for Sport (CAS) would come to the same conclusion. In March 2016, Kirdyapkin was retrospectively banned for doping and stripped of his Olympic win.

The CAS ruling meant that Tallent moved into the gold medal position and was the new Olympic champion. Sianfeng was bumped up to silver and I was declared winner of the bronze medal. It has been eight months since the court ruled that I should be awarded bronze from London, but as I write, I still haven't got it yet. I've had to put the saga to the back of my mind though in order to focus on another Olympic Games, this time in Rio de Janeiro in Brazil. Still chasing my Olympic dream, this time I finished sixth in the 50km walk. Close, but still no medal.

My Olympic medal ceremony from London was officially organised for Cork in November 2016 but, at the time of writing the book, nobody knew where my medal was: they were still trying to track down the original medal from the Chinese fella who was third. In a lovely gesture, boxers Paddy Barnes and Michael Conlon both offered to lend me their London 2012 bronze medals for the ceremony if mine didn't turn up on time.

Pat Hickey, the chairman of the Olympic Council of Ireland, was supposed to have one for me, but his return from Rio was delayed by the Brazilian authorities who arrested him on suspicion of ticket touting and nobody in the IOC in Dublin seemed to know where it was.

It's just a little round, flat piece of metal, not much bigger than the palm of your hand or thicker than a couple of coins stuck together, but for me that bronze medal symbolises so much: the sacrifices that my wife, Marian, and my kids have made over the years to let me follow my dream, and the sacrifices people who helped me along the way have made over the years.

I have idolised the great Irish sports people who have won Olympic medals in the past; people like the late Pat O'Callaghan, Bob Tisdall, Ronnie Delany, Sonia O'Sullivan, John Treacy, Michael Carruth, Wayne McCullough and to join the current crop of Katie Taylor, Paddy Barnes, Michael Conlon, Cian O'Connor, Kenny Egan, John Joe Nevin, the late Darren Sutherland, Annalise Murphy, Gary and Paul O'Donovan is the culmination of a lifetime spent chasing my sporting dreams.

Hopefully by the time you read these words, I'll have finally got my hands on that Olympic medal. Sometime in the future, I want to gather my Olympic, European and World championship medals and frame them along with my Ireland singlets and photographs from each race before hanging them on the wall of the gourmet coffee shop I dream of owning. In the meantime, though, you can be sure that for the first few weeks and months after I finally get that Olympic bronze, I'll be gazing at it, checking it for scratches, polishing it, wearing it around my neck and looking at myself in the mirror – just like I did when I was a kid.

My name is Robert Heffernan and this is my story.

1

Tougher in Togher

'I'm an ordinary man, nothing special, nothing grand. I've had to work for everything I own.'

from 'Ordinary Man', lyrics by Peter Hame,
sung by Christy Moore

With unemployment rising in 1960s Ireland and fewer people willing to emigrate than in previous decades, the Irish government tried to combat a growing housing crisis by building high-rise accommodation in some of the worst-hit areas of the country. The Ballymun Flats on the north side of Dublin became synonymous with this type of social housing of the time, but high-rise blocks were also built in other areas of Dublin, Limerick, Waterford and Cork.

While Ballymun's seven skyscrapers saw lifts installed to aid access to the dizzying heights of the fifteenth floor, a set of concrete stairs was deemed sufficient to get tenants to the third and highest floor of Cork's equivalent in Togher.

It was here, in a diminutive two-bedroom flat on the Deanrock estate in Togher – a perhaps fittingly sawn-off equivalent of the Ballymun towers – that I spent my formative years.

In Cork, the Deanrock flats quickly gained a reputation to match those in Ballymun, while those living outside Togher soon saw the whole area as bandit country. Like most people who grew up there, however, I have only good memories of the place.

Ireland's John Treacy was still a month away from being crowned world cross-country champion while Swedish band Abba were number one in the Irish charts with 'Take A Chance On Me' when I came into this world on 28 February 1978. I joined my father Bobby, whom I was named after, my mother Maureen and my big sister Rhonda in number 39 on the second floor of Block B a few days later.

At first my arrival was a novelty to Rhonda, who was a full nine years older than me. But having been used to getting all the attention from my parents up until then, the novelty soon wore off for her when she not only had to share an already cramped bedroom with a baby brother but was also expected to pitch in with the babysitting.

I was only one and a half when my younger sister Anthea arrived in July 1979. Anthea was followed by my brother Elton in August 1981. The addition of three new siblings must have given Rhonda plenty of sleepless nights, not to mention plenty more chores to do around the now overcrowded little flat. Although there were now six of us crammed into the flat's two tiny bedrooms, Elton was two years old and walking before Cork Corporation moved us to a slightly more suitable three-bedroom house in nearby Argideen Lawn.

Literally just a few hundred yards across the green from our previous home in the flats, three rows of six houses each formed a U-shape in the little cul-de-sac of Argideen Lawn, with ours the first gable end on the right. My earliest memory of the house itself is of the cubbyhole under the stairs. Normally used as a play den by my siblings and me, we would all scramble for shelter in there whenever we heard a clap of thunder.

In the centre of this U-shaped mini-estate, in front of all the houses, was a multipurpose tarmac court where the kids played and residents parked their cars, if they had one. That square of tarmac was my boundary at the time. Too young to be allowed across the road to the green, any time I stepped outside the estate I was usually in the company of designated babysitter Rhonda, who would shepherd me past the groups of lads smoking or drinking in the alleyways on the way to school or Mass.

Although St Finbarr's GAA club was right behind my house and future Manchester United legend Denis Irwin lived just a few doors down (Rhonda hung around with his sisters), sport was never on my radar in Togher. In our house, sport was never on anyone's radar.

A plasterer by trade, my dad would spend all week on the building sites, covered in dust and knobs of plaster, to provide for his ever-growing family. His brother Josie had trials with Manchester United as a teenager and my dad won various trophies and Munster titles for darts and road bowling, but both pastimes were regarded as a way to let off steam with his mates at the weekend. As far as Dad was concerned, sport wasn't going to help anyone pay the bills.

Bad language and littering were Dad's pet hates. If you left so much as a sweet paper behind you anywhere you would be eaten alive for the offence. A small but strong man, with plasterer's biceps and hands the size of shovels, calloused from working on the building sites in all weathers, my dad never laid a hand on me growing up, but there was always the fear there that he could if he wanted to.

But if my dad was tough, my mam was tougher. A stunningly good-looking woman with a wiry frame that belied her strength, my mother had no qualms about thumping me around the house whenever I did something wrong. For some reason, it never bothered me when it was my mam clattering me but the threat of 'telling your father' was often enough to stop my bickering siblings and me dead in our tracks.

Mam hailed from a very tight-knit community on the north side of Cork city, where nobody had very much but they'd all give each other whatever they had. I can remember walking around her home area as a child on visits to my Nana's house and thinking that my mam was famous. We couldn't walk 20 metres without her being stopped for a chat by one of the locals and it would take us all day to get from one end of the street to the other. While she had lots of friends and family on the north side though, my mam never really settled when she moved to the opposite side of the River Lee. For some reason she didn't mix with people as much on the south side and it's probably why we were soon on the move again.

I was eight years old when we got a transfer to a bigger three-bedroom Corporation house on Derrynane Road in Turners Cross. When I say Turners Cross, technically we were on the Ballyphehane side of Derrynane Road so our address was actually Ballyphehane, but Turners Cross had a much better reputation and, like the Dublin kids of the time who were told to give their address as Santry instead of Ballymun, Mam told us to tell everyone that we lived in Turners Cross.

With three bedrooms upstairs and an entrance hall, a kitchen, two living rooms and a toilet downstairs, the house on Derrynane Road was like a mansion to us kids. Bunk beds were wedged into the smallest room in the house, the tiny box room over the stairs, and myself and Elton shared the room's confines with a solitary locker and a rack behind the door to hang our clothes.

Rhonda and Anthea had a slightly bigger room beside us while Mam and Dad slept in the back room, beside the aptly named bathroom. This was literally a room with a bath in it and nothing else. If you needed a pee in the middle of the night, you had to go downstairs in the cold to the toilet.

Although we had only gone about three kilometres from Togher, Derrynane Road was much quieter and a lot posher than what we had been used to, and our arrival onto the street soon gave our new neighbours a rude awakening from their suburban slumber. On one side of us we had the O'Sheas, who had three boys older than me – Paul, Michael and Aidan – and a daughter, Anne-Marie, who was a year younger. Six feet two inches tall when he was fourteen, Aidan absolutely towered over me and pretty soon became my big brother from next door. When I found out that he played underage football for Cork and had medals for sprinting and hammer throwing I was fascinated with him, and 'Shazer', as he was known on the road, was my first-ever real-life hero.

On the other side of our house was Mrs Ryan, an elderly woman whose husband had died and whose family had grown up and moved on. Mrs Ryan was very prim and proper. Her house was spotless and her front and back lawns were trimmed meticulously. Our gardens, on the other hand, were soon overgrown and quickly became home to various pets while a dilapidated van, once used to carry my dad and his plastering equipment to work, was abandoned in our front driveway for years. Mrs Ryan couldn't understand our way of living and she and my mam could often be seen bickering back and forth across the garden wall, with my mother never giving an inch, whether she was right or wrong.

Looking back now, our arrival probably upset quite a few of our neighbours. Although I never did anything malicious as a youngster, I was always hyper. 'Runaway knock' and 'hedge hopping' were two of my favourite pastimes on the road. Runaway knock is pretty self-explanatory, while hedge hopping involved me and my friends – usually the Healy brothers, the O'Driscoll brothers, the Conways and Pa Barrett – lining up at one end of the street and racing to the other, using everybody's front garden hedges as hurdles on the way. A mistimed jump mid-race could take lumps out of someone's prized hedge and leave the owner on the warpath for a few days afterwards.

The nearest green area was about 400 metres away in Ballyphehane Park but most of us were too young to be allowed down there, so we made do with the little road that divided the two rows of houses on Derrynane, using front gates or jumpers for goalposts and kerbs for tennis court tramlines. While the real Wimbledon is often stopped due to rain, on our road it was only ever briefly halted to allow a neighbour's car to pass by.

My youngest sister, Lyndsey, arrived when I was nine and joined Rhonda and Anthea in their room. Lyndsey's arrival added an extra mouth to feed and although we had now moved into a bigger house, in a more sought-after area, we weren't suddenly well-off. Not by any stretch of the imagination.

My mother was always thrifty when it came to spending money and our weekend trips to the Coal Quay in the city centre soon became a thing of dread for Rhonda and me as we got older. Back then, the Coal Quay was where all the second-hand shops and market stalls could be found in Cork city and it was Mam's favourite haunt. She'd chat with everyone as she bought second-hand clothes, school uniforms and shoes from the various stalls as Rhonda and I pleaded with her to hurry on before somebody saw us.

For Rhonda and me, being seen shopping in the 'poor shops' of the Coal Quay by any of our friends or enemies resulted in instant mortification and at least a week's slagging in school, where the words 'I saw you down the Coal Quay' were seen as a slur on your family name and an invitation to fight (which, more often than not, I accepted).

In an effort to save a few pence, Mam would drag us into one particular shop where she would spend ages perusing the out-of-date cans and jars as Rhonda and I hid behind whatever we could find in case anybody saw us. Often we would trudge the 2 or 3 kilometres home laden down with plastic bags full of tins and jars so filthy dirty that you'd have to guess what was in some of them.

In the summer, Mam would round up us kids and we'd spend our entire school holidays shacked up in a battered old mobile home in Youghal while my dad, who still had to work in Cork during the week, would come down to us on Saturdays, stay for the weekend and be gone again for work on Monday morning.

The first day of summer would usually be spent crying that we had been dragged away from our friends although, slowly but surely, we'd get used to it and inevitably we would all be crying again two months later, on the day we had to go home. There was nothing much to do in the caravan park in those days so we had to make our own fun. When I was nine years of age, I got so bored that I went around to all of the nearby farms with Joseph Buckley, a friend I'd made in the caravan park, and got a job to pass the time.

We were only nine and on our holidays, but having a job on a farm was great because it opened up a whole new world to us. We'd get a lift with the farmer up through the fields on a tractor each morning to milk the cows and we did the same again in the evening. In between jobs we'd pretend we were cowboys and try and rope the newborn calves with a home-made lasso, or sneak into the hay barn and jump off the bales.

Because there were five of us kids in the mobile home during the week, you only got your breakfast, your dinner and your tea. There was no such thing as coming in and raiding the cupboards for a snack because there was nothing to raid, so getting dinners and teas from the farmer's wife was a massive bonus for me.

I'd work away all day with my new friends and at the end of the week I got paid a couple of quid, which meant I could go to the shop and stack up on sweets and chocolate bars, which I hid under my pillow until they ran out and I got paid again the following week.

When I was eleven, I worked on another farm, picking poppies for £4 a week during the summer. Then my dad would come down at the weekend and give me another £2 pocket money. I was loaded. I had more money back then than I had in my early twenties.

On the poppy farm I made friends with a guy called Anthony O'Shea from Knocknaheeny and got him a job picking potatoes. But Anthony did so much messing that there'd be nothing done. While I was happy enough with my wages, when Anthony's pay packet arrived at the end of each week, he'd say that we were being exploited and give out to the fella in the shop on the site, who would relay this information to the farmer and I was then tarred with the same brush as Anthony for hanging around with him.

After making my first Holy Communion in Togher National School, I moved to Scoil Chríost Rí in Turners Cross in the middle of second class. I was the smallest – and youngest – in a class of forty-four pupils. By the time I got to fourth class, I was behind the rest of the class academically and as I had been the youngest in my class I was made to stay back a year. Although my new classmates were all still taller than me, I was now surrounded by kids my own age. In my head though, I'd already done fourth class and figured that I should be better than them at something. I had no interest in my schoolwork so instead put all my efforts into being better than them on the sports field.

I'd never even seen a live sporting event while living in Togher but the move to Turner's Cross meant that Musgrave Park, the home of Munster Rugby in Cork, was just down the road from my house, as was Nemo Rangers GAA club.

Nemo were, and still are, a massive club, known throughout the country. A school friend of mine, Michael Buckley, played for them at the time and when they began to hold street leagues for the local kids to try and attract them into the club I went along.

Nemo's pitch was about 2km from my house so I'd run to training and home games. After a while I was made captain of my under-eleven street league team and I began to get very serious about my football and sport in general.

Around the same time, Ann Marie from next door, who was a very good sprinter, ran with Togher Athletics Club so I tagged along with her big brother Aidan and the rest of her family one day when they went to watch her run in an open sports day in Riverstick, about 15km south of Cork city. After seeing Ann Marie race, I decided to enter the 600m race for my own age group and, to my surprise, won it.

Although I did no running other than at football training, off the back of that performance I entered the school mile in Scoil Chríost Rí in sixth class and to everyone's surprise, including my own, went home with the massive winner's shield, having beaten the best runners in the school. I have a vivid memory from that day of one of the teachers saying 'well done, Robert' as they presented me with the trophy. It struck me that it was the first time in my life that I'd ever earned praise from any teacher.

Winning the mile in Chríost Rí was huge for any pupil and it earned me superstar status in school at the time. I was finally good at something and suddenly everyone in school wanted to know who this little fella Robert Heffernan was.

Another friend of mine in school, Mark Cogan, was also a sprinter with Togher Athletics Club and had a won a few All-Ireland underage medals. He trained twice a week with the club and after I won the school mile, he encouraged me to join him.

The club in Togher was based across the road from my first primary school and the clubhouse consisted of two dilapidated prefabs that had been previously used as school classrooms. The prefabs ran parallel to each other with a little open space of about the same area in between them. The interior of each prefab was sparse, to say the least. Painted white inside with plywood floors, there was no heating, no dressing rooms and no showers. If it was winter you could see the fog trails of your breath as you entered the buildings and while they have been home to some of the best athletes in Ireland for a long time now, the prefabs were never really fit for anything other than storing hurdles or other equipment.

On Wednesday evenings we'd go to the Mardyke track for training. Although I was seen as more of a distance runner when I first joined, I didn't want to be split up from my fast friends at those first sessions so I began my athletics training under Togher's sprint coach, Michael Devine, who gave me separate sessions from the others to encourage me to keep at it. I didn't race very much that summer because my family went to Youghal as usual, but I ran on the beach most days in an effort to get fitter.

When I completed my primary school education, however, instead of following the others to the mobile home in Youghal for the summer, I went to work on the building sites with my dad before joining the rest of the family in the mobile home at the weekends. At twelve years of age I was earning £7 a week helping another labourer mix plaster. Working on the sites meant I was forced to miss training so, to keep fit, I'd play handball off a wall on my lunch break or if the tradesmen sent me to the shop for messages I'd run there as fast as I could.

Although the attention I got from winning the mile in school had piqued my interest in athletics and I had joined Togher Athletics Club, I had no real interest in running as a sport. Gaelic football was my first love and I simply ran everywhere in the hope that I would stay fit enough for that. When I entered secondary school in Coláiste Chríost Rí, also run by the Presentation Brothers, just down the road from Scoil Chríost Rí, my main aim was to get on the school's Gaelic football team.

At only 4 foot 6 inches tall, I was the smallest first-year pupil in school but I was now playing regularly for Nemo Rangers and had progressed to captain my under-thirteen street league team, so I was disgusted not to be selected for the school's under-fourteen squad which was chosen from first- and second-year students after trials were held on the school pitch. At the time, I couldn't understand why I was left off the team, which contained mostly six-footers from second year and, having missed out on selection, I decided to try and show the Brothers who were in charge of the school team that they had made a huge mistake by leaving me out.

Every evening after school I would go to up to the school's multi-gym, which was basically another dilapidated indoor hall containing a few pieces of gym equipment and a climbing rope. Knowing that the Brothers who selected the football team were watching everything that went on in the hall, I would flog myself on the bench press, hamstring curls and lat pull-down machines every evening and was the only one that could climb all the way up the thick rope that dangled from the ceiling.

At the end of each night we'd have a game of football with a tennis ball and, for me, these sessions were an opportunity to flake into fellas and show the Brothers that it didn't matter what size I was, that my lack of height was no disadvantage and that I was good enough for the school team. While some lads went to multi-gym once or twice a week, I went every single night until the summer holidays forced me back onto the building site, where I now laboured for my dad.

Multi-gym also introduced me to other sports. As the athletics season approached, the Brothers would organise various events. One evening in second year they ran off long-jump, triple-jump and high-jump competitions, after which they organised a walking race. The walking race consisted of heats, where pupils lined up and race-walked up and down the hall. The winner of each race went through to the next round and although I knew absolutely nothing about the sport, I got to the final and won it.

Compared to football, race walking wasn't the most attractive sport in the world for a teenager to take up and I thought briefly about the slagging I might get if I was seen walking around Cork with my elbows swinging and hips swaying. Those thoughts didn't last long: I had probably built up enough credibility among my friends and peers as a footballer not to get slagged too much. However, I really began race walking because another pupil, Trevor Murray, encouraged me to. Trevor was very good at football and most other sports. He was one of the brainier kids in school and was hard as nails too, so I figured that if race walking was cool enough for Trevor Murray, it was cool enough for me.

After winning the race in the hall, I discovered that the school had a very strong walking team and a long history in the sport. Having missed out on selection for the Gaelic football team, I suddenly saw another window of opportunity to represent the school and, after trials, was picked for the walking team.

Tiny compared to most of my adversaries, however, I didn't win anything in my first year walking with the school, but overhearing Brother Colm telling someone that 'if Rob Heffernan was taller, he'd be the best walker in the country' spurred me on even more to prove that my lack of height was not a disadvantage.

Although I never thought of myself as small, my size often meant I was looked upon as easy pickings and I got into plenty of scraps in both Turners Cross and Togher. Having inherited the wiry 'greyhound breed' of both of my parents, though, I never shied away from a row.

After watching a Bruce Lee film on television, the kung fu legend's biography was the first book I ever read and it had such a big influence on me in those early teen years that I started tae kwon do lessons in Nemo's clubhouse and a few years afterwards I would walk all the way across town to another club in Shandon Street on the north side of Cork city for extra training. There, I'd work on the punchbags, stretch and do my patterns but I only ever got as far as a blue tag because I missed a load of gradings – probably because we didn't have the money to pay for them.

In the summer I could earn money on the building sites to pay for my own lessons but during the winter my mam would give me the £2 required for each class. As Christmas approached though, instead of going to tae kwon do, I'd keep the money for presents for my family and simply walk around town to pass the hour or two before going home.

I spent a third summer back on the building sites, this time shovelling enough sand and cement and hauling enough buckets of water and wheelbarrow-loads of plaster to keep my dad, my uncle and another plasterer going. Despite my wages going up to about £70 a week, I became more and more bitter about having to miss out on my sports. Every minute I got in the evening was spent kicking a football or training with Togher Athletics Club. Towards the end of second year, however, that all ground to a halt when I got my first real sports injury.

Osgood-Schlatter's Disease is a common knee injury that can cause a painful lump below the kneecap in children and teens who take part in sports. It usually happens during a growth spurt and is the result of bones, tendons and muscles all growing quickly but not necessarily at the same time. The good news is that, while it can last for what seems like a long time, you literally grow out of it.

But at fourteen years of age I didn't know any of that when a doctor diagnosed the ongoing pain in my knee. All I heard was 'You have a disease in your leg' and that I needed to be seen by a sports specialist. Given that my only access to the medical profession was by virtue of a state-issued medical card, that meant an agonisingly long six-month wait.

'What do I do until then?' I asked the doctor.

'Nothing,' was his reply. 'You rest.'

With the internet yet to be invented and no other way to find out about my condition, I went home that day believing I had a disease in my leg. As far as I could make out from talking to the doctor, if I did any sport in the next six months, my leg could fall off!

Those next six months crawled by and with nothing to be good at any more, I got really low. Although I had nothing else to distract me, I put no effort into my schoolwork and homework was rarely done. In our house, there was no incentive: stoic in the belief that I was going to follow my father's footsteps and be a plasterer and that school was just a place where you went until you were old enough to get a job, my parents never went to a single parent/teacher meeting and couldn't have cared less if I failed every exam.

I never skipped school but would spend half the time hiding in the toilets when I got there, just so that they couldn't suspend me for being seen outside the school during school hours. I'd get thrown out of some classes for messing but if I was being taught by one of the athletics or football coaches, like Brother Colm or Brother Sweeney, I'd pay attention. More often than not I would get good grades in their subjects, which showed that I could have done well in school if I'd put my mind to it.

When I eventually got to see a specialist in Cork Regional Hospital six months later, he took one look at my knee and told me that it was fine, that I'd grown out of it. After doing nothing for six months, I was so happy I ran all the way home from the hospital that day. I was sore for a week afterwards, but once I got back to full fitness, I was winning running races in Coláiste Chríost Rí without training for them and people were beginning to tell me that I could have a future in athletics. At home, though, nobody paid any attention. Like I said, sport was never on the radar in our house.

After passing my Junior Certificate in the summer of 1994, I got away with another few months in secondary school before the family prophecy was finally fulfilled and I left Coláiste Chríost Rí and the academic life behind for another career. I was off to serve an apprenticeship as a plasterer with my father.

2

Scholarship Material

The only advantage of working full-time with my dad was that I was soon deemed old enough to be able to stay at home when everyone else went to Youghal for the summer. This really annoyed my older sister Rhonda who was now twenty-three, had a full-time job and had fought much longer and harder for the same privilege.

Finally free from her babysitting duties, at the weekends Rhonda would still have to tidy up any mess I left behind me at home before Mam and Dad got back with Elton, Anthea and Lyndsey on Monday morning. Although Rhonda and I were extremely close growing up, like any other siblings we could fight like cat and dog, with Rhonda, more often than not, coming out on top.

With Mam and Dad away in Youghal every weekend, I was oblivious to the fact that my presence in the house encroached on Rhonda's blossoming relationship with her new boyfriend, Aidan from next door. When she came home from work one Friday evening to find the house looking like a bomb site, with a tent pitched out the back and all of my friends from Ballyphehane drinking in the garden, it was the straw that broke the camel's back.

She chased me upstairs where, having made it to the bathroom at the top of the landing before her, I managed to lock the door behind me and began taunting her even more. My smug sense of security vanished abruptly when Rhonda promptly kicked the door in and clattered me around the bathroom.

My plastering apprenticeship meant that my running was confined to the odd open sports day during the summer but I continued playing football with Nemo. Although my parents never once came to see me play, Michael Buckley's father Sean had a huge influence on me and made sure I always had a lift to matches.

I improved to the point where I was captain of Nemo's under-sixteen team and dreamt of a place on the Cork minor team. Because I was right half-forward and still a foot smaller than most of my opposition, I had to concentrate on getting space and finding a way to get to the ball before they did, so I rarely had time for banter or physicality with my opponent At one under-sixteen league game against Ballinore one day, the lanky half back marking me kept laughing and sneering at me the whole way through the game because I was so small. Most of the time I ignored this kind of thing and just got on with my game but for some reason this guy really bugged me. The fact that we were getting beaten only added fuel to the fire.

Sick of the constant name-calling and taunting, towards the end of the game I suddenly snapped and jumped up and grabbed him in a headlock. I was kneeing him in the face when one of my teammates ran over.

'Heffo, relax, boy! You've won the fight, get on with the game.'

But the ref had a different take on the incident.

'You haven't won anything. The two of you are off.'

That fight was the only blemish on an otherwise decent Gaelic football career but football was to take a back seat to athletics shortly afterwards. I was now training in Togher every Tuesday night, where I had moved on from the sprinters' group to the distance group and was now under the watchful eye of coach John Hayes, or as I have always called him, Mr Hayes.

John Hayes is small in stature but physically fit and very strong. He lived not too far away from me and took an interest in me as soon as I moved up to his distance group for training. He loaned me a running singlet and told me to look after it because it was possibly the club's only remaining singlet from the 1960s. When my mother washed it with one of my sister's tops, though, it turned bright pink. I did my best to avoid him for as long as possible afterwards. To keep fit, John ran around the park in Ballyphehane where I played football with my friends, so there was never much hope of evading him for long and he soon persuaded me to go back to training.

Like Sean Buckley, John Hayes became a father figure to me and was a really good influence in those early years. He held me back at first but always believed that I would do well when I hit my growth period, like the other lads my age. I was a really late developer, though: by the age of sixteen, I still hadn't hit puberty and I was beginning to get worried. The rest of my teammates had hairy legs and hairy armpits by then and I remember asking my mother one night if there was something wrong with me. She'd had a few drinks that night and when I put the question to her, she started crying and I'll never forget the words she said to me.

'Maybe if you were taller, people would start taking you serious.'

I couldn't believe it. Even my own mother thought I was too small.

She told me that we'd talk to my dad when he came home but he too had been in the pub and just brushed it off.

Knowing I was a late bloomer, John Hayes held me back for a long time, only allowing me to run in local races at first. Although he didn't have a sports science degree, John had great common sense and always dangled the carrot just far enough in front to make me want to keep going and improve another little bit. Whenever I reached a goal or hit a target, instead of celebrating it, a new target was set. Compliments on my performance were always very hard earned.

At around the same time, the buddies I had made outside of sport would be down in Ballyphehane Park drinking. I had no interest in drinking but, to be fair to those lads, they never pressurised me into joining them and I'd still go down to the park with them whenever they went. Instead of drinking, I'd have a pair of shorts on underneath my tracksuit and I'd run ten laps of the pitch in Ballyphehane before

16

sitting down and hanging out with them as they drank and chatted. Once, when I was about seventeen, I did join them for a few cans but was unlucky enough to get caught by my mam and got absolutely walloped around the house afterwards for my trouble. The ever-present threat of telling my father was acted upon.

While he didn't hit me, my dad's reaction upon hearing the news was just as bad. I remember cowering in my room as he stood over my bed berating me for drinking alcohol. Three times he left the room, only to return to emphasise the point even more and carry on the scolding. It took three days of absolute lambasting every time he saw me before it was finally out of his system and even though I never went near a pub, he had every barman in the area warned never to serve me.

To the left of the park, on the steps, was where the real tough boys hung out. While my friends might not have been model citizens as teenagers and were partial to the odd can of beer, these older lads were on something stronger altogether and the area was pretty well known for drugs at the time. Drugs frightened me. I'd heard of people in the area who had died from sniffing glue. There was something sinister about the lads on the steps and I was afraid to even cross over the road to that side of the park.

On training nights in Togher, I'd get a lift to the clubhouse with Mr Hayes and a huge group of us would run six or nine miles. The training was so hard that I'd be nervous in the car on the way over because I knew it would be torture. There was a pecking order in Togher and your status came from beating the other guys. Respect had to be earned and if you were at the bottom of the pecking order, then you got none. Those Tuesday evening sessions were as tough as any race, because every night was a race. There wouldn't be much talk out of me at those sessions, in fact I didn't mix much with the lads in the club at all back then because, to me, they were all my competition. After training I'd go home to my buddies in Turners Cross, where the competition didn't exist and I could be myself again.

While I often missed summer races due to working on the sites, in the autumn I began to run cross-country races in and around Cork when I was about fifteen. Even at those cross-country races, I never got that friendly with the lads in the club. Although this changed over time, the competition was so stiff back then that sometimes two-hour journeys would be spent in complete silence because we all knew that a bad performance could see one of us miss out on a place on the team. Only on the return leg, if we had won something, would everyone open up a bit and have a bit of craic.

The year after I left school, a cross-country race in St Aidan's primary school on the north side of Cork during the winter set me thinking about a return to education. I was still tiny compared to the rest of my teammates at Togher and at Nemo, even after a growth spurt that summer saw me go from 4 foot 9 inches to 5 foot 3 inches. There was a very strong field in that cross-country race, but I still finished sixth or seventh. Afterwards, a man came over and patted me on the back.

'Young man,' he said. 'You're scholarship material.'

Although I had never met Brother John Dooley before, his reputation as an athletics coach ensured that I knew who he was. A teacher at North Monastery, another secondary school in the area, Brother Dooley was regarded as a guru when it came to Irish athletics. A former All-Ireland champion at 1,500 metres, he had spent time in America, and was renowned for arranging athletics scholarships over there for promising Irish runners.

I couldn't believe that somebody like him would even notice me in the race, let alone go out their way to come over and compliment me. Having missed most of the summer due to work on the building sites, I knew I was nowhere near my best, yet here was this running guru telling me a scholarship to America was a possibility for me. I began to look into it a bit more and realised that the only way I could get a scholarship was to go back to school and sit my Leaving Certificate first.

After a lot of haggling with my parents, who couldn't see the point in going back to school, I rejoined Coláiste Chríost Rí halfway through my pre-Leaving Cert year. Once back at school, I regained my place on the school walking team and managed to finish second

18

in the Munster schools championships, which meant that I qualified for the All-Ireland schools championships. Although I finished last of eight walkers there, my second place in Munster was also enough to earn me an invitation to the Tailteann Games, which were held in Santry Stadium in north county Dublin that summer.

While my burgeoning athletics career had by then earned the support of my mother and started to turn me into the golden boy of the family in her eyes, my father wasn't impressed when I wanted to take time off my summer job labouring on the building site to go to walk in Dublin. He had seen it all before and was of the opinion that I was going to 'give up all this sport, like all the other young fellas', when I was eighteen.

I was already bitter about my dad's lack of interest in my sporting life when everyone else was beginning to take notice of me and that remark was the last straw. It drove a huge wedge between us and ultimately meant that it would be a full two years before I spoke to him again. In protest, I stopped working with him on the building sites so that I could train more and took a part-time job for two days a week in a book-binding factory just to have some pocket money.

The reality was that my family never believed I was going to earn an athletics scholarship. They thought it was fantasy stuff, and it was the same in school. When my career guidance teacher, Mr O'Loughlin, asked what I was going to do when I left school, I replied that I'd either go on and do a trade or go to America on a scholarship. He burst out laughing at me.

'You're too small to do either of them!'

Looking back, I can see where he was coming from but it was a terrible thing to say to a young lad and between that and my father's stance, I had a massive chip on my shoulder for a very long time.

Having ignored my father, I got the train to Dublin and the Tailteann Games with James Butler – who was a very good runner and was due to go to New York on a scholarship – and his father. With two walkers selected from each province for the under-seventeen walk, I was languishing in fifth or sixth place with a couple of laps to go but managed to work my way up to fourth place as we went into the back straight. One last spurt saw me kick for home in the last 100 metres and the guy in front of me was so tall that I actually went under his elbow as I passed him to snatch third and the bronze medal.

I crossed the line exhausted but absolutely delighted with myself when one of the judges suddenly pulled me aside and began to question me.

'Who are you? Where did you come from? Have you trained for this?'

After a couple of minutes of these random questions, I got disqualified for no apparent reason other than nobody knew who I was and therefore thought I shouldn't be able to beat the other guys, most of whom would have been known on the national scene for a long time. Returning home empty handed, I spent the entire train journey back to Cork crying.

In June 1996, I became the first person in our family to pass the Leaving Certificate. Passing my exams opened the door to an athletics scholarship in America but before I could run stateside I had to do another year in school in Ireland, this time in North Monastery where I would sit my SATs, which had to be passed in order to be offered a scholarship.

Under the watchful eye of Brother Dooley, North Monastery were renowned for their athletics team and had seven or eight All Ireland cross-country titles to their name before I joined the school. Having been one of the top dogs in Coláiste Chríost Rí though, at North Mon I was a mere mortal on a team that included the likes of Bryan Murray, Paul Carroll, Jason Foolkes, Kevin Lowe, Mark Cotter and Aaron Kearney, most of whom had won national medals, and it was a huge step up for me in terms of my sporting ability. For a long time in 1997 I was way out of my comfort zone.

Although the certificate we would be awarded at the end of the year was pretty much a made-up cert so that we could run with 'the Mon', we still had to go up to the Monastery every Thursday where we got homework to do for the SATs for America. Rather than actually do the homework though, Bryan Murray and I used to open up the answers at the back of the book and purposely get around 40 per cent of them wrong. We reckoned that Brother Dooley knew we weren't 'A' students and it would look suspicious if we got them all right.

Work experience was part of the year's course and I got placed in Cummins Sports, a local sports shop, where I stocked the stores and took in supplies.

In athletics, I focused on walking and did no running training but won the All-Ireland schools 3,000m on the track in Tullamore in County Offaly, beat all of the other lads on the running team to finish ninth in the All-Ireland schools cross-country, where we were second team, and was ninth in the inter-clubs cross-country championships.

Although I was still smaller than all of my competitors, after finally hitting puberty and growing three inches or so, to around 5 foot 6 inches, I really began to see improvement. I was now walking 60 to 80km a week in training, which was a huge step up and I went into the under-eighteen All-Ireland 10km walk in Tullamore in really good shape.

On the drive to Tullamore, John Hayes told me to sit on Mark Lennon from Kilkenny and stay there for as long as I could. Mark was a superstar at the time. He'd set all the national records for that age bracket but with two laps to go, I just went past him. I took well over two minutes off my personal best to record a 44' 40" for the 10km walk and caused the shock of the day by becoming national champion.

3

Who Are Ya?

Winning the under-eighteen national title gave me a great buzz. To have a national champion was huge for the club in Togher and the local papers soon began to take an interest in me, but I missed out on national duty that year as there was no Irish team selected for a major championship directly afterwards. I now had a new aim: I was the national champion, so I wanted to walk for Ireland.

That autumn, I was down the track one evening when I noticed another walker there. Olive Loughnane was two years older than me and had returned to her native Cork after studying in Galway. I can still remember the expression on her face that evening when what she thought was a twelve-year-old kid watched her train and then approached her with an offer she couldn't refuse.

'C'mere girl, I'm looking for a training partner,' I enthused. 'I want to qualify for the European Juniors.'

'Oh right,' she said, looking me up and down.

I was smaller than her, rake thin, had a skinhead haircut, an earring and a fringe.

'European Juniors are under-nineteen though. When are you hoping to go?'

When I replied 'next year', Olive nearly fell over, but soon after that we started training together, sometimes twice a day. Although our training was still pretty unstructured, my first year in the junior ranks, for under-nineteens, began well in February 1997, when I raced the National Indoor Championships in Nenagh in County Tipperary. The junior race was combined with the senior men and I walked 21' 30" for the 5km event, which was good enough for fourth place overall and victory in the Junior Championship. Not only had I won another national title, but this time I had beaten a lot of the more established senior walkers in the process.

Jimmy McDonald, who had been sixth in the Barcelona Olympics in 1992 and Irish internationals Mick Lane, Joe Ryan, Pierce O'Callaghan and Jamie Costin had all walked in Nenagh. Having put in a good performance against them, I was picked for an unofficial Irish national team to take part in a race in Folkestone in England a month or so later. By then, I had finally begun to develop, and mixing with the top athletes in North Mon day in and day out had changed my mindset to one of belief that I could do what they were doing.

Although I was steadily improving and beginning to turn a few heads on the race-walking scene, I still felt guilty whenever my dad and my younger brother Elton walked in, covered in plaster after a hard day's work on the building site and caught me watching TV in my tracksuit on the couch. As Dad and I still weren't talking, there was never anything said but I always felt uncomfortable, almost unworthy, sitting down beside them at the dinner table.

I was doing big miles on the road by then and felt that I was training as hard as they were working, but my soft little hands at the dinner table compared to their weatherworn palms and scraped knuckles told a different tale in Dad's eyes. Although we weren't on great terms, he still forked out to send me to England for my first international race and I got the bus up to Dublin, where I stayed with the O'Callaghan family before the boat trip to Holyhead.

Bernie O'Callaghan was the national race-walking coach at the time. A former international walker himself, his son Pierce had won everything on the domestic scene while growing up and, in my eyes, was king of the Irish race-walking scene, although he was a senior and didn't travel with the team that weekend.

A big Irish contingent boarded the ferry the following morning and then sat through the six-and-a-half-hour bus trip to Folkestone, where we could see the shores of France from the windows of our budget hotel. Among the travelling Irish party, I felt pretty intimidated. Unlike most of the others, I hadn't come to the sport through my family and was the only one travelling on my own. Most of the others had their parents or coaches with them but I was the only fella from Cork, the only fella with no coach, the only fella with no parent with him and the whole trip was like one long version of the silent drive to cross-country races with the lads from Togher.

The race in Folkestone was my first ever 10km walk and I did pretty well, finishing in the top five in a time of 47' 20". The result saw my confidence grow and I began to realise that if I put the work in and improved by just a couple of minutes over the next few months, I could actually qualify for the European Junior Championships that summer.

Having done well in the race, I began to come out of my shell a little bit on the way home and Jimmy Costin, who had gone out of his way to make me feel comfortable on the trip, invited me down to Dungarvan to train with his son Jamie, who was a year older than me and had finished twelfth in the 10km walk at the Junior World Championships in Sydney in 1996.

When I arrived home from England and announced that my aim was to get on the Irish team for the European Junior Championships in Slovenia that summer though, it resulted in nothing but laughter.

'Slovenia! Where's that, boy? It must be over the north side!'

In fairness, most of my family probably thought Slovenia *was* on the north side of Cork. But the thing is, nobody believed me. Not even slightly. Representing Ireland and going to Slovenia, in their eyes, was the same as my talk of getting a scholarship to America – nothing but a pipe dream. Rather than put me off, though, my family's reaction drove me on, made me even more determined to up my training.

A week or so later I headed to Dungarvan and stayed with the Costin family on their farm for a few days. Here, I would milk cows

24

with Jamie and Jimmy before breakfast. Jamie and I would then go picking stones in the fields in between eating again and training together.

We got on well together in Dungarvan and Jamie then invited me up to Dublin for a weekend to train with himself and his best friend Pierce (son of Bernard O'Callaghan, the national coach). Pierce was only a couple of years older than me but was way more mature and very confident. Our backgrounds were worlds apart both on and off the track. While I had yet to finish my secondary education and was just back from my first trip outside the country, Pierce was studying in University College Dublin and under the tutelage of his father had already represented Ireland on numerous occasions.

I remember buying a shiny new luminous green and blue Sub4 tracksuit and a new sports bag for the trip up to Dublin on the train. Pierce and Jamie collected me from Heuston Station and we drove to UCD where Pierce shared an apartment with Meath footballer Trevor Giles, who was studying physiotherapy. Trevor had gone home for the weekend so I stayed in his room. For the next three days our little group, which also included Brian O'Donnell, who is now a Fianna Fáil senator in Donegal, and 800m runner James Nolan, ate and hung out in the apartment in between training on the college track and the local roads.

It was a big step up in company for me and after a tough weekend of training, the lads dropped me off at Heuston Station for the journey back to Cork. They had only driven out of sight when I discovered that I had lost my wallet over the course of the three days, which meant that I had no train ticket home or any money, apart from £4 that I found in my tracksuit pocket.

With no mobile phone back then, I had no way of contacting them or letting anyone know of my predicament, so I walked the 3km from Heuston to Busáras, the central bus station in Dublin, and asked how much the fare back to Cork was. Although I looked young enough to be given a half fare, I was still £1.50 short and was left stranded, with no prospect of getting home. After an hour or so of pacing up and down in the blind hope that my wallet would suddenly appear, I sat desolately on the kerb with my head in my hands wondering how the hell I was going to get home.

'What's wrong with you?' asked a gruff Dublin voice a few minutes later.

I looked up to see a middle-aged Dubliner looking down at me.

'Are you on the rob?'

'No.'

He looked me up and down. My skinny, gaunt appearance, with my head shaved apart from my fringe, combined with the shiny new tracksuit gave him the impression that I was one of the local gougers.

'Are you on heroin?'

'No. I'm £1.50 short of my bus fare back to Cork and I've no other way of getting home.'

Unknown to me, this excuse was also one widely used by local addicts to obtain money off unsuspecting members of the public outside Busáras, so he stared at me for a few minutes, sizing me up, before bringing me across the road to what looked like some sort of office building. Inside, he spoke to a man he seemed to know and handed me a form to sign.

The building turned out to be the home of the *Big Issue* magazine and after much deliberation the duo persuaded me that if I sold five magazines, I'd have enough money to buy my ticket home. Reluctantly, I signed the form, stuffed five copies of *Big Issue* under my arm and walked onto the street just as a woman approached.

'*Big Issue*?' I asked as she reached me.

She took one glance at me and instantly ended my career as a magazine salesman with the words 'Would you go on to fuck!'

I walked back to Busáras where there was another guy selling *Big Issue* outside. I'd been told that while you got your first five magazines free you had to buy your next batch, so I persuaded the man to buy my five magazines at a knockdown price of £2 for the lot.

Moments later, Pierce's sister, Roisin, walked past and after hearing my story, handed me another fiver. With a few extra bob in my pocket, I walked up to Supermacs on O'Connell Street, bought a double burger meal and returned to the bus station with time to spare before the next bus to Cork. As I waited, I told the driver my story and he let me on for nothing, so I ended up with a load of money in my pocket when I got home.

I tackled my first outdoor junior championships in Tullamore that June. Although the juniors were walking in the same race as the under-23s that day, I managed to beat them all too and won the race outright, earning me the title of 'Athlete of the Meet'. In winning the race, I had clocked a time of 44' 44", which was fifteen seconds inside the time needed to qualify for the European Junior race-walking championships in Slovenia, and had guaranteed my selection for the official Irish team. I was absolutely delighted. Until I found out the date that the Europeans were due to be held on that July.

By then, Rhonda was engaged to Aidan next door and, by my calculations, they were due to be married on the same day as I was due to walk at my first-ever European Championships. In my mind, there was no comparison between going to a wedding — even my big sister's wedding — and walking for Ireland at the Europeans. I was going to the Europeans. But it took me a while to break the news to Rhonda and the rest of the family. In the end, I sort of blurted it out at the dinner table one evening.

'Oh, by the way, I won't be able to go to Rhonda's wedding. I'm going to the European Juniors in Slovenia.'

While Rhonda didn't exactly take the news too well at first, everyone was happy for me and I set about getting my affairs in order for the trip. The first thing I had to do was get a passport, which would also solve another ongoing problem in my life. Although I had just turned nineteen, I still looked about fourteen and had difficulty getting into pubs or discos with my friends. At least now I would have some identification if I wanted to go out in Cork.

In order to get a passport I had to go through the usual process of filling in the forms, having a couple of passport photographs taken and sending in my birth certificate. It was during this process that I got the shock of my life. I filled in the forms and got my photos done pretty quickly but obtaining a copy of my birth certificate seemed to take a bit longer. Mam fobbed me off for a while before eventually handing it over. When she did, I was flabbergasted.

Not only was I flabbergasted. I was somebody else.

A quick scan down the sheet of paper revealed that my name wasn't actually registered as Robert Heffernan. Instead, my birth certificate said I was Robert Kiely.

My heart stopped. In that instant, the split second that it took to read my name, I had lost my whole identity. All sorts of things raced through my mind simultaneously. 'Who the fuck is Robert Kiely? Is that me? Why is my name Kiely? Am I adopted? Is this my real family? Has my whole life so far been a lie? What the fuck is going on?'

I was confused and immediately hit my mam with these questions. But her response left me just as dumbfounded. As if it was no big deal, Mam explained that she had been married to a man named Kiely before she met my dad and that when I was born, the nurses in the hospital knew her as Kiely and simply put my surname down as the same as hers. The fact that my mother had been married before and had a whole new backstory before she met my father came as a complete shock to me, but in typical fashion she just brushed it off.

'Sure it'll be grand.'

'No, it won't be fucking grand, Mam!' I said. 'My name is Robert Heffernan, not Kiely. You need to get this changed!'

There was no way I was competing in the European Junior Championships as Robert Kiely. I didn't know anything about this other man, apart from the fact that he definitely wasn't my father. I'd never met him and, as far as I was concerned, he had absolutely nothing to do with me.

Despite my pleas, all my mother would tell me was that there had been a mistake during the registration of my birth, which made me even angrier, especially when she brushed it off as if it was a minor incident. With no further explanation coming from either of my parents, I turned to Rhonda to see if she knew what the hell was going on.

Although neither of my parents ever gave her the full story either, as far as Rhonda could gather, my mother met a man called Noel

Kiely when she was around nineteen and working in a bar near where she lived. The two began dating and were married in Cork in 1968, when Mam was twenty. Their first child came along the same year and baby Rhonda lived with them in Fairhill on the north side of the city.

Soon though, Noel was spending more time in the bar than Mam was and the marriage began to go sour. By the time Rhonda was five years old, Mam had split up from Rhonda's father and had moved with her daughter to England where they stayed with an aunt for a while, before getting their own place.

Mam worked as a cleaner and Rhonda went to school for a year or two before they moved back to Cork when Rhonda was seven. They were given a Corporation flat in Togher, where Mam met my father in a pub whilst out socialising with a neighbour from the flats. Within the year, my dad had moved in and I came along the year after.

Although it all went over my head at the time, with no divorce allowed in Catholic Ireland back then, there must have been a huge taboo about both my mam's separation from her husband and then her living 'in sin' with another man despite the fact that she was still 'married'. The fact that she was brave enough to leave her first husband and then start a new life and have a family with another man shows how tough a cookie my mother really was, but it must have been very hard on both of my parents at the time. Still, it would be over a decade later, after another chat with Rhonda, before I even realised that my parents were never married at all.

'Work it out yourself, Rob,' she said. 'Why do you think there were never any wedding anniversaries? Have you ever seen a photograph of them on their wedding day?'

It was something that was never, ever spoken about in our house and my youngest sister Anthea only found out about it at Christmas time in 2013. Eighteen-year-old me didn't take anything else into consideration, however, apart from the fact that I needed a passport with my own name on it to walk for Ireland at the Europeans. Changing my name to Heffernan, though, was not as easy as I had imagined.

It was very messy at the time because Mam didn't get on with her former husband. When she asked him to sign the forms saying that I wasn't his son, he refused. I couldn't believe it. I couldn't understand how my mother let them put another man's name on the cert in the first place or how my dad could have let it drag on for so long without wanting to get his own name as my father. I was distraught and really angry with both of them for a long time.

With a stalemate ensuing between my mother and her former husband, I took the issue into my own hands and found out that the quickest and easiest way to change my name to what it should have been in the first place was to do it by deed poll. I marched my mother to a solicitor's office over by Shandon Street where she witnessed me signing legal documents to change my name. One of the main parts of the documents was that I had to denounce the name Kiely, which was ridiculous to me as I'd never been a Kiely in the first place.

To me, and everybody that knew me, Heffernan was, and always had been my name and the whole scenario was very awkward and embarrassing for me at the time. Like my parents, I have never talked about it since and even writing about it now, over twenty-five years later, makes me feel very uncomfortable.

When the deed poll form was signed and officially stamped by the solicitor, I had to bring it into the passport offices. My first passport arrived just in time for me to go to Slovenia so I rang the Athletics Ireland office and they agreed that I could fly to the race from Cork rather than making the trip up to Dublin beforehand.

After winning the 1997 Junior National Championships, I began to get bits of advice from one of the national coaches, Mick Lane, who phoned my house every so often. I had never flown before and one of the first basic bits of information I can remember him telling me was to take my shoes off and drink water on the plane.

Although North Monastery used to bring in a physio, Liam O'Reilly, every Wednesday for the school athletics team, I was now on the Irish national team for the first time and thought I might as well avail of their services before the Europeans. The team had a physio, Oswald Schmidt, who was based in Togher at the time. I had a niggle in my back that I thought he might be able to sort out so I rang his office, told them I was on the Irish junior team going to the European Championships and asked if I could get in for physio before we went. I got in for two or three visits and flew off to the Euros from Cork with Ossie for company.

In Slovenia I met up with the rest of the Irish team and was given my first Irish running singlet, a tracksuit, a few T-shirts and a pair of shorts. I was living the dream. The Irish team was made up of five boys and four girls, under the management of Jim Kilty and Michael Quinlan. I was delighted at having made the Irish team, but Kilty made me sit up and take notice when he announced at our first team meeting that 'statistically only one or two of you are going to make it to senior internationals'. That sentence stuck in my head and made me determined to be one of the ones who made it.

Slovenia was like a different planet for me. As a newcomer to the Irish team I was in awe of most of my teammates and felt like a fish out of water. The athletes were housed in local student accommodation and I shared a room with Dubliner James Matthews, a 400m hurdler and a lovely lad. As a squad, we kept to ourselves in the lead-up to competition and didn't mix very much with anybody but in the days before my 10km walk, I remember being down at the track and watching some of the other athletes warm up. One Italian walker caught my eye. I can distinctly remember watching him on the track and thinking 'well I'm definitely going to beat him anyway. He looks useless!' The same Italian not only won the race but lapped me twice in the process.

I had been getting a bit of a name around Cork, had been in the paper a lot and had won the National Championships at home, but Slovenia opened my eyes to the fact that there was a whole new world out there. Even though I finished second last, I learned a lot from that first international outing. Looking back, I can see I hadn't a clue what I was doing but I was aggressive enough and had the mentality to take the lead from the start. I wasn't fazed by the event and took it on, leading the race for 5km.

On a scorching hot day, I was beginning to get it tough at the halfway mark when a big German named Andre Hohne suddenly made a move. He elbowed me in the shoulder as he went past and I completely froze. I was totally intimidated. After that, the whole race went south for me. I saved that lesson in my memory bank and never let it happen to me again. At first, I went through a phase where I'd throw a dig back if there was any argy-bargy but then learned that I had to roll with the punches, not react, and concentrate on what I was doing myself.

My training was ridiculous compared to the junior internationals who were professionals at the age of nineteen, with coaches, physios and doctors behind them. They seemed so mature that I remember feeling like a child beside them and a picture from those champion-ships that I have at home would seem to concur. I'm half the size of some of my competitors in the photo.

Although I had been well out of my depth, I came home from those European Championships feeling different from everybody. I started to evaluate what I did compared to the set-up and support the other athletes had and the whole experience taught me that I could improve on a lot of things, so my whole thought process started changing. I was hungry to be better. I also felt very proud of having represented Ireland and my confidence also began to grow as a result. I had swapped an Irish top for a Swedish top after the race and wore it along with my new national team kit everywhere I went afterwards.

Having received physio from Ossie in the lead-up to the Europeans under the impression that it was part of the national squad's set-up, I was taken aback when he rang my house looking for £150 in fees. I couldn't believe it. I was back in school, earning little or nothing as part of my work experience and had no way of getting the money for him. I looked up to Ossie and was too embarrassed to tell him I was broke but pretty soon the phone calls were coming to Cummins Sports too. Eventually, I had to tell them to say I wasn't in but it took a very long time for the calls to stop.

In 2014 I met Ossie at the Cork City Sports where he was working in a tent on the track and I took the opportunity to remind him about the money I owed him.

'Ossie, I owe you €150 since 1997. It's out in the car, boy. Do you want me to go out and get it?'

'Ah Rob, leave it go,' came the reply.

Having done a little bit of work ahead of the SATs, I scored around 1,000 points in the exams, which wasn't anything special but was enough to see me qualify for a scholarship stateside. Soon, I was getting phone calls from Brother Dooley. Everything had been set up for me to go to America. But that was another phone call I wanted to avoid.

4

The Mystery Voice

Although I had won a national walking title and represented Ireland in the walk at the European Juniors, the coaches at Campbell University in North Carolina were more interested in the fact that I had finished ninth in the Irish Junior cross-country championships, ninth in the All-Ireland schools championships and ninth in the inter-county championships that year, despite little or no running training. They told Brother Dooley that they saw me as a 'sleeper' and because of my potential as a runner, they were prepared to slot me into their running programme as an endurance athlete.

Everything had been set up for me to go to college in America but the European Championships in Slovenia had blown me away and I had begun to realise that walking was a really serious sport, and one that I could potentially be pretty good at. I had spoken to John Hayes for advice after returning home from Slovenia and he convinced me that I could be the best walker in the country within a couple of years and that I could possibly go to an Olympics if I put my mind to it. Once the Olympics were mentioned I was hooked. Having experienced the Europeans for the first time, I could only imagine what qualifying for the Olympics would be like and that became my next big goal.

But instead of informing Brother Dooley about my decision and explaining the rationale behind it, I was really immature about the whole thing and treated the entire saga in much the same way as I had treated Ossie. I didn't deal with it properly at all.

I was getting phone calls to my house not only from Brother Dooley but from the coaches in America too. I wouldn't answer them and told everyone at home to say I wasn't in whenever the phone rang. The head coach in America was annoyed at Brother Dooley, who in turn was probably annoyed at me but I just buried my head in the sand and rode it out until it was forgotten about.

Having shrugged off a possible college education, I got a full-time job in Cummins Sports in 1998. I worked from nine to five and had to work every Saturday with a day off during the week instead. If I didn't train before work, I'd get an extended tea break of half an hour and get out walking for 6km then.

A lot of other athletes from North Mon came on work experience and one of them, Jason Foolkes, soon became a great buddy of mine. He was trying to get a scholarship to America that year and after training really hard in the mornings, we'd take it in turns to go for a nap down the back of the store while the other kept an eye out for the store manager, Tommy. More often than not, I'd go straight from work to the track to train again in the evening.

Although the job was cleaner and less physical than the building sites, and therefore better for training, it was pretty mundane so I did my best to liven things up whenever I could. In between deliberately sending the wrong stuff down the chute to other staff, we'd entertain ourselves by ringing Cork's 96FM and answering the Mystery Voice competition. One of our colleagues in the store, Noel Hartigan, had scored the winning goal in an FAI Cup final for Cork City and almost every week, we'd put on a woman's voice and ask the presenter 'Is it Noel Hartigan, by any chance?'

◄○►

My first year as a senior, 1998, began with the 5km walk at the National Senior Indoor Championships in Nenagh that February. The race began at an amble with all of the favourites watching each other but I was cocky enough to wait it out and when the hammer went down halfway around I was able to stay with the older, more experienced guys.

As the finish loomed nearer, I found myself out front with seasoned international Pierce O'Callaghan, who would represent Ireland at the European Seniors later in the year. Neck and neck for a long period, there was a bit of argy-bargy between us on the last lap but I'd learned my lesson in Slovenia and, despite the fact that I was only half the size of him, a nudging match saw me push him up the embankment of Nenagh's track into lane four in the final metres and I beat him by a hair's breadth. To this day, I still get a sense of satisfaction from winning that national championship as a relatively unknown young fella beating Pierce caused a huge stir among the crowd.

Although the year had begun well for me, my season went downhill for a long time after that and the step up to senior level proved more difficult than I imagined. For reasons unknown, I kept getting sick any time I got myself into any sort of decent form. With no such thing as individualised training plans back then, the staple Irish race walker's diet was whatever you could fit in midweek with a solid two- or three-hour walk on a Sunday. But every time I got up to any decent level I'd break down and get sick and never developed enough to be able to take on a 20km walk that year.

When I finally got around to talking to Brother Dooley again, he advised me to get my bloods done and they revealed that my iron levels were very low: I was anaemic, which at least partly explained my lack of results. Third place in the national 10km championships behind Pierce and Michael Casey, both of whom went on to represent Ireland at the European Championships in Budapest that year, saw a terrible season end on a decent note but after a rather poor introduction to senior racing I decided to make some changes, both on and off the track.

While I had some good times in Cummins Sports, the job soon became very mundane and I began to question the fact that I was getting paid less money than the store manager for doing the same job as him. I came to the conclusion that working in a sports shop wasn't going to bring me much in my life, so I opted to go back to college and do a sports injuries course in Coláiste Stiofáin Naofa, a Post Leaving Certificate college in Cork.

Although racing against the seniors hadn't gone anywhere near as well as I had hoped, I still harboured dreams of going to the Olympics one day and the idea behind doing the course was that if I ever did get to fulfil that dream and made a name for myself in the athletics world, as a former Olympian I would have a good chance of making a living as a sports injury therapist. If my walking career never went any further, the course would provide a safety net for the future.

Although I hadn't done biology in my Leaving Certificate, my walking results were taken into consideration and I did well enough at the interview to be accepted onto the course. While the course ran full-time from Monday to Friday, I was only interested in getting the sports massage qualification out of it, so I skipped all of the other classes. To me, business class and gym instruction were a waste of my time, time that would be better spent training.

One of the perks of going back to college was the free use of the college gym, where I spent a lot of time stretching and hanging out in the sauna with Ross Corcoran after training sessions while the classes I had no interest in were going on. As we were learning about sports massage we all had to receive massage ourselves a couple of times a week, an added bonus.

Giving up a full-time job to go to college meant a sudden drop in my income. This was something my mam wasn't too pleased about at the start, so I continued to work in the sports shop on Saturdays. Qualification for the European Juniors the year before meant that I had also received my first grant from the Irish Sports Council of £1,200 and I tried to make that stretch for as long as I could.

I thought more about my training and how I could improve enough to qualify for the Olympics. For the 1999 season I began to train under national race-walking coach Mick Lane, who had given me titbits of advice before the European Juniors. A schoolteacher and qualified accountant from Mullingar, County Westmeath, Mick had represented Ireland at a European Championship and had also coached Jimmy McDonald, who put Irish race walking on the map when he finished sixth at the Barcelona Olympics in 1992. While he could be stubborn at times, Mick was a really good disciplinarian and he created a good environment in Limerick, where most of the walkers on the national squad would come together for squad training weekends.

While I mixed college, weekend work and training at home, Pierce and Jamie had gone to Australia over the winter and were training full-time with Kiwi Craig Barrett and Aussie walker Nathan Deakes, who had won a bronze medal at the Commonwealth Games in Kuala Lumpur the year before. Every so often I'd get a letter from the lads telling me what training they were doing and some paper clippings about Deakesy's feats over there.

Those letters and the knowledge that the lads were training hard in good weather kept me very motivated over the winter and I began the new season well with victory at the 5km National Indoor Championships in February again. I had recorded the exact time as I had beaten Pierce with the year before but this time Michael Casey was the runner-up. Casey was at least ten years older than me and a very experienced international, so his was another big scalp for me to claim.

As part of Mick Lane's training regime, Olive Loughnane and I joined a group of walkers that he coached, including Bobby O'Leary, Gillian O'Sullivan, Deirdre Gallagher and Pat Ryan, on a warm-weather training trip to Fuengirola on Spain's Costa del Sol that Easter. Mick had a contact over there who owned an apartment, into which we were all lumped together.

Although I was now part of the 'elite' walking scene in Ireland I still felt almost unworthy, or at least, very uncomfortable among the group so I brought a friend of mine from Togher Athletics Club with me. Martin 'Dealer' Byrne was a 'Del Boy' character who earned his nickname by wheeling and dealing his way around Cork at the time. 'Dealer' was a decent runner but more importantly to me, having him around helped me feel more at home over the next two weeks. He slept on the couch in our apartment and we generally took things less seriously than everyone else, even managing to sneak out for a few pints the odd night.

While some of our sessions were done on the local track, most of our fortnight in Fuengirola was spent walking up and down a one-kilometres stretch of beachfront promenade all day. On longer walks we'd go a bit further but would more often than not end up trying to avoid holidaymakers and old people as we trained, which didn't make much sense to me but Mick was the coach and, to everybody else in the group, what he said was gospel.

Shortly after that training camp, I took on my first ever 20km race at the Irish National Championships, which were held on the South Ring Road in Cork. As the course was local, it was one of the rare occasions when my mam and dad came to see me race and I can still remember my mother giving out to me about the state of my clothes when she saw how well presented Pierce O'Callaghan and Jamie Costin looked, the duo dressed from head to toe in matching kit sponsored by Reebok and looking tanned and fit after their training stint Down Under.

The lads took gold and silver on the day with me finishing third and taking the bronze medal. Although my time of 92 minutes wasn't quick enough to qualify me for the Race Walking World Cup in Mézidon-Canon in north-west France the following month, the national coaches recognised that it was my first 20km and that I was progressively getting better. As the World Cup was a team championship they put a case to Athletics Ireland that, for my development, I should be sent to France with the lads, and Athletics Ireland accepted their proposal.

Ray Flynn from Sligo was the Irish team manager in France, with Pierce's dad, Bernie, and Mick Lane for support. Although I had seen Ray around the domestic scene as he officiated at events in his standard attire of duffel coat, wellington boots and clipboard, I had never really spoken to him before. He soon took an interest in me and we hit it off almost immediately, not least because he told me I was going to win the Olympics one day!

In race walking, the World Cup and European Cup are run on alternate years and apart from the World Championships, European Championships or Olympic Games, are the biggest races on the calendar. Based on a 2km circuit on a road thronged with thousands of spectators waving national flags, the World Cup in Mézidon-Canon was huge for me, by far the biggest thing I had ever competed in.

While I was completely raw, Pierce and Jamie were used to big events and knew all of the top international walkers. From their stories, I had begun to see these guys as superstars but one of the things that struck me as I lined up alongside them for the first time was that most of them weren't much taller or bigger than me. I was fascinated by that and immediately knew that any chip I had on my shoulder about being small had to be brushed off forever. If they could do it, I could it.

On the start line, someone shouldered me out of the way but, remembering the intimidation I felt at the European Juniors, I threw a puck back at him and went off hard from the gun. I stayed at the front for a few kilometres before the big guns took over and even though I covered the course in the same time as I had for the nationals, I had drifted to seventieth place by the finish, which emphasised the gulf between me and the best walkers in the world.

After the race there was an official banquet that night and after a few hours of free food, drink and music I wound up at a party with some of the Irish contingent in one of the houses in the local village. Here, I noticed the reigning European champion, Ilya Markov, among the partygoers and, star-struck, I introduced myself and asked him for his autograph. The Russian had obviously had a few drinks and was only too happy too oblige, but I couldn't believe it when he swapped tracksuit tops with me as well.

Having seen the top walkers up close and personal in Mézidon, I began to realise that they were no different from me or anybody else and I came home from that World Cup unbelievably motivated to improve enough to be able to compete against them and take them on in the big events.

A schoolteacher from Killarney, Irish international Gillian O'Sullivan was based in Cork at the time and I started training with her soon after Mézidon. Gillian is very level-headed and training with her was a big step up for me. We would train together in the morning and evening and if I was one minute late she wouldn't speak to me for the whole session. Gillian was so disciplined that it rubbed off on me and taught me how to manage my time properly.

While I had still been improving slightly, for much of the early season I found myself fading dramatically towards the last third of a 20km walk and even any time I did a long walk in training so I knew something was wrong somewhere. A trip to the dentist revealed an abscess underneath one of my teeth and he recommended a short course of antibiotics followed by an extraction of the decayed tooth. Within days of getting my tooth out, I started to feel as if I had more energy and was no longer feeling as drained after long training sessions.

My next race came a month or so later in England, where Pierce, Jamie and I paid our own way over to take part in a Grand Prix race in Leamington Spa. Here, representing Togher, I finished fourth behind British Olympian Chris Maddox, Pierce and Jamie, and set a new personal best time for the 20km walk of 86 minutes. Our times also saw Jamie and me qualify for the European under-23 championships in Gothenburg in the process and my Sports Council grant went up from £1,200 to £3,600, so the night was spent celebrating in a local pub with the lads.

Jamie and I went back to England a week later for the British under-23 championships, a 10km race held on the track in Bedford. Up until then I had never beaten Jamie in competition and he reminded me of this fact as we played pool in our budget hotel the night before the race. With the game balanced on the black ball, Jamie chalked up his cue while I leaned over the table ready for my shot.

'This is it, Heffernan!' he said. 'Me and you on the last lap. Who has the bottle?'

Although the game had nothing to do with race walking, I took the next few minutes very seriously and went to bed very pissed off when I fluffed my final shot and Jamie potted the black to win the game. While it was probably said in jest, the remark rattled around in the back of my head for the whole race the next day and was foremost in my thoughts as Jamie and I went neck and neck after pulling clear of the others at the halfway mark.

Still stinging from the pool game, I put the boot down again and, to my surprise, began to pull away from Jamie on the last lap. For the first time ever, I beat him by a couple of seconds to win the British title race.

Delighted, a huge celebration ensued again that night and the partying continued when I got home to Cork, where a night out with my friend Barry ended with me falling asleep on the table of the local Abrakebabra before a bouncer picked me up and fired me out the front door, damaging my back in the process. When I realised that my wallet was still sitting on the table, I tried to get back in but they wouldn't let me so I kicked at the door in anger only to be chased down the street by two bouncers. Although they didn't catch me, they phoned the Gardaí and a squad car pulled up alongside me as I sat on a bench at a nearby bus stop. I was arrested and spent the next few hours in Togher Garda station. I woke up the next morning completely ashamed and when Gillian saw me coming out of the station I told her that I had crashed my dad's car and had to go down to pay for the damages caused.

A week later I tackled the Irish under-23 championship, but the late nights and lack of recovery saw the wheels begin to fall off and Jamie got his revenge by beating me into the silver medal position. At the time, I saw no correlation between my defeat and the late nights, and partied again after I broke the Irish record for 3km at a National League race the following weekend. I finished second to Pierce in the National Senior Championships again a week later and after racing every weekend and drinking and partying after each success or failure, I left Cork for the European under-23 championships in Gothenburg a week later.

Jamie and I both stayed in Pierce's house the night before we left for Sweden and, as young guns tend to do, we stayed up half the night talking about how great we were going to be. Jamie was sure he was going to win a medal at the Euros and had me convinced that we were all going to win medals. The two lads were way more mature than me at that age and I was hanging on their every word and starting to believe them.

'When you go over there, you realise you've got there on credit,' said Pierce, pulling me aside just before I went to bed. 'You got no favours. You deserve to be there . . . and you can beat Jamie as well!'

Here was Pierce O'Callaghan, the star of Irish race walking, telling me that I could beat Jamie Costin, his best friend. Jamie had been twelfth at the Junior World Championships a couple of years previously. I did the maths and went to bed thinking that if Jamie was going to win a medal at the Euros then maybe I had a chance too.

By the time I got to Gothenburg the next evening though, I was shattered. To make matters worse, I twisted my knee a little bit dragging my suitcase up the hotel stairs and it filled up with fluid. The race itself was held on a hot sunny day on a 2km loop around a park. Even though I had done everything wrong in the weeks building up to the championships, things started well for me and I was in the lead group with the Russian, Spanish and German walkers for the opening kilometres.

Two nights before, Jamie had been full sure he was going to win a medal in the race but he was nowhere to be seen in the group as we went past the 5km mark and I was surprised to see him sitting on the side of the road as we came around a corner shortly after. Although Jamie was out, things were still going well for me and I stayed with the leaders for the opening 10km. Around then, though, the late nights, the partying and the week-after-week of racing before the Euros caught up with me. My legs went and I blew up. You could probably hear the bang in Togher. As my legs turned to jelly, I fought to hang on to every walker that passed me on the way to the finish but I was walking on empty and ended the race in second-last place, with a time of 96 minutes.

I was absolutely disgusted with myself but with the season over, decided to forget about walking for a while and went on holiday to Torremolinos a few weeks later. While I was in Spain, the World Championships were being held in Seville, so I took a three and a half hour train trip over to watch Gillian O'Sullivan and the rest of the Irish team in action. I hung around the stadium in forty-degree heat for most of the day and after the women's race, stayed on to watch the first half of the men's walk. But as the last train for Torremolinos left before the finish, I had to phone Pierce back in Ireland for the results.

'Ilya Markov won,' he said. 'He wore your top on the podium!'

I was so gullible back then that I actually believed him for a minute but the fact that Markov had become world champion that day flipped a switch in my head. A few months earlier I had seen him at a party in Mézidon. He was just as small as me. He'd given me his top. He'd had a few beers. As far as I could see he was just a normal fella. If he could win the World Championships, then so could I.

Although I still was on holidays, I began training again the next day. The Olympics were less than a year away and I badly wanted to go to Sydney.

5

Sydney in Sight

As the 2000 season approached all I could think about was qualification for the Olympics. I reckoned that I needed to win the National Championships over 20km, that if I was number one in Ireland then even if I didn't make the 'A' standard automatic qualification time, which was 83 minutes back then, I might get to the Olympics on the 'B' standard time of 85 minutes.

Training and diet were really beginning to interest me but my own training was still mainly based on hearsay, from what other fellas said they were doing. As ridiculous as it seems now, my obsession at the time was about doing 100 miles a week (or 160km in today's money) and I can remember coming home from one of Mick Lane's training camps in Limerick and totting up my mileage to realise that I only had 99 miles done. I got changed back into my gear and literally went the extra mile to get the hundred done.

My fastest time for 20km up until then was 86' 30" but after the improvements I had made the year before I thought it was realistic that I could improve a minute and a half and get the 'B' standard in almost a full season.

A lot of the older, more experienced guys with the same Olympic dreams as everyone else were back on the domestic scene at the start of the year but when I won the 5km National Indoor title for the third year in a row that February, it told me I had the beating of all of them, over a short distance anyway.

Shortly afterwards, I flew to the Isle of Man with some of the Irish walkers to compete in my first 20km walk of the year. We organised the trip ourselves, staying with local families to keep the costs down. As usual, I lined up with a blank stare on my face, so focused on my own performance that I was borderline aggressive to anyone who even looked crooked at me. British walker Chris Maddox, who had been to five Olympics and beat us all in Leamington Spa the year before, was the biggest name on the start sheet and I was absolutely intent on showing him who was boss and nailing him to the road. But he completely threw me when he came over and patted me on the shoulder before the start.

'You're the future,' he said, with his hand outstretched for me to shake. 'You're going to be great!'

As it turns out, Chris is a lovely guy, a gentleman, but his gesture that day surprised me.

'Fuck!' I thought as I reluctantly shook hands with him. 'He's after throwing me here. Why is he so nice? I'm not meant to like this fucker!'

As usual, I started off fast and ended up walking 84 minutes, lapping Maddox on the short 800m circuit, beating all of the British seniors in the process and getting my 'B' standard time for the Olympics.

Even though I still didn't record a time fast enough to qualify automatically for Sydney when I won in the National 20km Championships in the Phoenix Park a few weeks later, in beating Jamie and Andy Drake who had come over from England in search of an Olympic qualifying time, I had now beaten all of the other Irish walkers and most of the English guys. I was only twenty-two, and was hoping to get selected off the back of those performances.

Some of Mick's group went back to Fuengirola for another warm-weather camp around Easter with Gillian and I training really hard on a loop around our apartment block. On one of those walks under the scorching Spanish sun it was so hot that I took my singlet off and dropped it on the ground beside a wall in an effort to stay cool.

Back then I only had one or two singlets, so I was devastated when I got back to find it was missing. I searched all around for it but by the time we went out to dinner that evening there was still no sign of it. As we were walking along the promenade though, I noticed a big hairy street seller squeezed into my singlet. He was that big, it looked like he had sprayed it on.

'Gillian,' I said, growing animated. 'He has my fucking singlet on!'

Gillian had been around long enough to know what was coming next so she continued walking as I went over to him.

'That's mine,' I said gesturing to the singlet he was bulging out of. 'No!'

'That's mine. My top. That's my top. Take it off!'

The longer he denied the fact that he was wearing my training top, the more animated I became, until I was almost jumping around him like a Jack Russell at his ankles. Although he was probably three times my size, he eventually gave in and peeled it off and handed it to me. The singlet was so smelly that I threw it in the bin on the way to dinner but I sat down to eat satisfied with the fact that I had got it back.

In June, Gillian, Olive, Jamie and I made up the Irish team for the European Cup in Eisenhüttenstadt, Germany. Pierce was suffering from chronic fatigue syndrome at the time but came over to support Jamie and the rest of us.

Having experienced Mézidon-Canon and Gothenburg, I began to take these big international races very seriously and about a week before any big race I would completely shut down, get nervous and was like a briar to be around. I was on edge all the time and every effort was made to save energy in the days leading up to an event, even down to the scenario where, for some reason I can no longer remember, I wouldn't have a hot shower the day before the race for fear it would zap my energy. By the time race day came I was like a coiled spring and as soon as the starter's pistol fired, all of that energy was unleashed and I was gone like a rocket.

Nowadays, people sit down and talk about sports science: numbers, heart rates and lactate thresholds. Back then I had one tactic: go! And go hard! My thinking was that if I went off fast in every race then, bit by bit, I would last longer and longer at the front and eventually I would still be there at the end of the race.

My plan was to build endurance onto speed as I got older. I couldn't understand the big mystery. If I could stay with the leaders for 10km now, I thought, then next year it'll be 13km, the following year it'll be 16km and after that I'll win a medal. People were telling me I was stupid but year upon year, slowly but surely, my times began to drop.

The first few kilometres always give me a buzz and in Germany I walked the opening 10km in a new personal best of 40 minutes, not far off the leaders, the best walkers in the world. I knew that my good start meant that, if I could keep it up, I had a great chance of getting an Olympic 'A' standard time but while I was getting stronger and could hold the top guys for 10 or 12km, when the crunch came in the last quarter of the race I still hadn't developed enough to be able to stay with them and began to fade dramatically.

As Pierce was out injured, he was helping team manager Ray Flynn on the table at the side of the road and was handing me drinks but back then I didn't know how important fluids were and didn't drink as much as I should have.

Although an automatic Olympic qualifying time was touch and go, there was no such thing as advice from the Irish coaching staff apart from the odd roar of 'Go!', 'more arms,' or 'faster!' from Ray. After 15km I knew that a minute or so would be the difference between my going to Sydney and watching the Olympics at home in Cork on television, so I fought to hang on inside the top ten walkers. But I died another death in the last few kilometres, drifting down the field to seventeenth place. With 2km to go I was suffering like a dog but another glance at my watch told me that if I didn't collapse between there and the line, then I was almost certain of a qualifying time for the Olympics.

Those last 2km were absolute hell. I was hanging on for dear life. I was shattered as I crossed the line, completely broken up, but I had finished fifteen seconds inside the 'A' standard required for an automatic place on the start line in Sydney. I'd often seen fellas collapsing and falling on their knees after a race and always thought, 'Have a bit of respect for yourself. I'd never do that.' But I came very close in Eisenhüttenstadt.

It was hard to take it in at first; that there could be no question marks, no politics, no 'B' time needed. There were no 'ifs' or 'buts' about it. I had met the 'A' standard criteria for qualification and was going to the Olympics. I had done it and I had done it myself. It was an unbelievable feeling. I remember thinking afterwards, 'This is it. There is nothing else I can do in life. I'm after achieving everything. I've made it!'

Gillian put in a marvellous performance to finish fourteenth in the women's race and both she and Olive also earned Olympic qualification that day. To have three walkers qualify for the Olympics was monumental for the sport in Ireland and a big group of us hit the town and partied the night away afterwards.

We didn't get back to our rooms until around four in the morning, but the buzz of Olympic qualification mixed with the alcohol in my bloodstream meant that the next two hours were spent staring at the ceiling in a blissful stupor until it was time to get up. In spite of having just done the 20km walk and qualified for the Olympics, I had planned to train the next day and as I lay there I thought to myself, 'Why not train with a bunch of people around you?' Thus, with no pre-planned intention, I found myself lining up for the 50km walk at around eight o'clock that morning, still drunk.

At the start line I was physically wrecked, but so happy with myself that I was still on a complete high. I was extremely hyper during the warm-up, whooping and chattering as I paced up and down among the other athletes. I thought it was hilarious but others obviously thought, 'This guy is absolutely crazy.' Although there was no malice in it, I probably drove Jamie mad as he tried to get into the zone and focus on getting his own qualification time. Maybe the laughing and joking relaxed Jamie a little bit though, because he brought the Irish contingent in Sydney up to four when he became the first Irish walker ever to qualify for the 50km race. When the race started, I led for a good 15km, still drunk and buzzing from the night before, before eventually dropping out exhausted.

I was at the finish when Jamie crossed the line, where best friend and now coach Pierce was waiting for him. When he came through the line Jamie was in an awful state. He was wheelchaired off in floods of tears, put on a stretcher and put on a drip in the medical tent where Pierce, who was also crying, stood by his bed for the next two hours.

The duo were like brothers but while it was very emotional to see them crying with joy after Jamie's qualification, I thought it was hilarious. Big fans of *Father Ted*, they would call each other Ted and Teddy and I couldn't stop laughing when they started blabbing through the tears.

'Good man, Ted. You did it!'

'This one's for you, Teddy!'

That night we went out again, this time with the rest of the squad, but while Jamie and Pierce were getting very serious and philosophical about things and how they would approach the lead-up to the Olympics, I hadn't even thought of any of that and was just out for the party, which continued when I came home from Germany. Back in Cork I joined my buddies from Ballyphehane – Gordon O'Mahony, John Costelloe, Kevin Ward, Barry O'Donovan and Paddy Maher – in Youghal for a few days.

Like the *Father Ted* episode where an over-exuberant Father Noel Furlong, played by Graham Norton, takes a youth group on holiday, we all bundled into the little caravan usually reserved for our family holidays in the summer. Here, I spent the next few mornings walking and the evenings partying. We lit bonfires on the beach and went on the beer most afternoons and for a while it was nice to be just one of the lads again.

A week later, though, I was back training really hard and gone to ground. My qualification was big news for my club in Togher and they put on a fund-raising night for me, which took the pressure off me financially and enabled me to focus more on my training. With a few quid more in my pocket I didn't need to worry about paying for the extra squad training camps that Mick Lane held in Limerick or any equipment I needed in the run-up to the Olympics.

Having coached Jimmy McDonald to sixth place in Barcelona and now with three more athletes qualified for Sydney, Mick's stock was rising dramatically in Irish athletics. The environment and the people I was around on those camps was great and a lot of the training was really good but soon after we all qualified for Sydney, Mick upped the ante and we started doing different sessions, some of which I didn't entirely agree with.

We usually trained twice on a Friday. In the morning, he had us doing 20 x 800m efforts on the track where, in between each repetition, he'd have us lifting weights, doing press-ups and other mad stuff. Whenever I questioned him as to why we were doing anything he would simply reply, 'You'll see!'

All the runners would be on the track looking at us as if we were lunatics. Even though I wasn't that clued-in to training programmes and knew nothing about periodisation — building training sessions towards a specific target — I knew this was crazy stuff and was half-embarrassed to be doing it. We'd do another session in the evening with weights strapped on each wrist until we hit the last 3km. Even on these last sessions, sometimes I'd be banging out those last 3km in 11' 20", which meant I was setting a new Irish 3km record in training most weeks. I would then go to a competition the next morning and walk a 10km race, or if there was no competition Gillian and I would do a two-hour walk for training.

On a Saturday in June, just seven weeks or so before the Olympics, I entered a 50km walk in the Phoenix Park in Dublin, with the aim of completing the first 35km for training. After lapping the whole field, I went through the 35km mark in a time of 2 hours 31 minutes. Knowing that I was very close to world record pace for the 50km, I wanted to carry on and go for the record and Mick Lane had to literally drag me off the course for fear I would do damage to myself.

When I got home that night I went to another fund-raiser in a local GAA club, had a few pints with my friends and fell into bed at around three in the morning. I got up four hours later, drove to Tullamore and broke the Irish record for 3km in a race on the track there. The following Sunday I smashed the Irish under-23 10km record in the National Under-23 Championships in Tullamore again.

It was my third Irish record in a week and I was absolutely flying but my training was all over the place and, with little time for rest and recovery, I broke down and got sick after the Under-23 Championships, which meant I couldn't walk in the Senior Championships in Santry the following week.

With the Irish team due to fly to Australia the following day, I had to turn up at the National Championships and tell the head of the sport's national governing body, Bord Lúthchleas na hÉireann (BLE), Chris Wall, that I wasn't able to compete.

I was gutted but at the time but there was a massive rift between BLE and the Olympic Council of Ireland (OCI) so my withdrawal didn't go down too well with Wall, who totally dismissed me.

'You're Hickey's boy now,' he sneered, referring to Pat Hickey, the then chairman of the OCI. I was livid but had to bite my lip and hang around the track all day as the other events went on.

That night I went out drinking with Jamie and Pierce and we arrived in Dublin Airport the next morning, hung-over, ahead of the long flight to Australia.

When we arrived Down Under, the OCI put all of the Irish athletes into a holding camp in Newcastle, 160km north of Sydney, for three weeks prior to the start of the Games. We all got vouchers which entitled us to eat in the local restaurants for free and the whole team would head out on a Saturday night for a few drinks. It was like a holiday for me.

I was twenty-two years old, with no idea what to do in the lead-up to the Games. The journey to Australia hadn't been kind to me and for a long time I found it very tough getting over the jet lag and found it hard to gauge my form. Not having a proper day-to-day training plan didn't help either. In fact, I had no training plan at all while I was there.

Mick would tell me on the day what I was to do, or sometimes I'd jump in on one of Gillian's sessions. I trained very hard but with nothing else to go on, I worked off her plan. Looking back now, there was too much distraction in Newcastle and we spent way too long there. Still unsure as to whether I had recovered from the jet lag, my first way of testing whether I was over it or not was to walk in a 5km running race on the local track. After doing a pretty good time in the race, I persuaded myself that I had recovered but in reality I had just mangled myself and dug myself into a deeper hole.

A week or so before the Games began we took a two and a half hour bus trip to Sydney and entered the Olympic village for the first time. The first thing I noticed about Sydney was the heat and humidity there compared to the cooler climate of Newcastle. The village itself was very impressive but we were all staying in prefabricated Portakabin-type accommodation with no air conditioning and it was boiling in the rooms.

I was rooming with John McAdorey, a 100m sprinter from Ballymena, a lovely fella. We had to sleep with the windows open every night and still woke up stuck to our beds the next morning.

Even though it was my first time to be there, being in the Olympic village never fazed me. Some of the lads went off one day to meet Mohamed Ali, who was a big hero of mine, but I didn't go with them because I was focused on my race. The only famous person I recall seeing was Ethiopian long-distance legend Haile Gebrselassie in the athletes' dining hall and I remember thinking how small he was.

Just days before the Olympics, I walked a 10km session alongside compatriots Mark Carroll and David Matthews, who were both running. I walked that 10km in 41 minutes, which is ridiculously fast for the week of an Olympic race. The next day, on the Thursday before the Olympic walk, Mick had me doing a 6km split session on the track, where the first 3km were done fast and the final 3km were done as hard as I possibly could, at Irish record pace.

In the days before the race itself, I went into shutdown mode and can remember chastising myself for feeling ungrateful as I stood among the Irish athletes at the opening ceremony in the Olympic Stadium. Rather than savouring the atmosphere, saving as much energy as possible before the race was my top priority and all I wanted to do was go to bed and rest instead of standing in the middle of the track watching the ceremony.

On the morning of the race, Mick brought me into a room on my own underneath the Olympic Stadium and lay me down on a massage table. In an effort to calm me down and get me ready, he began doing these sort of hypnotic relaxation techniques he had picked up somewhere along the way but as I lay on the table I was thinking, 'I don't want to be doing this at all. I'm getting ready to go to war.' My mind wasn't open to it at all and all I wanted to do was get out and warm up.

I eventually got out onto the road outside the stadium and was warming up when I heard a familiar voice calling my name. I turned around and saw 'Dealer', my old club mate from Togher, behind a fence waving an Irish flag. I went over and chatted to him and immediately felt like I was back in Cork Institute of Technology or the Mardyke, racing at home. Chatting to Dealer calmed me down a bit and made me feel like it was just another race as I lined up for my first Olympics.

When the starter's gun fired, I took the lead in the stadium. After 3 or 4km I was involved in a bit of a fracas with a fella from Belarus who clipped off me and nearly fell over. He threw a few obscenities at me but got as many back, which made me feel a bit more like I belonged in the race.

With the temperature soaring, I hung off the back of the lead group for about 10km but just 2km later was really starting to struggle. Just getting to the finish line that day remains one of the hardest things I have ever done. I still hadn't learned the importance of drinking during the race; the heat and humidity of Sydney absolutely drained me and I just didn't have anything left in the tank.

I thought I was going to die in those last 2km, which probably took me ten minutes to complete. Absolutely shattered, I crossed the line in a time of 86 minutes, a full three minutes slower than my best time, twenty-seven places and seven minutes behind gold medal winner Robert Korzeniowski of Poland. I was in such a state physically that I was put on a drip immediately and kept in the medical centre for hours afterwards until I rehydrated.

Later that evening, people were congratulating me on a good performance, reminding me that I was young, that it was my first Olympics and that I would improve on my twenty-eighth place over time. But I didn't want to hear it. For me, that was a cop-out. I knew I was capable of far better and something had gone wrong in both the race itself and in my planning for it.

It dawned on me that while I had spent time at training camps with the Irish squad, nobody really knew what I was doing when I wasn't on those camps. While I had a huge hunger to train and get better, I had no direction, no accountability to anybody in BLE or anywhere else. All it would have taken was for someone to sit down and chat to me in the lead-up to the Olympics to realise that I actually hadn't a clue what I was doing.

By the time the closing ceremony came around I had relaxed a bit and upon seeing Robert Korzeniowski – who had also won gold in the 50km walk – in the track centre, I approached him, asked him for his autograph and got my photograph taken with him. Up close, the Pole was the toughest-looking competitor I had ever seen. He was even a little bit smaller than me, which inspired me to come back to the Olympics again.

In typical Irish fashion, I stayed on in Australia for a few weeks afterwards, doing the backpacker thing and going to Fraser Island with 400m sprinters Rob Daly, Paul Opperman and a few others. But pretty soon I started to feel unfit, so I changed my ticket to go home early and start training again for the 2001 season.

6

Korzeniowski and the Kid

Having stayed on in Australia and partied for a few weeks, my instinct kicked in after a while and with a World Championship coming up at the end of the new season, I began to feel guilty.

My mentality at the time was that I needed to punish myself back into fitness and so, overweight and only off the plane two days, I decided to enter a 5km road race around the Marina in Cork, where I would be way out of my comfort zone, thinking it would humiliate me enough into copping myself on and knuckling back down to training.

My plan backfired when I actually won the race and, thinking I was invincible and didn't need to train as hard as everyone else, I celebrated with another night out. I won a 4km race in Belgooly, north of Kinsale, on St Stephen's Day that year. First prize was a microwave, which I sold, and spent the hundred quid I got for it on another couple of nights out in Cork.

Now that I was the big Olympic superstar around town, I also decided it was time to move out of my parents' house. With the Olympics over, I think my dad was expecting me to see the light and take up a 'proper' job and it seemed that every time he came home from work, I was still lying on the couch recovering from training.

Qualifying for the Olympics saw my Sports Council grant go up from €3,000 to €12,000 for 2001 so I moved into an old Georgian house on Newenham Terrace, just a few kilometres away from home and a bit closer to the city centre. The three floors of the house had been converted into apartments and mine had two rooms, a kitchen-cum-sitting-room and a decent-sized double bedroom with an en-suite bathroom.

I was very organised in those early months. Everything was spotless and, with no distractions, I trained properly and used my newly qualified skills as a physio to make a few extra quid in the evenings. I won my first walk of the year, the National Senior Indoor Championships, for the fourth year in a row in February 2001 but even though I was now an established senior walker, I still had no real plan or training programme for the rest of the year.

Shortly after that race, I was looking for training tips on race walking when I came upon the website of Olympic champion Robert Korzeniowski. Innocently, I reckoned that as I had met him at the closing ceremony in Sydney and had my photo taken with him, Korzeniowski would remember me so I set about sending him an email.

Email was still pretty new in Ireland at the time and as I didn't know much about it, I got one of the lads from Cummins Sports, John Mullen, to set me up with an email address. As 'plumsucker', among other things, was one his favourite terms of endearment for me, John opened an account for me at plumsucker@yahoo.com.

Thinking nothing of this, plumsucker from Cork then sent the double Olympic champion a long email telling him that he was a big hero of mine and asking him for some advice. I never really expected him to answer my email, let alone phone me, which is exactly what he did that Valentine's Day.

'Hello?'

'Haylo, Robert,' came the thick Polish accent down the line. 'This is Robert Korzeniowski.'

'What?'

'This is Robert Korzeniowksi . . . '

'Will ya fuck off! Who is it, boy? Pierce, is that you?'

'No. It is Robert Korzeniowski.'

'It is yeah, come on, boy, who is it?

'It is Robert Korzeniowski. I got your email . . . '

It took a while, but the penny eventually dropped that it actually was the Polish legend on the other end of the line. I was on the phone to the double Olympic champion!

After some innocent questions about how fast and how often he trained, Korzeniowski told me that he was going to be based in Johannesburg in South Africa with the Polish athletics team that March.

'You are welcome to come along and train weeth us if you like?'

I couldn't believe it! If I could have bitten his hand off down the phone line I would have. Training with the Olympic champion? I didn't even know where Johannesburg was or how much it would cost to get there but I knew I was definitely going.

The following week, I went back to the Isle of Man to race in a 20km walk. The day before the race, I told Mick Lane that Korzeniowski had phoned my house and invited me to train with him in South Africa. Mick burst out laughing and no matter what I said, he wouldn't believe me. I think he spent the next few days asking the others which one of them was winding me up.

In the hope of setting a new personal best, I roped British walker Andy Drake into being my pacemaker for the first half of the race, completely sucked him in by telling him how fast he was, and he tore off from the gun before he completely blew up after 10km.

Andy was a doctor, a really intelligent guy but when his legs went and he drifted down the field, I remember laughing to myself, thinking that he was supposed to be the smart fella. I lapped Jamie two or three times and beat him by ten minutes, setting a new Irish record for 20km while Gillian did the same in her race.

Shortly after I got home to Cork, there was an email from Robert Korzeniowksi waiting to see if 'plumsucker' was coming to the training camp a couple of weeks later. I went to the travel agent, arranged my flight, changed my email address to a slightly less moronic one and sent him back confirmation that not only was I coming over, but both Gillian and Jamie would be coming too. Because I changed my email address, though, he never got the correspondence telling him that we were coming so the three of us arrived in South Africa a few weeks later with absolutely no idea where we were supposed to meet up with him.

Having landed in Johannesburg, we found out that the Polish athletics team trained in Potchefstroom, two or three hours' drive away. After hiring a taxi, we arrived at the training centre in Potchefstroom to find that all of the Polish athletes were based there, except the walkers. After much discussion, one of them rang the Polish Federation for us to find out where Robert Korzeniowski was training and conveyed the message that three Irish walkers had just arrived looking for him.

A series of phone calls back and forth to Poland followed and ended with Korzeniowski telling them to give us his address in Melville, a suburb of Johannesburg, two hours back in the direction we had just come from.

A few minutes later we were standing outside the centre with no idea how we were going to get to Melville when we saw a guy get into a car nearby. Although he wasn't driving a taxi, we wandered over and asked him if he would drive us to Johannesburg for a hundred quid. While Jamie and I thought nothing of this, Gillian was way more mature than us and wasn't keen on jumping into the back of a strange car with a strange man in a strange country.

At the time, Sacha Baron Cohen's Ali G character was really big on television and Jamie and I started asking the guy questions from the show as we drove along, one of which was whether it was okay to shoot somebody in South Africa. In answer to our question, our new-found chauffeur leaned down and reached under his seat as he drove, pulling out a huge shining machete with his left hand.

'No it's not legal but . . .'

While the sight of the blade terrified Gillian, Jamie and I thought this was hilarious. When our driver suddenly stopped outside a random house on the way, Gillian was convinced we were going to be kidnapped and murdered, never to be seen again, while Jamie and I joked and laughed in the back seat.

As it turned out, the guy simply came out of the house a few minutes later and continued the journey until we eventually arrived in the little town of Melville, where a couple of minutes later we spotted Korzeniowski walking down the main street. I can only imagine what he thought of me pulling up alongside him, with two extra 'guests' complete with bags and baggage, but he took it in his stride.

He brought us to the house the Polish walkers were staying in and squeezed two single beds into a tiny room for me and Jamie while Gillian was given a bed in the same room as Korzeniowski's sister Silvia, another walker. Robert and the rest of the Polish athletes had their own rooms and there were also two coaches and a physio staying in the house.

We stayed in Melville for twenty-two days and I learned more about training, technique, diet and recovery in those twenty-two days than I had done in my entire walking career up until then. The Poles had a complete training programme tailor-made to their requirements and every day was fully planned out with everything done for a reason. Breakfast was at eight every morning, after which they all went back to bed for an hour. There was a meeting of coaches, physios, athletes and helpers every morning before training at ten to explain the purpose of each day's session.

At home, I had been used to doing three-hour walks with no drinks and just some emergency money in my pocket. I'd get complete sugar crashes and go into a shop to buy a bar of chocolate to get me home. I thought this made me tough but I soon learned that it was all misdirected stupid stuff.

The Poles had drinks made up before every single walk, with people organised to hand them out along the route. They had somebody doing video analysis of their technique every time they trained and had coaches following them on bikes. In the afternoon the whole squad went back to bed. Even for easy 6km and 8km walks in the evenings they were doing drinks and video analysis again.

Korzeniowski was meticulous about the importance of hydration, nutrition, rest and recovery and it soon rubbed off on us. When he saw us train with no drinks for the first couple of days, like we did at home, he went crazy.

'This ees ridiculous! You need to keep the tank full,' he said. 'You don't let a car run out of petrol. Your body is the same.'

Keen to learn as much as he could, Jamie hit Korzeniowski with a barrage of questions every evening over dinner. Within days he had made great friends with all of the Polish athletes. I had no interest in making friends. I just wanted to be better than all of them. In my head, training with Korzeniowski was my ticket to getting better. He was the reigning Olympic champion but, to me, he was old and slow. I was faster than him over 5km and I wanted to take him down over the longer distances too. I was mad to impress him and did every training session he did, but while Korzeniowski and the rest of the Poles had a long-term plan, every single day was a race to me.

I did a 30km walk with him one day and never opened my mouth for the whole session. After 28km I suddenly put the boot down and went off, dropping everybody. Jamie was laughing at me while some of the Poles who had finished shorter sessions were waiting on me coming in and they were clapping and taking the piss.

'Well done. You beat the Olympic champion. You are our new champion!'

I couldn't understand it. In my head this was what I needed to do to get better but the Irish trio were considered to be Jack-the-lads on the camp and I was soon seen as the loose cannon and the lunatic of the group. Jamie thought it was the funniest thing ever but in the back of my mind I was thinking, 'You'll see who has the last laugh' and vowed that Jamie would never beat me again in a race.

Korzeniowski was measuring his effort off heart rates and blood lactate and slowly building a foundation upon which to stack the blocks of more intense training. I had no idea about any of this and simply went flat out, all day, every day. Sure, I could go out and drop him in some of those 30km sessions, but, in hindsight, my lactic was probably 6.1 at the end of it while his was maybe only 2.2, which meant that while my legs were burning from lactic acid build-up and I was gasping for breath at the end, he had been walking within himself, at a purposely comfortable level, so he didn't allow that to happen.

While he was developing himself, putting all of his training blocks together scientifically to build a foundation, I was destroying myself and it wasn't long until my house came crumbling down. In our first week in South Africa I walked 120km. In the second week I did 180km but after 77km of the third week I was in bed for three days on antibiotics.

The biggest thing I learned over there was that anyone could handle the first couple of weeks' training but the last week was when the real quality came in. By then, when all of the aerobic work, all of the middle-ground stuff is done, when you're fully adapted, the last week is where you had to put in four-minute kilometres and do the hard work.

By that stage though, I was on the broad of my back in bed, having totally overcooked it in the first fortnight. Even though I wasn't able to finish off the camp, Robert could see how driven I was and how badly I wanted to learn. A rough diamond, I had put myself out there and if the lads laughed at me, then big deal. I showed him that I had the appetite to work and wasn't afraid to go hard, and he invited me to train with him again later that summer.

A couple of weeks after coming home from South Africa, I travelled to Sligo, where I stayed in Ray Flynn's house ahead of the 20km National Championships. I won the title race in a time of 83 minutes, beating Jamie by around four minutes in the process, with youngster Colin Griffin third a couple of minutes further back while Gillian beat Olive and Ann McGill to take the women's championship.

Two weeks later I raced in Leamington Spa again, this time beating world record holder Julio Martinez and recording a time of 81' 11", lopping a minute and a half off Jimmy McDonald's old Irish record. Not only had I set another new Irish record for the 20km walk but I had also won £1,000 sterling in prize money, which would help me get to my next training camp, so I celebrated with a few pints at the banquet afterwards. In the summer, I travelled to the

French National Altitude Training Centre in Font-Romeu to train with Robert Korzeniowski and the Polish national squad again.

As in South Africa, Gillian and Jamie tagged along too but this time Mick also travelled with us. Even though the nucleus of the Irish walking team was represented in Font-Romeu there was no support from Athletics Ireland. As usual, we all paid our own way and basically piggybacked on the Polish squad's camp.

Although our coach Mick had now jumped on the bandwagon, he was too stubborn to ask questions and learn from the Polish squad while we were out there, possibly for fear of looking stupid as national coach.

First opened in 1967 to allow French athletes to train at altitude ahead of the Mexico Olympics, Font-Romeu is surrounded by woodlands and countryside. As well as a running track, gym and swimming pool, it has loads of trails and circuits to walk on but with Mick there, we were soon back doing some of the stuff we did at home.

When I saw Robert Korzienwoski laughing when he saw us doing weights on the track one day, however, I knew something was wrong.

'You know, Robbie, eighty-one minutes is very good but, for you, this is not your potential,' he said one day out of the blue. 'You need a plan. I don't know what plan, but any plan.'

I had continued to improve slowly every year but I couldn't believe this guy who had achieved everything, who wasn't Irish and therefore had no agenda, was telling me that I could walk even faster. With his base work done earlier in the year, Korzeniowski had gone up another level in training while we still seemed to be doing the same old stuff.

I came home from Font-Romeu, raced the National 10km Championships in 38' 44", the fastest time in the world so far that year, and in May went into the European Cup in Dudince, Slovakia in really good form. After a fast start I had covered the opening 10km in 39' 30" and was lying in eighth place among the best walkers in the world. But I had raced too much in the run-up to the Europeans and blew up again, drifting to eighteenth place by the time I crossed the finish line in 83' 57".

While my placing was an improvement on the previous year, I knew I was capable of way better and was distraught at the finish. Pierce, though, couldn't understand my reaction.

'You have to be ecstatic that you were up there with the best walkers in the world for 10km,' he said. In my head I was thinking, 'What a fucking idiot.' I was genuinely gutted. Pierce and Jamie always had this thing about being in the lead group, being seen on TV with the lead group, being seen with the stars. I walked back to the changing rooms with Andreas Erm who had just finished third and was telling me that he lost concentration in the last few kilometres and should have finished second. The lads couldn't believe the German, who they had built up as a superstar, was talking to me.

Having seen me race and train, Korzeniowski began to take more of an interest in me, started to take me under his wing and give me snippets of advice whenever he saw something wrong. The World Championships were held in Canada that year and as Edmonton was at altitude, he advised me to get out there eight or nine days early so that I could adjust to the different time zone and acclimatise to the altitude before the race.

I informed Athletics Ireland of my plan but they told me that they wouldn't be paying for any of that, so I booked my own flights and, a week and a half before the championships, jumped on a plane to Canada. With no accommodation booked prior to my departure, I had no idea where I was going to stay. I had requested an aisle seat on the plane so that I could get up and stretch whenever I needed to. Seven and a half hours later, we landed in Toronto.

Resplendent in a white Athletics Ireland top (which I had spilled coffee down the front of during the flight), I stood on my own in the arrivals hall and waited for my connecting flight to Edmonton. All of my luggage had gone through, however, and I had nothing else to change into. I had also left my wallet in one of my checked bags. My Visa card didn't work in the restaurant so I was stuck in the airport on my own for the next six or seven hours with nothing to eat or drink.

By the time I got on the connecting flight I was tired, hungry and looking a bit the worse for wear so I was in no mood for conversation when this big Canadian guy sat down next to me.

'Hey man, you're from home!'

His accent saw me dismiss him straight away.

'No, boy. I'm from Cork . . . in Ireland.'

He didn't take the hint.

'Yeah! I'm Irish as well!'

In foul humour by this stage, all I wanted was to be left alone, so I pretended to nod off. But the Canadian kept asking questions.

'Do you mind if we swap seats? I have a problem with my back.'

In my head the answer was 'Look, I'm having a shitty day. I've to walk in the World Championships next week. I reserved this seat especially, paid extra, so that I can get up and stretch, so NO, you can't have my fucking seat!' but what came out was typically Irish.

'Yeah, no problem.'

The Canadian began to tell me how his ancestors came over from Ireland and settled in Newfoundland, a place I hadn't heard of before, and he asked me what I was going to Canada for.

'I've the World Athletics Championships in Edmonton.'

'Man, I'm from Edmonton.'

'Oh, yeah? Will it be tough for me to get a hotel when we land at two or three in the morning?'

'Man, you don't need a hotel. You can come stay with me.'

Having matured just a little since hitching a ride with a complete stranger in South Africa, I began to wonder why this guy would want me to stay in his house and couldn't come up with anything that didn't involve duct tape and a shallow grave in his back garden.

As soon as I ate something, I pretended to go to sleep and hoped he'd forget about it by the time we got to Edmonton. When the plane landed I waited for him to get his bag out of the overhead compartment and gave him a few minutes' head start on the way to the luggage carousel. I had just grabbed my bag off the conveyer belt when I got a tap on the shoulder.

'Man, it's all okay. I just spoke to my wife. We have a spare room.'

For a few seconds I stood there wondering what I was going to do. I sized him up and asked myself whether I would be able to get away from this over-friendly giant if anything happened in the car.

Ken O'Neill turned out to be one of the nicest guys I have ever met and I stayed in his house for ten days before those World Championships. He and his wife fed me and looked after me and brought me to tracks in the area to train while their son came out with me on his bike and did my drinks. I even gave him my camcorder and he taped my training so that I could keep an eye on my technique. In return I got them tickets to the closing ceremony and brought them to meet the Irish team.

After walking so fast over 10km earlier in the season, I was convinced I would be able to stay with the leaders until the end of the race but when things heated up in the last quarter of the race I didn't have the change of gears to stay with them and found myself in a savage personal battle with a Belarusian and an Italian for a place in the top fifteen.

I finished fourteenth in Edmonton, the best result of the Irish athletics squad and a big improvement on my twenty-eighth place in Sydney the year before, but at the end of the race, I collapsed and vomited pure black. The Irish team doctor on the day told me that that I had pushed myself so hard that I had emptied the contents of my stomach.

My fourteenth pace saw me heralded as the 'great young Irish fella' again but when Robert Korzeniowski saw me afterwards he asked me what had happened, what had gone wrong. Up until then, I thought I had got a decent result but Robert had trained with me, knew what I was capable of and said that he thought fourteenth place was rubbish. I told him that I had walked 38' 40" for 10km in the National Championships a few weeks earlier – a phenomenal time – but he just brushed it off, absolutely dismissed it.

'Speak to me about the World Championships,' he said.

At first I wasn't happy with his comments, but deep down I knew Robert was right and he made me have a close look at everything I was doing again. The message was loud and clear: nothing else mattered except the biggest race of the season.

When I went over everything in my head, I realised that I had peaked too soon, too early in the year. My periodisation was all wrong. Instead of one big block of really hard training, I was tapering off four earlier competitions, which meant I hadn't really got enough hard training in and had no base built up.

After Edmonton ended the season, we had an unofficial Irish team training camp in Limerick again, with the usual group of walkers in October. Only back in pre-season training two weeks, we had a 30km walk the day after doing 4km intervals on the track. I did my last 20km in under ninety minutes. Not many Irish walkers had done that in a race and here I was doing it after two weeks of training in the middle of winter, so I knew something was wrong with my whole training plan.

I questioned Mick Lane as to why I was able to do it that fast. It was wintertime and I could have been out roaming Cork with my friends at the weekends so if I was going to be doing 30km training instead I wanted to know why I was doing it in that time and what the reasoning behind it was.

I had plenty of questions: why 30km? Why not 20km? Why not 40km? Why had I walked 10km in 38 minutes in the summer but in Edmonton I could only do 20km in 85' 00", almost four minutes off my personal best time? Why was I training so hard in October?'

When he simply replied, 'You'll see,' I began to wonder if Mick actually knew the answers himself. I knew I was going way too well for the off season and decided there would be no harm in going out that evening.

That night, youngster Colin Griffin and I went to the bar in the hotel where we gatecrashed a wedding and had great craic. When we got back to the room in the early hours, Colin was in the process of getting changed for bed when I pushed him out into the hallway and locked the door. The commotion outside woke Pat Ryan, who opened his door and saw Colin standing there in the nip. There was war the next morning.

Mick brought us both into the middle of the track and gave us a bollocking. While Mick had been coaching me for two years, I felt he still didn't know anything about me. Apart from training camps, he didn't know how I lived day in day out, how I trained on my own in Cork like an animal for most of the year. Now I had come away for a weekend and for once I had let my guard down and was getting strips torn off me in the middle of the track while the others looked on.

That was a defining moment for me. I left Limerick that day determined to show those coaches how good I was. I never contacted them again afterwards.

7

Burning the Candle at Both Ends

With winter looming and no racing to be done, I began to realise that living on my own in Newenham Terrace wasn't all it was cracked up to be. Sitting around the flat all day on my own after training was slowly dragging me down and for a bit of company and someone to chat to, I had Dealer move in around Christmas time 2001.

Dealer was good company and really livened the place up, but maybe he was a bit too lively in the end. Up until his arrival, I had never been into the nightclub scene and if I went out, which wasn't often, it was usually for a few pints with my friends from Ballyphehane and I'd be home before closing time. Dealer, though, was a bit of a party animal. A trainee architect, he could survive on a few hours' sleep and pretty soon he had persuaded me to join him on his adventures in clubland.

Within weeks, I had easily slipped into Dealer's routine of going out and partying all night and for the next three or four months, the weekend started on Thursday and ended on Monday. I knew this wasn't the lifestyle of an Olympic athlete but to compensate for my late nights, I'd stay in bed until midday, making sure I got ten hours' sleep before going training, often for very hard 30km sessions, in the afternoons.

With no coach any more, I tried to copy some of the stuff Robert Korzeniowski did on his training camps but I didn't understand how to put all of the different phases of training together and my 'training programme', if you could call it that, was merely a case of throwing a lot of muck at a wall and hoping some of it would stick.

Even though I was burning the candle at both ends, my season didn't suffer unduly at first and I continued to get decent results. In February 2002, I took another indoor national title, setting a new Irish record of 18' 53" in the 5km walk in Nenagh. This of course persuaded me that what I was doing was okay and with nobody around to tell me otherwise, I carried on.

I had met a girl on one of our nights out and had been meeting up with her for a few weeks but that wasn't the reason that Dealer got his cards a month or so later. With the European Championships coming up in Munich that July I needed some peace and quiet in order to knuckle down and get some proper training in. I told Dealer that the landlord wanted him out as there was supposed to be only one person staying in the flat.

In April, I competed in a Grand Prix race in Naumburg, Germany, against a world-class field that included Sydney Olympic silver medallist Noé Hernández of Mexico. I put in a great performance in Germany to smash the Irish record and finish second behind Spaniard Juan Manuel Molina in a time of 80' 25". Molina, who would go on to become European under-23 champion that July, only got away from me with a lap to go and, as the result was my first on the world stage, people were now starting to take notice of me.

A few weeks later, on the recommendation of former German 800m runner Stephan Plätzer, who was coaching his wife Kjersti Plätzer, a Norwegian race walker who had taken silver in Sydney, I went to Salzburg to train with Gillian O'Sullivan. Stephan told us Salzburg was a lovely area for training, so Gillian and I ventured out there on spec, much like our trip to South Africa a couple of years previously. We stayed in a hostel in the city centre for a couple of days before finding a farmhouse in the foothills of the Alps next to where Salzburg Football Club trained. We remained there for a couple of weeks, training in the fresh Alpine air and beautiful scenery.

We came home for the Dublin Race Walking Grand Prix on 15

June, which also counted as the Irish National 20km Championships, and I managed to win in a time of 81' 31" from Italian walker Alessandro Gandellini, with Jamie Costin third in 82' 45".

Having spread the word at the nationals about how nice Salzburg was, Gillian and I were joined by Jamie, Olive Loughnane, runner Mark Carroll and massage therapist Liam O'Reilly when we returned to Salzburg ahead of the European Championships. Mark Carroll had already been European champion over 5,000m, European indoor champion over 3,000m and had missed out a place in the final at the Sydney Olympics by just one place so he was the big star in Irish athletics at the time. The fact that he was from Knocknaheeny in Cork and had also gone to North Monastery made him an instant hero of mine.

I also knew Liam O'Reilly from his time at North Monastery, where he would arrive at the school every Wednesday to give the athletics team massage. A Garda by profession, Liam was renowned throughout Cork and further afield for his 'healing hands' and athletes and GAA players from around the country swore by his massages, or to put it correctly, swore at his massages. Originally from Bandon, Liam worked out of the front room of the Garda station in Passage West, where he was based. Dressed in full Garda uniform, he'd have the walkie-talkie strapped to his belt in case of emergency as he massaged whoever was on the table while six or seven lads lined up on chairs waiting their turn. Liam would torture every single one of them but he was very good at his job, which is why Mark always used him. If he was good enough for Mark Carroll, Liam was good enough for me. Liam was also good craic to have around and the dynamics of that group in Salzburg made that training camp one of the best I'd ever been on.

Just before the Europeans we all raced at the National Track Championships in Santry. For me, the nationals are the best event of the year in Ireland. Commentator Brian Maguire really got the atmosphere going and I always thought it was the day to showcase your event to the Irish public. There is always a good crowd in Morton Stadium.

Having left Mick, I was making out my own training programme and was still on an upward curve. I had broken the Irish 5km indoor record and the 20km outdoor record already that year and on a lovely summer's day in Santry, I won the 10km walk in another new national record of 38' 37", which was another big jump.

Mark won the 5,000m on the same day and we both ended up in Sidetracks, a nightclub in Cork, in our shorts and tracksuits later that night. The next day, out of guilt, we went down to the beach in Youghal and ran it off. Even though I hadn't done much running I tried to impress Mark and stayed with him as he ended the session with five-minute miles for the last couple of miles. It was, of course, totally the opposite of what I should have been doing only a few weeks out from the European Championships but I was feeling pretty good that year and, if Mark was doing it, I was doing it.

Before leaving for Germany and the European Championships in August, I was hit with the bombshell news that the girl I had been seeing on and off for the previous month or so was pregnant. I was going to be a father.

Still only twenty-three and never having been in a serious relationship before, the news took my breath away. I was in total shock for the first few minutes but the more I thought about it the happier I became and resolved there and then to stand by her and do everything I could to help raise the baby.

Having walked 80' 25" in Naumburg, I went into the Europeans confident that I could get a good result and took the race on from the gun. I mixed it with the Russians, the Spanish and all of the big athletes for most of the race but towards the end, Spanish walker Francisco 'Paquillo' Fernández blew the field apart and was heading for gold with Olympic bronze medallist from Sydney, Vladimir Andreyev, in clear second.

After 17.5km I was still in the fight for third and a bronze medal, but while I had been able to cover a lot of the earlier moves, when I tried to go towards the end of the race I just didn't have the pace or the power to challenge. The chase group began to splinter soon after and I finished in eighth place, just eighteen seconds off a medal.

That European Championship was a good one for our little training group from Salzburg: Mark took sixth in the 5,000m and Gillian fourth in the women's walk. Eighth place in the European Championships was a huge jump for me. I was still very young and had improved enough to be in the mix at the head of the race for almost the whole 20km. I can remember Irish team manager Patsy McGonagle giving me a big hug in the tunnel afterwards and telling me, 'You're there, you're there. You're up with them now.'

I still went home hopping, really annoyed that I got dropped out of the group in the last kilometres and it ate away at me for a couple of nights afterwards. I went out for a few drinks in Cork a night or two later and ended up going into an Internet cafe on the way home at around 3 a.m.

I was still trying to figure out why I was dropped. I had set good times all year and was beginning to think I didn't have the balls for the big championships. Andy Drake had been in the same race but finished maybe ten minutes behind us. He had a big write-up on some race-walking site explaining how the race went for him and what happened. It was very well put together and brilliantly written and he described in minute detail how his technique let him down and how this didn't happen and that didn't happen for him.

I'd had a good few pints in me and I decided to respond to Andy's article, dismissing it totally, which maybe wasn't the brightest idea. But it was inconceivable to me that he could write something to make his race look so good when he wasn't even in contention. I had mixed it with the medallists and came home pissed off after finishing eighth.

Unknown to me throughout this whole period was the fact that the girl I had been seeing in Cork and who was now carrying my baby had been on the rebound from a previous boyfriend of five years. Shortly after my return home from Germany she informed me that she had decided to go back to him and pretty much broke off all contact with me.

With the season over and nothing to stay in Cork for, I took up an invitation from Mark Carroll to go to America and, for the next six weeks or so, I lived with him in Rhode Island where he housed me and fed me and I did his massage while he trained for the New York Marathon. Having come from similar backgrounds and grown up just a couple of miles apart, Mark and I got on brilliantly. Mark was completely driven. Better known as a 5,000m runner, he was also the Irish 10km national record holder. He was beginning to step up in distance and now had a contract to run in New York. He was training with fellow Irishmen Keith Kelly, Gareth Turnbull and a few other runners over there so I ended up training as well but with very little structure. I could do 10 miles in the morning and then go running with Mark in the evening but still had my thing about doing 100 miles a week.

When we weren't training we spent our time watching running movies and running videos. Mark was very well organised, while I still did mad things over there, including running a 5-mile road race in 24' 20" and getting friction burns on my legs for my trouble. When my legs came around again, Mark and Keith dropped me down to the start line of the Rhode Island Marathon, which I had intended to walk in for training, until I saw the entry fee.

'Lads. It's seventy dollars to enter. I'm not doing it!'

'What are you on about, boy?' asked Mark. 'You're only training, sure just jump in at the start and say nothing.'

Without really thinking it through, I lined up among the throngs of entrants with no entry fee paid and no race number on. I started very easy and was ticking along, just enjoying being able to walk in the middle of a big crowd on a nice route with plenty of supporters on the roadside.

Slowly though, I began to come through the field and after about three hours and with a mile to go I found myself walking alongside the leading local woman runner. Because she was running and I was race walking, the television cameras on motorbikes began to focus on me and followed me the whole way in to the line.

Because I had no number on me, the television commentators had no information on me apart from the fact that I was race walking, which they wouldn't have been accustomed to. I crossed the line in

3 hours 10 minutes and there was a lot of hype about how fast I had walked, even though it was just a training walk for me. As an illegal entrant to the race, I started to get worried when I was swamped by the press while the race organisers threw a medal over my head. Scouring the place for the nearest exit before somebody asked me for $70, I glanced across the barriers to see Mark and Keith falling around laughing.

I came back from America in October and I went straight back into the rut I had been in before. As I hadn't seen my friends in ages I partied with them at first but would then feel guilty for drinking and run another road race to punish myself, while the bills were mounting up in my apartment. Although my result in Edmonton had seen my Irish Sports Council grant increased to €12,000 for the 2002 season, these grants were always broken into four payments, the first of which usually didn't arrive until April, which meant that I was barely able to pay my bills for the first three months of every year.

To combat this, I got a Visa card, borrowed whatever I needed on that and paid the Visa card bill when the first instalment of the grant came through. More often than not, though, the grant would be delayed and my Visa card would be maxed out by the time it arrived, so I was robbing Peter to pay Paul for the rest of the year. When I got home from Rhode Island I was waiting for the next instalment of my grant, knowing that even when it did come I couldn't do anything with it as I still had rent, electricity, heating and a huge Visa bill to pay.

At one stage my electricity got cut off so I got an extension lead and ran it out into the hall to use the electricity from the other part of the house. My grandmother had to come in and pay my bill of around €500. Even though it was winter, my heating was rarely on as I simply couldn't afford to turn it on. In the middle of all of this, I was a couple of months away from becoming a father to a child that I had no financial means of taking care of. While I had no emotional ties any more to the girl who was about to have the baby, I was still determined to do the best for the child but couldn't see any light at the end of the tunnel.

When Liam O'Reilly called in and saw how down I was he came back a few days later with his solution.

'That's it now, Heff,' he said. 'We're gone. Florida in December, with Mark.'

'Liam,' I said. 'I can't go nowhere, boy. I've no money. I genuinely have no money.'

'No. I've the ticket bought,' he said.

Even though Mark Carroll had invited me to train with him again, in the sunshine of Florida this time, I didn't want to go to America because my head was all over the place. Liam wasn't taking no for an answer, though, and I found myself on a plane to Florida on St Stephen's Day. While I was sat in Florida knowing that a girl at home was about to have my baby a few weeks later and that the bills would still be there when I got home, my head might as well have stayed in Ireland. I felt like a complete pauper in America. I trained every day but had no interest in what I was doing and picked up an Achilles injury which only made things worse.

Unknown to Mark, Liam had also invited Jamie Costin out to train with us but Mark didn't get on with Jamie and, assuming I had invited him, went ballistic with me when he heard he was coming. Not wanting to squeal on Liam, all I could do was deny that it was me who invited Jamie without asking him, but the argument escalated until Mark and I were squaring up to each other like bantam weights and we nearly came to blows as Liam looked on. When things eventually cooled down a bit and Mark left, Liam came over to me.

'I tell you now, boy, I wouldn't have let him talk to me like that,' he said, having started the row in the first place. 'It's a good job I'm going home in the morning.'

This was news to me.

'What do you mean, you're going back to Ireland?' I asked. 'We're here for another ten days. Jamie's arriving tomorrow. I can't stay here on my own. I don't even want to be here. I'm only here because of you!'

After another argument, I eventually persuaded Liam to change my ticket and a couple of hours after Jamie arrived in Florida at Liam's invitation, to train with me, I was boarding a plane to make my way home.

8

Meghan

Upon arriving home from Florida in January 2003, I got a text from the girl I had been seeing to say that she had given birth to a baby girl. It was bad enough having to find out by text but it was the last line of that message that really ripped the ground from under my feet. '*She might not be yours.*'

Having spent the months beforehand worrying constantly if everything was going to be all right and about how I was going to be able to a proper father to this child when I could barely look after myself, I was absolutely incensed with the news. While I now had absolutely no emotional ties to the child's mother any more, I had this gut instinct that this baby was mine and that the text was just a way of fobbing me off so that I wouldn't be 'interfering' in her new life with her ex-boyfriend.

I stormed across town to my mother's house and told her the news and we decided that the only way to find out for definite whether I was the father or not was to get a DNA test, which proved easier said than done. It would take a full five months for those test results to come through and in the meantime my world was slowly unravelling.

In an effort to ease my money worries, I had moved into a two-bedroom apartment opposite the River Lee with my brother Elton at the tail end of 2002. The logic behind the move was that we could share the bills between us and that Elton would be company for me when I wasn't training. As usual though, the first three months of 2003 were spent racking up my Visa card bill as I waited for the first instalment of my Sports Council grant to come through, while Elton spent the days working and most evenings out with his new girlfriend.

As well as heating, lighting and rent, I now had solicitor's bills to pay and by the time it came to March and the first training camp of the year, I simply couldn't afford to go. I went into the local Allied Irish Bank and explained my situation: told them I'd competed at the Sydney Olympics and that I needed a small loan to tide me over until I got my grant the following month. They pretty much laughed at me.

With no money, I had to stay in Cork as most of the Irish walkers went off to altitude camp in Mexico with Robert Korzeniowski and the Polish squad on the link that I had opened. It felt like my life was over. Disillusioned and stressed out about the impending DNA results, I'd lie in bed in the morning after Elton went to work and was so depressed that I found it very hard to get up. It would have been great to get away to camp and have the routine of training every day to keep me occupied, but at home I was lost and on a rapid downward spiral. Despite my having missed the camp, nobody from Athletics Ireland lifted the phone to find out how I was doing, what I was doing, or what my plans were. Before, I had never noticed it because I was always moving forward but now I was stuck in a rut and finding it hard to move at all.

After coming home from Mexico, Jamie went to Germany at the end of April and at the Naumburg Grand Prix qualified for both the World Championships that year and the 2004 Olympics in the 50km walk. A week or so later he came down to Cork to meet his sister who was studying nursing in University College Cork. He rang me and asked to meet up with him for a drink but while I wanted to congratulate him on his Olympic qualification I had eventually got back into a decent training routine, had received the first instalment of my grant and was due to walk my first race of the year in San Giovanni, Italy, three days later, so I purposely went out with just €2 in my pocket so that I could have only one soft drink before making my excuses and going home.

When I walked into the bar, though, Jamie had a pint on the counter waiting for me. I told him I had money for one drink and that I only came in to say 'well done' but one pint led to another and we ended up going to a nightclub and then back to my house where we downed the remains of a bottle of whiskey we found in a press, despite the fact that I don't even drink whiskey.

We talked complete rubbish for the whole night and soon everything came pouring out and I got very emotional. I missed a planned training session with Gillian the next morning and having ruined my decent run-up to the race in Italy, woke up feeling so low that I might as well have had a rope around my neck. I spent the morning on the verge of tears before forcing myself out of the apartment and into town, where I bumped into Gillian. She could see that I had been out the night before and I remember feeling ashamed when I saw the look of disgust on her face.

The race in Italy a few days later pretty much summed up my whole year. In savage heat, I walked 83' 01" for 20km, finished sixth and missed Olympic qualification by a single second. Although I was extremely frustrated at getting so close to a place in Athens, at least I had shown that I was back on the right track and decided to go to the European Race Walking Cup in Cheboksary, Russia, two weeks later.

By now, the baby was four months old but as the DNA test results hadn't come back I still hadn't seen her. I was still dealing with solicitors and trying to find out if I was a father, a niggling back pain had begun to get worse on my training walks and the first instalment of my grant was spent. I was an emotional mess by the time I got to Russia. While I might have looked okay from the outside, all of those problems were simmering under the surface and the pain in my back soon saw my technique fall apart.

The rules of race-walking are fairly straightforward. Your leading foot must land on its heel and your leading leg then has to stay straight at the knee until it passes directly under your body while one foot must remain in visible contact with the ground at all times. Although freeze-frame or photograph any race and you will see walkers with both feet off the ground for a split second, the visible contact rule is judged 'to the human eye' by numerous judges placed around every circuit. A yellow paddle from a judge is a warning to keep an eye on your technique. If you don't heed the warning, then a red paddle follows from the same judge. Three of these red paddles from different judges and you're disqualified, while the chief judge can also disqualify a walker inside the finishing stadium or in the final 100m of a race, even if they have had no previous warnings.

Injuries, fatigue, dehydration and lack of concentration are the main reasons otherwise strong technical walkers suffer disqualification and, in Cheboksary, my problems all came to a boiling point and suffering from most of the above, I was disqualified from the race for lifting for the first time ever. To drown my sorrows, I went out that night, drank straight Russian vodka for the first time and apparently caused mayhem over there. I say 'apparently' because I don't remember any of it, but Irish team manager Ray Flynn said I was going 'absolutely mental', whatever that means, and that the Russian police were called to the hotel. He had to bribe them not to lock me in a cell.

With my bills mounting up and knowing that the next instalment of my sports grant was almost spent before I got it, I decided to call an early halt to my season and go on holiday. With no money to go anywhere else, that holiday consisted of a week's drinking in Cork with Stephen Macklin, a runner and friend from Togher. University College Cork had just broken up for the summer and we piggybacked on some of their nights out, swilling bottles of beer in a cancer research lecture of all places one afternoon. The week consisted of waking up, going on the beer and going to sleep. It was great while it lasted but by the end of the week I genuinely thought I was going to die.

I'd never treated my body as badly in all my life and I was rattled so much from being out all week that I spent two full days in bed drenched in sweat. I had heard people talk of being 'in the horrors' from drink but never really knew what they meant until then. With Elton gone to work, I woke up one morning to see demons jumping out of my apartment window into the River Lee opposite my house. While part of my brain knew that what I was seeing couldn't be real, I was completely terrified and afraid to lift my head from under the covers for most of the day.

Dying of thirst, I eventually had to crawl on my hands and knees to the fridge where I gulped down a half bottle of orange juice that Elton had left behind him. When I came out of the horrors, the guilt set in again and it was time for my penance. As usual, my way of making up for my sins was to murder myself in a race of some sort so, two days later, I jumped into the John Buckley 5km race, walking with the runners down the marina.

Far from winning the race as I had done on previous guilt-ridden punishment sessions, this time I got an absolute pasting and when I saw my time afterwards I was so disgusted that I ripped my number off my singlet before anybody could see me. The back pain was killing me after the race so I arranged to see Dr Johnson McEvoy in Limerick who sent me for a bone isotope scan. The scan revealed two stress fractures in my back, which required six weeks' rest. Once I found out I had them, I knew that I wouldn't be ready for the World Championships in August and, with everything else that was going on in my life at the time, my 2003 season was written off.

When I got injured and had no money, everyone disappeared. After Edmonton and Munich I had been like the Pied Piper, everybody flocking around me, but now suddenly nobody apart from my family and Ray Flynn, who consistently rang to check how I was doing, seemed to give a shit whether I was dead or alive.

I was confused and couldn't understand where all my friends had gone. I'd never had a shortage of people to go out with before when I came home from a championship or won a local race, but because I hadn't done much going out when I was younger I was naive when it came to who my friends really were. As well as Ray Flynn, who became a really good friend through his constant contact with me at the time, Mark McManus, a Scottish friend who was based in a gym in town, also tried to keep me going. Mark was working with Munster Rugby at the time and he'd pick up the phone and persuade me to go down to the gym by telling me that Donncha O'Callaghan or somebody would be in there training. When I'd get there, he'd tell me I'd just missed him and get me laughing by telling a few jokes and, unknown to myself, I'd end up doing a couple of hours' training, with him getting me to do exercises I was able to do without aggravating my back and I'd go home afterwards in good form.

At the end of June, the DNA results proved conclusively that the baby was mine and the definitive news that I was a father jolted me out of the rut I was in. I realised that I needed to move house. I couldn't be living in the city-centre apartment with a baby. The city had too much distraction. It was bad for my training, bad for my head and I had to break the circle. Upon receiving access to the baby from the judge, I left the courthouse that morning and cycled from there to my sister Anthea's mobile home on the beach in Youghal, 50km away. I stayed with her, her husband and two young babies for the rest of the summer. From then on my life revolved around getting to see my daughter.

The first time I ever laid eyes on her was in the first week of July 2003 in her grandmother's house, where she was living at the time. Meghan was five and a half months old by then, but the moment I picked her up she smiled at me and an unbelievable feeling washed over me that first time I held her. It's hard to describe it now but it was a powerful, life-changing feeling. The house could have been burning down around us and I wouldn't have noticed. I fell in love with her instantly and only just held in the tears of joy that were welling up inside me.

One of the first things I noticed about Meghan was her long eyelashes, a family trait on my mam's side. She was gorgeous; small and petite but strong and wiry like the Heffernans, with beautiful big blue eyes and a head of short light-brown hair. I hadn't seen her for almost the first six months of her life, but I felt as if she knew me immediately. Meghan's birth was seen as a scandal around Cork and the club in Togher at the time. You could almost feel everyone saying, 'Look at your man. That's his career over. He's ruined his life.' But it did the exact opposite. One of the first things I did was get her name tattooed across my back to show everyone that I was proud of her, that I was going to look after her and that I was going to get on with things.

Meghan being born was one of the best things to happen in my life. Having her to look after made me stronger, gave me something to walk for and it definitely changed my life. I was determined to get back to another Olympics to be a good example to her. The Jack-the-lad Rob Heffernan who went out with his friends was gone. I was back, really focused, and everything I did from then on was to provide a better life for my daughter, to give her opportunities that I hadn't had.

With no satellite dish in the mobile home in Youghal, I couldn't watch the World Championships on TV that August so I relied on messages from the Irish contingent in France to tell me what was going on. I was absolutely delighted when Gillian won silver in the women's walk in Paris but when the Australian Luke Adams, who was around the same level as me at the time, finished fifth in the men's 20km race, I couldn't help but wonder what might have been.

Meghan, though, was more important to me than any World Championships or Olympics and getting to see her every week gave me a new lease of life. I had responsibilities to her and my goal from then on was to see Meghan as often as I could so that I could form a bond with her as soon as possible. Every time I saw her it was like Christmas Day so I went to court for a second time that August to get more access to her.

Awarded more time with Meghan – every Thursday and Friday – on these days I'd train in the morning before driving the 50km to Conna to pick her up. I'd then do a 'confirmation run' to get her around to my mother, my brother and sisters and the rest of my relations so that she could get to know them and form a bond with them too. After leaving her home, I'd try to train that evening and again the next morning before making the same 100km round trip again. This routine continued for years afterwards and, while it wasn't ideal as regards my training and racing, it was worth it to have the relationship I have with Meghan now.

83

9

Athens – A Greek Tragedy

lthough I was now paying maintenance to Meghan's mother and wasn't any better off financially, I had a new focus and something to work for so I trained really well over the winter before heading to Mexico for my first race of the year, the opening round of the IAAF Race-Walking Challenge, a seven-event series leading up to the 2004 Olympic Games in Athens.

As an Irish team but paying our own way as usual, Colin Griffin, Gillian and I spent eight days in San Diego with national coach Mick Lane, acclimatising to the time difference and humidity before driving across the border to Mexico and the race.

We were a real mixed bag going on that trip. Gillian was a world silver medallist and in with a great chance of winning her race. Colin was carrying a shin injury when we arrived but hoped it would be cleared up before the race came around, while, for me, it seemed as though my whole life was riding on the race in Tijuana.

I still hadn't qualified for the Athens Olympics in August that year and knew that I would maybe only be able to afford to have one more chance to get the time after Mexico. I also knew that if I didn't get to the Olympics I would be off funding the following year and my career could be over.

In extremely hot conditions, I lined up against Olympic gold medallists Robert Korzeniowski, Jefferson Pérez and the rest of the top names in world race walking. In stark contrast to my previous qualification attempt for Sydney, though, I had no interest in trying to compete with those guys. My only goal in that race was to get a fast enough time to qualify for Athens. I didn't care where I finished as long as I got the Olympic qualifying standard of 83' 00".

I started well and was on pace at the halfway mark but I tried not to make any impulsive decisions, didn't try to stay with the leaders like I had in Eisenhüttenstadt. In Tijuana, my walk was a lot more measured and a lot more controlled. With 4km to go, I still felt very strong and knew that once I didn't fold and just kept it together I would be okay.

Even though I was walking within myself a little bit, I just wanted to tick the box, get the job done and qualify for Athens. In the end, I walked 82' 30" and finished sixth, one place behind Italian Ivano Brugnetti. Afterwards I knew I probably could have done better but instead of berating myself like I normally would have, I was very happy. The sense of relief afterwards was overwhelming and I broke down in tears.

It felt as if I had managed to clean up my whole life and was in a really good place. The worries of the past year had been wiped from the slate and I was back on track. I had just finished sixth among the best walkers in the world and was going to the Olympics again. I had my second chance.

Although Colin was still injured and missed his race, he came with me to the hotel bar afterwards for a celebratory drink. Colin is from a strong athletics family background: his mother, Patricia, ran for Ireland and just missed out on an Olympics while his father, Padraig, was a former president of BLE and a former Irish Olympic team manager. Colin himself had broken junior national records at every distance.

I enjoyed hanging around with Colin because he was from a completely different environment. He was well educated, very smart and very serious about his training and racing, with everything he did researched and analysed to the last but he wasn't in the least bit streetwise. Because he'd never met a character like me growing up, we rubbed off each other, had a bit of a laugh and got on very well. I had shaved IRL into his head at the European Cup in Dudince in 2001 but he never had the body language to carry it off and just looked like a complete lunatic.

After spending a few hours chatting to American walker Curt Clausen at the bar in Tijuana we got back to our room late and overslept the next morning, missing the bus to the airport and our flight to Prescott, Arizona, where we were to spend the next three weeks at an altitude training camp with the Irish crew. By the time we dragged our bags down to the hotel lobby, the Polish squad were heading out training and, having seen Gillian and Mick leave earlier, they were laughing at us.

We scrambled to the airport and got our flights changed before sitting down and making our plans for the upcoming training camp. Because Colin couldn't walk with his shin injury and knowing that both of us had already got the camp off to the worst possible start, I made out a cycling programme for him. I figured that cycling would have less impact on his injury and it would keep him fit until he was able to walk again.

Although I was no longer being coached by Mick, he was still national coach and was still coaching Gillian so we were expecting a bollocking when we arrived at our training base, a holiday home owned by former Irish race walker John Kelly, who had competed at the Mexico Olympics in 1968. Instead, we got the silent treatment from both Mick and Gillian when we arrived. They saw us as complete wasters and there was a definite tension in the house from then on.

Even so, training was training and I got up early the next morning and went for a walk with Gillian while Colin stayed in bed. It didn't matter to me that Gillian still wasn't talking to me. As far as I was concerned, I was there to train, Gillian was there to train and work had to be done. Once we did our training I didn't care if they never talked to me. After a good session that morning, Gillian turned to me as we walked up the driveway.

'That young fella better have gone out on the bike this morning.'

Seconds later, I entered the sitting room to see Colin panned out on the couch, covered in muck and blood, with his jersey in shreds and looking as if he'd been dragged through a hedge backwards. Although he was obviously in a serious state, the sight was too much for me. I turned on my heels before bursting out laughing in the hall so that he wouldn't see me. It took me a couple of minutes to compose myself before I could ask him what had happened.

Colin had a habit of speaking with his hand over his mouth and in a very serious tone he began to mumble that because the brake levers were the opposite way around on American bikes, he had pulled the front brake instead of the back brake as he rounded a corner and had been catapulted over the handlebars into the middle of the road. As well as the shin injury he had been carrying, he now had a dislocated shoulder.

Colin was so precise about things that he was able to tell me what his heart rate was when he was lying on the ground but I was so giddy that I had to leave the room again and nearly passed out with laughing before we got him to the nearest hospital, where he was put in a sling and given very strong painkillers. Thanks to the generosity of the Kelly family, Colin didn't have to pay a penny and was released back to the house later that night.

By the next afternoon those painkillers had turned Colin into the complete alter ego of himself. The ultra-serious athlete was replaced by a delirious, sleepy, out-of-his-brains young lad and I was delighted. I trained so hard that when I got back to the house I just wanted to switch off completely and now I had this fella who was high as a kite to have a bit of craic with. At the time, the American soccer team had posed for a nude calendar and it was big news over there. So Colin and I decided to copy it. We'd pose in the nip and take photos of each other in our room, before getting them blown up and sticking them on the fridge each morning. Although we always had our bits covered, the others would go mad every time they came down for breakfast and went to grab the milk, while Colin and I fell around the place laughing and tried to think up a better pose for the following morning.

Within days Colin had a stationary bike in the front room and with music pumping through the house, he trained like an animal with his arm in a sling and the sweat dripping off him. The two of us had great craic on that camp and, in fact, he asked me to be a groomsman at his wedding years later.

But having put in a solid winter in Youghal, qualified for the Olympics again in Tijuana and then done some serious training in Arizona, I almost screwed the whole lot of it up as soon as I got home and was greeted by the buddies I hadn't seen in months as I came through the arrivals doors in the airport. They had come to the airport with only one thing on their minds: to celebrate my Olympic qualification straight away.

Having purposely moved down to Youghal to get away from the culture of going out drinking to celebrate success, I hadn't seen many of the lads since I'd first got to visit Meghan and had kept the whole background story to myself. When you're young you think you're the only one in the world that has problems but when I went out drinking with the lads I discovered they all had their own problems too, and the more we drank the more problems we had.

I never got down or depressed when I was out drinking with them. I'd always have good craic but sooner or later we were all wallowing in each other's problems and telling each other how great we were. I spent the weekend on the beer, got sick and was on antibiotics in the days before my next World Cup race in Naumburg, Germany. Having gone off with the leaders at the start of the race, I convinced myself that I had the training done and that I'd be all right, but by the time I got to 18km I was in bits. I actually stopped race walking and began walking normally for a few minutes, as if strolling around a shop perusing my next purchase, to try and pull myself together.

I was well off the pace by then but Jamie Costin wasn't too far behind me and my pride couldn't let him beat me. I ambled along for a good few minutes to give myself enough of a break so that I could finish the race off at a pace that wouldn't allow Jamie to catch me. I was in such a bad way that beating Jamie was the only thing I had left to fight for. In the end, I finished ten seconds and three places ahead of him in twenty-seventh as Ecuador's Jefferson Pérez beat Robert Korzeniowski and Nathan Deakes of Australia in a cracking time of 78' 42".

A month after Germany, I had fully recovered and competed in a World Grand Prix race in La Coruña, Spain, at the beginning of June. Just over two months out from Athens, I finished fifth in a very strong field and was back to my best.

In July I returned to Font-Romeu in France for my second altitude camp of the year. The Polish squad and Robert Korzeniowski were also there and as Jamie had kept the lines of communication open between them, we jumped on their bandwagon again and even though Mick was there as Irish national coach, we used their coaches to give us bottles and their athletes to train with.

Mick drove me mad in Font-Romeu. He was supposed to be there for everyone but in reality he was only interested in Gillian and was really coaching only her by then. I trained with Korzeniowski as much as possible. I wanted to learn as much as I could from him.

'Robbie, you need a plan,' he would say. 'I don't know what plan. But you need a plan.'

I came home and finished second at the Dublin Grand Prix in Phoenix Park that July. Nathan Deakes of New Zealand won the race in a really fast time but, having tried to follow him, I blew up and only walked 83' 30", so I was down in the dumps for a while after it.

On 25 July, I set a time of 39' dead in the 10km Nationals on the track in Santry after a hell of a battle with Jamie. We'd been training a lot together that year but I hadn't been beaten in four or five years in Ireland so when we were neck and neck with 2km to go, I remember looking at my watch and wondering how he was still with me.

We both kicked at the same time and it was balls-out racing to the line but with three laps to go Jamie started retching. Out of the corner of my eye I could see his head jerking. A few seconds later I looked over and his shoulders had gone. Then he started getting sick all over himself. I put the boot down and did my last 2km in 7' 38", beating him by just nine seconds.

In the month before Athens, Elaine Fitzgerald was Athletics Ireland's new high-performance manager and asked everyone what she could do to help them ahead of our three-week pre-Olympic holding camp in August. As world silver medallist, Gillian got to bring her coach Mick and her sports injury therapist Mick Cotter. While Mick Cotter was a bit of a character and worked on me as well, I felt that Mick Lane was there just for Gillian and, whether that was true or not, I always felt a bit isolated whenever I went away with the Irish team.

I told Elaine that I got homesick when I was away if I didn't have somebody that I could have a chat with. I felt different, inferior even, to most of the team and told her that I'd love to have somebody around who had my back. Having had Ray Flynn as national team manager back in my first World Cup race in Mézidon in 1999, I thought he would be a positive guy to have around so I asked if he could come with me, and Elaine agreed.

The Irish team had a holding camp in a hotel on a promenade in Ioannina in Greece for three weeks before the Olympics and with the whole camp paid for, we didn't want for much. The camp was similar to our pre-Sydney Olympic camp, but with Ray alongside me to keep me company and provide a few laughs it didn't seem nearly as long as it had in Australia. Training went very well for me and I did a 20km session, eight days ahead of the Olympic race, that would have seen me finish in the top twelve in Athens. Things were going well in the Irish camp until we got the shocking news that Jamie, who had continued training with the Polish squad instead of joining us in Ioannina, had been in a serious car accident and had broken vertebrae after taking a loan of Robert Korzeniowski's car and hitting an oncoming water tanker one afternoon.

Jamie had been in great shape that year, had set the second-fastest time ever by an Irishman over 10km when he finished ten seconds behind me in the Nationals and was raring to go in Athens. When I went down to the hospital to see him, though, he looked horrific. They were deciding if he needed metal plates in his back and for a while it was touch-and-go whether he'd ever walk again, let alone race walk. He was on the broad of his back in bed, with tubes and wires coming out of him left, right and centre. Seeing him in that state really shook me up.

With Jamie out of the Olympics, things went rapidly downhill for the Irish walking team: Gillian was forced to withdraw from the women's race due to a leg injury and I got gastroenteritis a few days later. I don't know if it was something I picked up on my visit to the hospital or something I ate in the village but for the next couple of days, in the words of Peter Kay, it was 'coming out both ends'. I was put into quarantine in the Olympic Village, and spent two days in bed away from everybody for fear that the bug would spread.

After a couple of days in bed I started to come around a little bit but felt as weak as water when I tried to train. With the race only a few days away, I rang Robert Korzeniowski for advice.

'The only hope you have of competing is if you speak to the doctor and get him to put you on intravenous fluids,' he said. 'Your stomach isn't working and you wont be able to absorb anything if you don't get this done. You are going to be dehydrated in the race and if you don't do this, I am sorry, but it is not possible to race.'

I went to the Olympic Council of Ireland doctor and told him 'Robert Korzeniowksi said I need to be put on an intravenous drip to stay hydrated.'

The doctor started laughing at me.

'You could start two or three kilos heavier!'

I said, 'Look, this is Robert's advice. He has won the Olympics twice already and he says I won't be able to race if you don't put me on a drip to replace the fluids I've lost.'

'I can give you Dioralyte,' was his answer. That was the extent of our medical backup with the Irish Olympic team in Athens: something you give a child to drink if they have the runs.

The day before the race my heart rate was over 170 bpm whilst doing five-minute kilometres and I knew things weren't looking too good. On the morning of the race I felt like muck but convinced myself on the start line that I had the training done and everything was going to be all right.

91

I competed well enough for a while and was maybe in the top fifteen and coming through the field when I got my first red card for lifting after about 8km. Nowadays, if I get a red card, it's like a check, a warning to get yourself in line and remember your technique. Back then it sent me into a panic as it was only the second time it had happened to me, and I had neither the experience nor the strength to deal with it.

My power had already started to dissipate by then and unknown to myself I was so weak that I had started leaning back. My technique, something I had previously been renowned for, was shocking and soon I was all over the place. Another card a couple of kilometres later left me worse off and by kilometre 11, I got my third red, was disqualified and was out of the Olympic race. My aim going into Athens had been a top-twelve finish and from my session the week before I was well on target for that. Now I was disqualified, a non-finisher, nothing. I was absolutely distraught.

I was so disgusted after being disqualified that I immediately grabbed my gear bag and went to a bar in Athens, with Ray following me. With my Olympic race number still pinned on my singlet and another one stuck on my kitbag, I stayed out drinking and drowning my sorrows for the rest of that day until, with nowhere else open, I found myself in a corner of a strip bar later that night with Ray trying to convince me not to give up walking altogether. When we went to leave after two bottles of Heineken each, the barman tried to charge us €80 for each bottle. I can still remember Ray putting his two hands out and saying, 'No. I'm not paying that!' It was late at night. We were in a dodgy strip bar in the middle of Athens. Nobody knew where we were and I remember thinking that we were going to get killed that night. The manager appeared and argued with Ray but he stood his ground and ended up giving him the regular price for a drink before we walked back to Ray's apartment. I slept on his floor rather than face the Olympic Village.

I went out for a run the next morning to try and process stuff but when I went back into the village I felt like a second-class citizen, a piece of dirt. I felt I wasn't an Olympian because I'd been disqualified.

I kept myself to myself for the next few days, simply waited it out until it was time to go home. Back in Cork, people were sympathetic, told me the judges had it in for me, were out to get me, but when I rang Korzeniowski, who had won a second Olympic gold in the 20km walk that year, he gave it to me straight.

'Robbie, I feel sorry for you but it was the correct decision.'

Afterwards, I stayed in my sister's mobile in Youghal again for a while. In between collecting Meghan and driving her around to the rest of my family, I spent my days walking the beach and my nights sitting in the bar across the road reading a newspaper with a pint.

Instead of getting metal plates in his back, Jamie opted to let things heal naturally and after being flown home from Athens in an air ambulance, he was back in his parents' house in County Waterford six weeks after the Olympics. I went down to visit him and spent a lot of time with him that winter. I'd drive down and collect him and bring him to Cork to stay in the mobile home with me.

While I was contemplating giving up the sport after my Olympic disaster, Jamie was in a body cast and couldn't move very much but was still very positive and was talking about training again. His injury put things into perspective and made me realise that being disqualified in the Olympics wasn't that big a deal in the grand scheme of things.

10

Pensioners in the Pool

At the end of 2004, Robert Korzeniowski announced his retirement from the sport so I sent him another email, this time thanking him for all his encouragement and advice during the year. With four Olympic gold medals, three world titles and two European Championships to his name, Korzeniowski began coaching other walkers when he retired, including the top two competitors in the world at the time, Spain's Francisco 'Paquillo' Fernández and the Russian Ilya Markov.

The Pole was on a contract with the Spanish federation, worth around €30,000, to make out Fernández's training programme, while former world champion Markov was operating on his own, outside of the Russian system, and as world number one had an agreement with Korzeniowski where he would give him a small fee and a percentage of his prize money as payment for his coaching.

After my latest email, Korzeniowski offered to take me on and coach me too, even though I was still broke and had no money to pay him. I was delighted, really excited at the prospect of learning from the best race walker in the world but also completely terrified of the Polish legend. Just as I had been in South Africa when we first met, I was overly keen to impress him when he invited me to a pre-season training camp in his native Spała in central Poland in December 2004.

After organising a cheap flight to Poland, I arrived in Spała without a penny to my name and was put up in a house near the local sports centre, alongside Fernández and his female coach, Montsé Pastor Martínez. Fernández had World and Olympic silver medals to his name and, with Korzeniowski now retired, was the hot favourite to take over where the Pole left off. Although I'd raced against him loads of times, we were on opposite ends of the walking spectrum and I'd never spoken to him before. In Spała, I was now suddenly rooming with the Spanish star.

'Paco', as he was known, had no English and I had no Spanish so for the first couple of nights I felt so uncomfortable in the room that I went to bed at nine o'clock and prayed that I'd go to sleep first. But after a couple of nights we'd sit down and try to communicate with each other as Montsé dished up our evening meal. I soon realised that while Paco was the big star of international race walking at the time, he was just the same as me and we had a bit of craic together and got to know each other over the following week.

Training-wise, I was super-motivated to have a good 2005 but was still very naive in my approach to the season. With most of the workload just basic training and conditioning, anybody can train with the best in December or early January but while Paco, Ilya and the Polish guys who were also there were all looking at the bigger picture and the season ahead, I was keen to show them what I could do straight away.

After a few days of running myself into the ground in the freezing Polish winter, I got a head cold. But instead of taking it easy I pushed on through it, continued to train hard and probably went into the next camp in Guadix in southern Spain a little bit tired. Carved into the rock of the Sierra Nevada mountains that surround it, the town of Guadix looks like it's stuck in the middle of a mini Grand Canyon. Its elevated position of around 3,000m above sea level and the fact that it is home to the Andalucían Race Walking Centre of Excellence mean that a lot of European race-walking nations use it as their training base during the year.

It was here that my new training partners and I had our first serious altitude training camp in February 2005. The first thing I noticed was the amount of race walkers in Guadix. On the track, nobody ran or jogged. Everyone, from kids to pensioners, race-walked. Robert made sure we had everything we needed there, from food to physios and technical coaches. The weather was great; there was an outdoor athletics track and an indoor sports complex with a gym and a pool not too far away but this time around the training was lot harder.

Paco Fernández lived in Guadix at the time so while I stayed in a nearby hotel with Ilya Markov, Paco spent most of his time at home and, apart from during training, pretty much kept himself to himself. Markov on the other hand was very friendly. Hard as nails during training and racing, Ilya was a gentleman off the road, polite to everybody, and we became good friends.

I was now training with the world's number one and two walkers, as well as Spanish walkers Davide Dominguez and Jorge Silva and the Polish squad. Each training session was harder than the last and I woke up most mornings with sore legs. Afternoons were spent in bed, sleeping for a couple of hours in the hope of recovering enough to tackle the evening's training session.

We went out for somebody's birthday on one of the nights and I asked Paco whether he ever went out during the season. 'I like to go out sometimes, yes,' was his reply, 'but it's not possible with Robert's training.' At least I wasn't the only one who found it tough.

While I could just about handle the workload of the training, by the end of the third week I was really struggling with homesickness and not seeing Meghan. Whenever I had a few minutes to spare I'd go down to the payphone at the end of the road and ring my mam to see how she was and how things were going at home. International calls were costly and most evenings I barely had enough money to say hello. I was supposed to stay in Guadix for twenty-one days but I missed Meghan so much that I left three or four days early to go home and see her.

By then Elton had moved out of the four-bedroom semi-detached we now rented in Carrigaline, and the girl who owned the house moved back in. She was a corporal in the navy and decided to rent two rooms to a couple of Polish lads, while I took the other one. After a couple of months back in Ireland, in April I was selected for the Irish team and went back to San Diego with Ray Flynn and Colin Griffin ahead of another race in Tijuana. While there, I got word from Athletics Ireland that my grant was going to be cut back from the €20,000 to €12,000, which meant I would be under huge pressure financially to get through the rest of the year.

While trips to big international races were paid for by the national federation, none of my training camps were, so Ray helped me put a case forward, explaining that as well as trying to fund my training, I now had a daughter to support. But Athletics Ireland put me back in my box by telling me that my grant was for sport and not to support my personal life.

After a few days in San Diego, my hip started suddenly snapping when I was race-walking. It was getting sorer with each day leading up to the race but with prize money to be won and the possibility that my grant might go back up if I finished high enough in a world-ranking race, I kept on training and took anti-inflammatory tablets before the race. I struggled to finish in the top ten, completing the 20km in 84 minutes and, crucially, missed out on the prize money by a few places. If I'd been sixth I would have got a grand, which would have only paid for my trip over there in the first place.

As a result of the effort and the anti-inflammatories, I was shitting blood that evening and spent the next day in bed. Thankfully, it began to clear up and I was back to normal within a couple of days, when I travelled with the Irish team to Querétaro in Mexico to train at altitude for three weeks afterwards. By then Jamie Costin had made a great recovery from his accident and he joined us and got back into training over there. In fact Jamie did more training over there than I did as I still had the snapping problem with my hip whenever I race walked.

I tried walking normally for the first couple of days and even managed a bit of running without pain but as soon as I went back race walking my hip was at me again and I couldn't follow any of Korzeniowski's training plans for longer than a day or two before having to stop for a couple of days due to the pain. I spent a lot of that camp in the pool and the gym, trying different types of training but my hip was so sore that I didn't get any proper walking training done at all.

With nothing else to do on training camp apart from train, I had a lot more time on my hands and again I missed being at home and especially missed Meghan who was now one year old. If Ray had not been on that camp I would have cracked up. He got up at seven every morning and went for a run on his own and would then come out with me whenever I tried to train or just hung around and chatted whenever I couldn't.

The Polish and French teams were based nearby so I went to the Polish physio for treatment a couple of times a week and by the time I got home and back down to sea level, at the end of April, my hip felt a bit better and I was able to start walking again.

Although I hadn't race-walked that much in Querétaro, the three weeks of swimming, running and gym work at altitude had kept me in decent shape and at the European Cup in Hungary a month later, I was walking in the top eight for most of the race. Without enough specific training done, though, things began to fall apart for me and I faded dramatically in the last 4 or 5km, drifting back to fifteenth in a time of 84' 05" while my new training partner, Ilya, finished over three minutes ahead of me, taking victory ahead of Juan Manuel Molina of Spain and Vladimir Stankin of Russia.

After Hungary, my hip flared up again and, unable to train and with no money to do anything else, I began to get really down and found it very hard to stay motivated. Korzeniowski was still on the other end of the phone for advice but he didn't really know what was going on with me at home so he brought me over to his house in Poland at the end of June, where he had a plan that would see me through until the World Championships in Helsinki that August.

'Look,' he said when I arrived, 'the way that your year has gone, because you don't have all of the blocks of training done, you only have one big competition in you. You're going to be finished for the year after Helsinki. It can be a big competition for you, but you have to be smart.'

After light training each morning as Robert went to work in Warsaw, I had no choice but to take it easy. I had nowhere else to go and nothing else to do bar spend the rest of the day in his apartment, which was brand new and still had no television or phone set up. Robert was very good to me and made me rest and recover and even organised a Polish friend of his to give me massage and physio during the day. He'd then come home in the evening and I'd do some more light training with him for company.

Robert reckoned I had too many distractions in Ireland so, because I was still injured and couldn't train at altitude that summer, I went straight from his house to Spała in Poland ahead of the World Championships instead.

My daily routine in Spała consisted of going to the pool every morning at seven for a rehab session with some of the local pensioners. The class was for people who'd had strokes or just wanted to do a bit of gentle exercise and although the pool was absolutely freezing, I couldn't really complain when there was an eighty-year-old Polish woman doing the same exercises next to me. After breakfast I'd do a shorter, tailored training version, the minimum needed to keep me fit with the emphasis afterwards on recovery. I'd get massage in the sports centre, stretch and then use the centre's renowned cryotherapy chamber in an effort to recover.

My body fat percentage is around 6 per cent, so cryotherapy was absolute torture. Every day I'd don a pair of white clogs, knee length socks and a hat and gloves to cover my extremities before walking into the smaller first chamber, which was kept at between minus forty and minus seventy degrees Celsius. After half a minute in there I was already rattling but this first chamber was just to allow your body to adjust before moving into the main chamber, which was around 8 foot square.

With the temperature in there kept at between minus 120 and minus 160, I had to keep walking around in a circle and found myself singing songs out loud to keep myself alert during my three- or four-minute treatment. On leaving the chamber I then had to walk around for another few minutes in case my body shut down before going on an exercise bike or a treadmill for a few minutes to get the blood flowing again. The goalkeeper at West Bromwich Albion was there at the time and the Welsh rugby team used it before getting to the World Cup semi finals in 2011. After lunch I was tired from the recovery so I slept for a couple of hours before training again at half past five.

With my credit card now almost maxed out and my credit union loan growing instead of shrinking, I couldn't afford to stay in the Olympic Sports Centre so I stayed in a nearby B&B for €7 a night, full board. Ilya was going out with a Polish girl and living in Poland but he had no money either and had to do the same. During my month in Spała, Robert's plan for me seemed to be working and I rang him to tell him I was feeling better.

'Robert, I'm actually feeling pretty good,' I said, after a few weeks.

'Robbie, thees ees normal,' he replied. 'You train, you rest, you have no deestractions, you recover!'

I managed myself well enough to be able to come home and win another National Championships off my reduced training programme but while it probably looked as if everything was going fine, the pain in my hip was killing me the whole way through the race and it was sheer determination to get to Helsinki that kept me going.

By the time Helsinki came around, I was feeling pretty good again and things seemed to be going to plan in the first half of the race. The pressure of a big international competition meant my hip was very sore again but when I was still inside the top eight walkers with 4km to go, everything was looking rosy. As the course turned back onto itself, I looked along the road on the opposite side of the cones and counted back through the field behind me until I came to the guy in twelfth place.

If I finished ahead of him, finished top twelve in the World Championships, I knew that my Sports Council grant would be upped to €20,000 again for 2006. That was enough incentive to push myself through the constant pain and I knew that even if I lost a few places, I wasn't going to die enough to drop out of the top twelve between then and the finish. After a pretty shitty season, I realised that

I was heading for a good result and that I would also win a few thousand euro if I stayed where I was.

As I headed towards the line, I started calculating how much the result would earn me. I added the prize money to the grant I would get for the following year and worked out how much would be left over after I cleared my Visa card, my loan from the credit union and another one my mam had given me to tide me over. After doing the figures in my head, I reckoned I'd have around €11,000 left to survive on for the following year, which was a huge sum of money for me.

Five hundred metres later, I was disqualified and had lost it all. I had been completely distracted by the thoughts of finally being able to clear my debts instead of focusing on my technique.

After being disqualified in the Olympics the year before and now again in the World Championships, the last race of my 2005 season, not only had I lost all hope of my grant being upped to €20,000 for 2006, but I had failed to get any sort of result during the year and now wouldn't qualify for any Sports Council funding at all. I would have no income in 2006. No income meant no sport. No sport meant no life.

I was distraught by the time I got home to Cork. I was totally depressed and was now so broke that I had to walk around the corner to my sister Rhonda's house every morning for breakfast. Rhonda had suffered post-natal depression a few years earlier and could see how down I was. She knew what I was going through. She was always there to talk to and every morning would invite me back over that evening for dinner. 'I've loads made,' she'd say. 'I'm only going to be throwing it out.'

Although he didn't say anything, I could almost hear what my dad was thinking at the time. 'Robert's after walking in two Olympics but he hasn't a pot to piss in.' The only reason that drove me absolutely bananas at the time was because it was true.

My off season was consumed by going to physios and doctors, all of whom told me something different from the others. I went to Dr Noel McCaffrey, who told me I had a leg length discrepancy. I got orthotics made for my running shoes but when I went back training with them in, they did nothing.

After that I was being treated for osteitis pubis, an overuse injury that affects the pubic joint and surrounding ligaments, but by October my injury still wasn't getting any better and every visit was costing me money. To make ends meet, I got a few days labouring on the building sites for Elton and got a part-time job with my brother-in-law Aidan, which meant the locals had a two-time Olympian as their coalman. Now, at my lowest ebb, I thought about packing the sport in altogether.

Then Marian came along.

11

The Chicken Walker

The Chicken Walker. I didn't know it at the time but that's what
they called me when they first joined Togher. Her and her friend. I
was seventeen back then and busy trying to qualify for the
European Juniors and even though Marian Andrews was one of only
two girls in the club back then, she was four years younger than me,
so she wasn't even on my radar screen.

The first blip appeared one night in October 2001.

I was in the passenger seat of my friend Pa Murphy's car, cruising
around in the twilight of Cork city's streetlights when I noticed her
standing at an ATM with her friend. Pa pulled the car in along the
kerb and beeped the horn at the two girls, who turned around and
waved.

Marian was wearing white jeans, a white crop top and a pink
jacket. She looked absolutely stunning.

Blip.

Pa rolled down his window and shouted a few obscene words that
barely passed as chat-up lines, even for him, and the pair, having
retrieved their money from the hole in the wall, started to totter over
to the car in their high heels.

Blip. Blip.

Obviously a bit the worse for wear after a few drinks, the girls
spent a few minutes exchanging smart comments with Pa as I just sat

there, almost speechless, staring into Marian's big brown eyes before she turned on her heel and headed for the nearest nightclub.

Blip! Blip! Blip!

Although she will tell you that it was just a few fleeting moments on a night out for her, from then on, I couldn't get Marian Andrews out of my mind. She was absolutely gorgeous: a vision in white. And fluorescent pink. I was mad about her from the start.

Although I'd been to the Olympics in Sydney by then, I was still training with my club in Togher during the week. I found out that Marian lived just a couple of kilometres away in Deer Park and was soon calculating my route to training so that I could deliberately bump into her on the way and get chatting to her. Marian was a sprinter, so not long afterwards I found myself doing my long sessions on Saturdays, which meant that the next day I could do a hill session, walking alongside the sprinters' group as they trained, just to see her.

Still dipping in and out of running races back then, I was second in the Cork County Cross-country Championship about a month later and when Togher won the team prize for the first time in its history, the club night out was hastily arranged in Redz, a local nightclub, that same evening.

Marian was there and by the end of the night we were dancing to the slow set. We saw each other every day for about a week after that. I'd walk home from training alongside Marian as she jogged and found any excuse I could to meet up with her, until a friend of mine told me she was seeing someone else. I'd had very little experience with girls up until then and can remember being absolutely heartbroken upon hearing this news.

Instead of asking her about it, stubbornly, I stopped talking to her for about two months instead, blanking her completely. In fairness, Marian probably didn't think much about it, probably thought I was a bit strange. All over her one minute and not talking to her the next. But I was proper gutted and even though we'd only been 'going out' a week or so, it took me a long time to get over it.

Although I eventually started chatting to her again and never stopped fancying her, we began to move in different circles and drifted apart soon after. While my life was consumed by training and racing and I had begun to go abroad for warm weather and altitude training camps, Marian didn't take her sport half as seriously. She rarely missed training with Togher during the week but had no problem with skipping a race, even a national championship, if it clashed with her job in Dunnes Stores.

While I spent my weekends resting up before races and recovering after them, Marian spent hers partying with her friends and enjoying life. Whenever we did see each other at training or around town, though, we got on really well and she was never too far from my mind.

Although it had been three months since my disastrous outing in Helsinki, by November 2005 neither the physical pain nor the mental anguish of that competition had fully dissipated. My days were spent carrying coal in an effort to pay my bills while most evenings were spent on Liam O'Reilly's massage table, set up in the clubhouse in Togher, in an effort to fix my hip. On one such evening, I decided to text Marian, on the pretence of having Liam look at an ankle injury that I knew she had recently picked up. In reality, I just wanted to get her to call in to the club so that I could see her. I hadn't really thought things through, however: she agreed to call in and then arrived at the clubhouse moments after Liam had finished treating me and met him walking out the door with his massage table under his arm.

With Liam gone out the door laughing to himself, I couldn't think of anything to do other than try and give her some advice myself. I cringe even now when I think of my woeful attempt at wooing her by having her sit on a Swiss ball and do some ankle rotation exercises in the prefabricated hut.

While my ploy to get her to the club that night wasn't great, I must have done something right because we met again the following evening and from then on we got on like a house on fire. It was the first time Marian had spoken to me without me being the Jack-the-lad around the club and for some reason I found it easy to open up to her about my problems. Like most people outside of my immediate family, up until then Marian had only seen Rob Heffernan the

Olympian or Rob Heffernan the National Champion so she couldn't believe how down I was when we first met and that after my disqualifications in Athens and then Helsinki I was actually contemplating giving up walking.

Having seen me as someone who was doing very well on the international scene she couldn't understand how my confidence had gone so low, how I was almost afraid to bump into people on the street. With my athletics gone for the season, I believed I was of no value to anybody and had no self worth. While my sister and my mam had always believed in me, they were family and I felt they had a duty to believe in me, but when Marian began to gee me up, telling me that I needed to get my injury sorted out, that I could win medals at European, World Championship and even Olympic level, it began to build my confidence back up.

We went out one night for a meal. When I went up to pay for it, my Visa card was declined but she still stuck around. After that, we ate in the house I rented a room in, in Carrigaline, and even though she told me years later that she didn't want to be eating late at night, Marian put on a brave face and tucked into my not-so-gourmet offerings.

Both a bit older and with more life experience behind us than when we first met, neither of us was ready to be infatuated with the other so we were seeing each other for about three months without telling anybody at first. Marian would tell her mam that she was going to her friend Tracey's house but would sneak off to meet me, while I would tell Rhonda that I was going to the club after dinner. It wasn't that we were being secretive: we just didn't feel the need to broadcast our relationship in those early days. I now had Meghan and Marian had a seven-month-old son, Cathal, so neither of us was looking for a relationship at the time.

After six months or so, though, we decided to take the next step and move in together. We'd been going out for months, had known each other for years and were a lot more mature than when we first met so moving in together didn't feel like such a huge step. Marian was still working in Dunnes at the time, and was supporting me rather than the other way around.

Her mam probably wasn't too happy when we first rented a house in Monkstown, out in the country, especially as I'd bring Cathal to her house every morning so that she could look after him while I trained. We had so little money at the time that I'd bring the rubbish over with Cathal because we couldn't even afford a bin tag. Still injured at the beginning of 2006, I was forgotten about by Athletics Ireland. Apart from Ray Flynn, who kept in contact with me as a friend, nobody in Athletics Ireland seemed to care where I was or what I was doing.

Every time I tried to go back race walking I'd build myself up and get motivated for training but it would only last for three or four days before I'd get hurt again and have to stop. With everything else that was going on in my life at the time, at one point I even wondered if I had a real injury or whether my injuries were psychosomatic, if I was just lazy, or what the hell was going on.

To take my mind off things, I spent a lot of time in the club that year helping to coach some of the younger athletes. Myself and Frank Doherty, a stalwart of the club, essentially looked after the club in Togher that year. I looked after the novices and the endurance side of the club and coached the cross-country team while Frank looked after the sprinters.

Coaching the lads in the club gave me a new lease of life and I put all of my energy into helping out and trying to develop them a little bit. Out of his own pocket, Frank had already bought a set of gym equipment, a squat rack and some Olympic lifts from a neighbour who'd had them in his garage and we got a few machines and an exercise bike together bit by bit. Marian was training with the club, too, so I spent a lot of time in that gym working out with the sprinters just to be around her. Even though I was injured, I was back motivated and there was great camaraderie in the club.

Frank and I built a little office in one of the prefabs and we would hold club meetings and set out training plans for the different groups in there. The endurance lads were a real mixed bag and we had everything from a science student who'd got 600 points in his Leaving Cert to a fella who'd been arrested for stealing a Garda car.

Stephen Macklin, who is currently head junior coach with Athletics Ireland, was also there, as was my friend Pa Murphy and even my brother Elton took up running that year.

Elton had never, ever been into sport. He'd done nothing in school, never kicked a football or even come to see me race, let alone tried athletics himself but he turned up one evening in a honky old pair of runners and a ripped tracksuit that was covered in blobs of plaster to take part in a mile race. Despite looking like Uncle Fester from *The Addams Family* with his shoulders all bent over, Elton came second. He ran 5' 20" for the mile without ever doing any sport before in his life. I couldn't believe it.

Even though the lads all came from different backgrounds I could relate to all of them and had great craic with them that year. They thrived on a bit of structure and that year the club won the National Indoors 400m, the 4 x 400m relay outdoors and the National Novice Cross-country Championships for the first time ever.

In February 2006 my injury was still dragging on and I still wasn't able to race walk. A local businessman, Robert McCarthy, the CEO of Biocell in Cork, offered to pay for me to go over to a specialist in Germany to get my injury checked out but I wouldn't follow up on his offer because I was simply too embarrassed to take his money.

After doing the rounds of various physios and doctors, I got to see Dr Johnson McEvoy in Limerick and he diagnosed a sports hernia. He explained that because I used my hips so much, the torque of twisting and turning in race walking had pulled continuously on the lining, which was okay if I'd built the area up enough to take it. In 2005, though, I had skipped some of my phases of training and didn't have the sufficient core strength to stop it and it was an injury that needed to be surgically repaired. Johnson contacted renowned surgeon and former Meath All-Ireland winning footballer Gerry McEntee and he booked me in for an operation in March 2006.

Hernia operations were way more invasive back then so I could barely move for four weeks afterwards. It was a success, though, and gradually I was able to do some easy race walking. By the end of April I had found a really cheap package deal to Gran Canaria and headed over with Togher club mates Steve Macklin and Tristan Druett for my first proper training camp in over a year.

Since moving in with Marian things had been going great for us but our little household was still relying solely on her income to keep us afloat, so I had also come up with a cunning plan to make some money while in Gran Canaria. Before I left Cork, I went around my friends and took orders for cartons of duty free cigarettes and other stuff that was either very expensive or very hard to get in Ireland at the time. I reckoned that after selling them on at a mark-up when I got home, my master plan would see me make around €500, which would be enough to pay for another two-week training camp later in the season.

On arrival home to Shannon Airport though, one of the most embarrassing scenarios of my life took place as I stood, dressed in my Team Ireland Olympic tracksuit, and watched as customs officers pulled 5,000 John Player Blue cigarettes and a dozen pornographic DVDs out of my Irish Olympic kitbag before waving me off. Having used my last bit of money to fund my new illegal cigarette and porn trade, I'd had everything seized by customs and was now in a deeper hole financially when I got home.

To make matters worse, when I started training hard in Gran Canaria I knew almost instantly that I had the same problem with my right side as I'd had with my left. I hadn't said anything about it before my first operation because I felt my left side was much worse so when I went back to see Gerry McEntee for a check-up, he was really annoyed with me because they could have both been done at the same time.

I didn't get my second hernia operation until June 2006, which meant the European Championships were gone for another year but by the time they came around I didn't really care. After the second hernia operation I was born again. I was finally healthy. I could put my bad years down to two hernias rather than just me being crazy. I had the double Olympic champion coaching me and I was in a very happy place living with Marian. I had a second chance and wasn't going to mess it up.

Robert couldn't give me any training plans until Athletics

Ireland's medical team were finished with me and satisfied I could go back training, so Mark McManus and Mary Gleasure were my strength and conditioning people at the time. I was only meant to have three or four visits with them but Mary went above and beyond the call of duty and really looked after me. She had me back doing rehab and activation work, very basic core exercises, three days after my second operation. After a week I was working on ladders, which kept me in a straight line as I couldn't go laterally. I was doing this three times a day and was going well until I woke up one night with green puss oozing from the wound and hallucinating.

Elaine Fitzgerald, Athletics Ireland's high-performance director at the time, told me to go to A&E where I was put on antibiotics and after a week or so it calmed back down. Once I knew I was healthy again and that my body was right, it didn't bother me if I could only walk four steps the first day, a kilometre the first week. It was progress and things were moving forward.

The last real mistake I made when it came to my training programme came a few weeks afterwards when I entered a National League race in Limerick. Marian was running there too so I drove down with her and threw myself into the 3km race. It was my first race since Helsinki and even though it was only a local race I was really nervous and anxious going into it.

I went out and hit the race so hard that I won it. My time of 12' 07" wasn't exactly world-record pace but I had only been back race walking for ten days after missing a whole year so in my head this was brilliant, even if my blood lactate was 15.2 and I was panned out at the side of the track afterwards.

Twenty minutes later I rang Robert Korzeniowski, keen to impress him with the news that I was back, and back with a bang. He absolutely bollocked me out of it.

'You are stupid,' he bellowed down the line at me. 'You have no respect for your body. This is a very dangerous thing to do. You know, Robbie, if you continue like this, I will not help you any more.'

After that conversation he didn't ring me for over a week and I was terrified he was gone, that I had blown it and lost my coach before I even had the chance to get fit enough to train properly under him.

From then on I had to account for everything I did each week and I had to stick to his training plan. There was to be no impulsive stuff any more and, like the Polish squad on their training camps, every training session or race was done for a reason and everything was aimed towards the biggest races in the world, the races which Korzeniowski had made me realise were the only ones that counted.

Although I had missed the Europeans in the summer, there were still a few smaller races left on the circuit at the end of the season. These were complimentary races, like exhibition events where some of the bigger international names in race walking could show their stuff to an appreciative home crowd for a few quid in appearance fees and most of them, especially the ones in Spain, attracted huge crowds to the side of the road.

Normally I'd have been on my end of season break like everyone else but as I was still trying to get back to fitness I raced in one of these races in Guadix in September. Among the thousands of spectators at the race were Ray Flynn, who had come out with his wife to watch the race, and Marian and Cathal, cheering me on. In the 10km race, I finished fourth behind Paco, João Vieira and another Spanish guy but I'd felt awful the whole way through the race. I hit a bit of a downer after crossing the line and just walked off. Marian thought I was gone straight to a bar but I just needed some time to pull myself together for an hour and got back training the next day.

I spent another couple of weeks training in Guadix before going to a 10km Grand Prix race in Krakow where I finished third behind Ilya and Paco and earned myself €1,000, which meant I could contribute something meaningful to the household and didn't feel like a complete pauper for once. Beating a few really good guys over there proved that my performance in Poland was much better so I decided to go to Copenhagen in October where, ten weeks after my second hernia operation, I lined up for my first 20km race of the year.

Having flown over on my own, I was joined by Ray the following day and Jamie Costin, who also competed. I won the race in 82' 30", beating second-placed Jamie by nearly six minutes and qualifying for the World Championships the following year. I was absolutely delighted.

I had to spend the night in London Stansted after the race and having gone through security, I sat down next to a power point, plugged my phone in and rang Marian. Qualifying for the 2007 World Championships meant I would be back on funding in January 2007 and could aim towards a place at the Beijing Olympics in 2008. I chatted to her for four or five hours and was almost in tears with joy. I had my life back.

12

Big Trouble in Little China

ecause my 2006 season had only got going after nearly
everybody else's had finished, I didn't take much of a break that
winter and began the 2007 season in solid condition. Marian was
still the main breadwinner at home but as well as working, looking
after Cathal and doing her own training with the club, she helped out
with my training as much as she could, which was a lot. After
working all day, she'd come home and put Cathal in a baby seat in the
back of the car and they would drive after me as I walked the country
roads on the dark winter nights. At the weekends Marian would run
alongside me without thinking about her own training requirements.

As part of my early season training, I was invited to Ibiza to walk
in the Spanish National Championships as a guest, where I finished
third behind Paco and Juan Manuel Molina. My time of 83' 03" for
the race saw me miss out on an Olympic qualification time for Beijing
by just three seconds, but I was still very early in my periodisation for
the year and knew that I was nowhere near my peak, so finishing third
was a good result. My prize money from the day was enough to cover
my next training camp.

As the biggest stars on the international scene, Paco and Ilya had
a Spanish racing agent, Alberto Armas, from a company called Alka
Sport. Alberto got them appearance fees to walk in various races and
organised their entries to the big races. As I was now training with

the two lads for periods of the season, I began to get thrown into some of these deals as an added bonus. Buy two world-class walkers and get an Irish walker free. While I rarely made any actual money out of these deals, it meant I didn't have to pay for the trips to these races, which was a huge bonus for me.

One of the first of those races came in China that March. With the World Championships due to be held in Osaka, Japan, that year and the Olympics in Beijing in 2008, the opportunity to race in China with all of my expenses covered was too good to turn down. Korzeniowski figured it would be a good way to get used to the time difference, experience the food and see how I got on, before tackling the two bigger events.

China was unlike anywhere I'd ever been before. We were based in Shenzhen in the days leading up to the race and I've never seen a place as busy in all my life. People were milling around everywhere like ants and I remember thinking that it made New York look quiet. Australian walker Luke Adams was also in China and staying in the same hotel. I'd got to know Luke after battling against him in various races and we got on well, so we hung around together over there. With a few days to go to the race we changed our money in the bank nearby ahead of our first venture outside the hotel, a shopping trip for DVDs and electronic goods.

After asking around a few people in the street market nearby, a little Chinese dude beckoned to us and we followed him down a back alley, where he told us to wait as he went to get some DVDs. He then brought us in the back door of a shopping mall and up five flights of stairs, into a corridor leading to the public toilets. When another fella appeared out of nowhere, I was beginning to think there was something dodgy going on but tried to play it cool. The guy wanted 100 renminbi for ten DVDs, which was the equivalent of around a tenner at the time, so we agreed and I handed him a 100 renminbi note for mine.

He looked at it for a second before handing it back to me.

'No, no,' he said, waving his hand in the air. 'Money no good.'

'The money is good, boy,' I said. 'I only got it out of the bank.'

'No, no, no. Money no good!'

I then took out a different note and handed it to him and Luke gave him one of his too but every time he handed it back saying it was no good. This went on for a few minutes before I eventually got pissed off.

'Luke,' I said, starting to walk around your man. 'Fuck this, boy. Yer man is making a langer out of me here, boy. I'm not dealing with him. I'm gone.'

Walking around him, talking way louder than usual, had made him wary of what was going to happen next and he took a tenner off each of us, gave us each a bag of DVDs and we went off happy.

As we went back through the shopping centre we spotted a massage parlour and thought it would be no harm to get the legs and back loosened out before the race. When we went in we were given two pink dressing gowns to wear as we sat waiting for our masseurs, who turned out to be two big fat Chinese men. With no oil or anything, the two boys, who stank of cigarette smoke and alcohol, knocked lumps out of us with their dirty hands. There was nothing we could do only piss ourselves laughing.

After our torture we got up to pay but soon found ourselves in the same scenario as when we were trying to buy DVDs, with the owner telling us our money was no good.

'The money is good,' I said. 'I only got it out of the bank half an hour ago.'

With no other cash on me, I had to bring your man with me, over to the Bank of China where we had withdrawn the money earlier. I went up to the same girl behind the counter that had served me earlier, took the money out and told her the story.

'You didn't get this money out of the bank,' she said. 'This money is fake.'

'I did get it out of the bank,' I told her. 'I only took it out a half an hour ago. You gave it to me!'

'Did you buy anything since then?'

'I did,' I said. 'But I didn't get any change. I paid the exact amount.'

'What about those?' she said as she looked down at the bag of DVDs.

115

'That's all I bought, but I paid for them with a 100 rinminbi note.'

The girl explained that, within the blink of an eye, the guy who sold us the DVDs had switched our real notes for fake ones and like two gullible magician's helpers, Luke and I kept handing them over. I'd just lost a hundred quid.

The next day, Paco, Ilya, Montsé and I went outside for a coffee and a stroll around the street and on the way back, who did I see only yer man that had sold me the DVDs. I couldn't believe it. He was standing in the middle of a group of people in a pedestrianised area. I told Ilya the story of the previous day and we went back to the bank to tell the girl behind the counter.

The cashier called the Chinese police, who arrived two minutes later in a paddy wagon and parked it about fifty metres from the pedestrian street where the guy was standing chatting to people, oblivious to them. As they made their way out of their van, I walked over to yer man, who was about 6 foot tall, put my arm around his shoulder and said 'How's it going, boy? DVDs good?'

His face drained of blood instantly and he turned on his heels and ran, with me running after him. Unfortunately for him, he had run directly towards Ilya. The stocky Russian saw him coming and hit him full on, locking his arms around him in an upright position. Ilya had only been clamped around him a couple of seconds when I hit him full on with a rugby tackle and both of us wrestled him to the ground in the middle of the bustling street as Paco and Montsé, who were unaware of any of the story, looked on in absolute bewilderment.

The police then came over, peeled the Chinese fella off the ground and arrested him as the whole of Shenzhen turned to watch. Cuffed, he was thrown into the back of the paddy wagon with a few other criminals while Ilya and I were also given seats in the van for a trip to the police station to give statements. Ilya was deadly serious as he sat beside the driver but I was bursting myself laughing in the seat behind him.

When we arrived at the station, the cops pulled the dude out of the van and I almost felt sorry for him because they began to slap him around the head as they walked him down the hall. I had to ring Luke

LEFT: Proud as punch: with my younger brother Elton and the huge shield I got for winning the school mile in sixth class in Scoil Chríost Rí.

BELOW: At the Munster Schools Championships with teammates from Coláiste Chríost Rí. I'm on the far right, aged sixteen but looking about ten.

My first senior international appearance came at Mézidon-Canon in France in 1997. (L–r): Ray Flynn, me, Jamie Costin, Pierce O'Callaghan and Bernie O'Callaghan.

Meeting my daughter Meghan for the first time. It was July 2003 but it felt like Christmas Day to me.

TOP LEFT (l–r): Me relaxing with Robert Korzeniowski and Paco Fernández in Matsui, Japan, ahead of the 2007 World Championships in Osaka; TOP RIGHT (l–r): Pat Ryan, Colin Griffin, Jamie Costin, Paco and me in Matsui; MIDDLE: training in 2007 for a Grand Prix race in Shenzhen, China; (l–r): Hatem Ghoula (who would win bronze in the 20km walk at the 2007 World Championships), Paco, Ilya Markov and me.

Looking a bit pasty on my wedding day in October 2009 after spending much of the night trying to avoid being kidnapped by the Spanish contingent. (L–r): My brother Elton, my dad Bobby, Marian, me, my mam Maureen and my sisters Lyndsey, Anthea and Rhonda.

ABOVE: 'Rob! Your dinner's ready!' Behind every good man is a great woman and Marian has been with me every step of the way. INPHO/ MORGAN TREACY

RIGHT: My son Cathal tries to cool me down with some ice-cold water after a tough 30km session Down Under in December 2011.

FACING PAGE: On the way to fourth place in the 20km walk at the European Championships in Barcelona in 2010. I would eventually be upgraded to bronze after Russian winner Stanislav Emelyanov was banned for doping. INPHO/MORGAN TREACY

FACING PAGE: On the way to another fourth place, this time in the 50km walk at the Olympic Games in London 2012. Four years later I was upgraded to bronze after another Russian winner, Sergey Kirdyapkin, was retrospectively banned for doping. INPHO/MORGAN TREACY

RIGHT: So close, yet so far. Patsy McGonagle (right) tries to console me after I finished fourth in London. I thought it would be the closest I ever got to winning an Olympic medal. INPHO/MORGAN TREACY

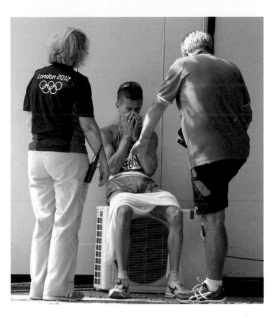

BELOW: I was on my hands and knees after the 50km walk at the London Olympics. Earlier I had been in the same position before the race, vomiting with nerves. SPORTSFILE/ STEPHEN McCARTHY

LEFT: Racing in front of friends and family spurred me on to a new national record of 11:11.94 for the 3km walk at the Cork City Sports in 2013.

BELOW: Playing it cool in the early stages of the 50km walk at the World Championships in Moscow in 2013.
SPORTSFILE/STEPHEN McCARTHY

to get him to come down to the station, as a second witness to the DVD scam, and reluctantly he joined me and gave a statement. The guy was a well-known conman in the area and we were both due to go back to the police station a couple of days later but we didn't bother. Like the time I got my singlet back in Fuengirola, I was happy to have had the last word, so he probably got off.

A few days later, Paco won the race and I finished one place ahead of Ilya in ninth. I'd had a good, solid, controlled performance and my time of 82' 06" qualified me for the Beijing Olympics the following year.

Robert Korzeniowski was delighted with me. Every race I went into now I was a little bit more controlled, I was starting to get better and was more professional. At the banquet that night, I sat down at the back with Paco and Ilya for the final speech, which turned out to be given by none other than Pierce O'Callaghan. He had the place eating out of his hands and we ended up drinking a traditional drink like *sake* afterwards and getting drunk with the Chinese coaches before Ilya carried me up to bed.

Always trying to come up with quick-fire ways to earn a few extra bob, I'd gone to China with an empty gear bag and the day after the race, with Luke in tow again, I filled it to bursting point with stuff ranging from MP3 players, memory sticks and other electronic gadgets, to Converse runners and even silk kimono-type pyjamas. After being caught out a few days earlier by the guy with the DVDs, there was nobody in China who could haggle better than me that day. If someone asked me for €10, I'd offer them 50 cents. In my mind I had to make up for the money I'd lost in my previous deal. By the time I was ready to fly home I'd filled the bag for half nothing.

When I got home though, I sold none of it. Instead, friends that called over were asked, 'Do you want an MP3 player?' before they left the house. I gave most of the stuff away for nothing so Marian put the clampers on my impulse buying after that trip. To this day I never buy anything when I'm away.

While I'd been almost depressed at the thoughts of going home to an empty house and facing up to my bills in previous years, now I couldn't wait to get home to see Marian, Cathal and Meghan. Marian was a fantastic influence on me and meeting her was the best thing ever to happen to me in my life, even if she had to knock the corners off me at first. Still broke and struggling to meet the bills, my last hare-brained scheme came shortly after that trip.

In desperation to dig ourselves out of the money pit we seemed eternally stuck in, I persuaded some of my family and friends to give me a loan of €2,500 to invest in a new scheme I'd heard about from my brother-in-law, where a €5,000 investment earned a €20,000 return. I didn't know much about it at the time but this pyramid scheme, or pyramid scam as it should have been called, relied on each individual introducing two or more people into the scheme and this 'endless' supply of new members provided the get-out cash for those who had gone before them. Needless to say, I never saw my €2,500 again, which probably wouldn't have been so bad if I hadn't persuaded Marian to take out a credit union loan for the other half of the money. Instead of making twenty grand, we had thrown away five grand and had more bills to pay than ever before. When Marian didn't leave me after that, I knew she loved me.

When my grant came through in April 2007 it was time for altitude camp again but with everywhere at altitude in Europe frozen over at the time, it looked like our only option was to head to South Africa again, until Korzeniowski had a brainwave. Since retiring from race walking after the Olympics, my new coach had also become head of sports for Polish television and was due to fly a crew over to Morocco to interview Hicham El Guerrouj, who had won two gold medals in Athens and still holds the world record for the mile, the 1,500m and the 2,000m.

Ifrane in Morocco is at altitude of over 1,600m and so, to kill two birds with one stone, Korzeniowski decided our next altitude camp would be in Morocco. After my pyramid scam fiasco, I didn't have any money to waste so I couldn't even afford to book a suitcase on the plane and arrived in Morocco with just a little 10kg carry-on rucksack of clothes and training kit to do me for the three weeks.

As well as Paco, Ilya and myself, Jamie Costin and Colin Griffin came to the camp too and I roomed with Colin for the duration. Accommodation was very basic in Morocco, with no Internet or phone, and the weather was pretty hit-and-miss while we were there. Some days we were freezing cold and the training was very tough. Paco had a Spanish physio with him so we got physio every day and ate all of our meals in the hotel. The odd night we'd go down the backstreets into an Internet cafe to contact home but with no money to do anything else, most days all I did was train twice a day, eat in the hotel and stay in my room afterwards.

At the time Morocco had bit of a Wild West reputation and rumours had begun to circulate that several top athletes from the country had doped in order to gain their international success. Possibly because Morocco was out of the way, there wasn't as much anti-doping testing being carried out there at the time and the subject came up one night as Colin and I headed for bed.

Afterwards I lay on my bed and couldn't help wondering what something like EPO would do for me. I'd already done 80 minutes for 20km at that stage and reckoned that if someone with my ability took EPO, they could knock three minutes off that. I'd been getting decent results for years but was still stone broke and scraping my way through each year. If I was doing 77 minutes regularly, I'd be loaded. I'd be getting start money, prize money. I'd be a star. But apart from the obvious ill effects and your life being ruined if you were ever caught, I knew I'd never do it. When I was a kid, I was in Lifestyle Sports with a fella from school one day when he suddenly robbed a football jersey off the rails and walked out of the shop. He was caught just down the street in McDonald's afterwards and I ran all the way home roaring crying. As soon as I got in the door of my house I blabbed the whole story to my mam through my tears and then, even though I hadn't done anything wrong, I got walloped around the house for hanging around with a fella who robbed stuff.

I don't know if it was the upbringing I got from my parents – being made go to Mass every Sunday, getting walloped for dropping papers on the ground, berated for drinking alcohol and clattered for being in the same shop as a guy who stole a football jersey – or if it was the influence of my former mentors, from Michael Buckley who drove me to football matches as a kid, to my tae kwon do instructors Dermot Walsh and Ann Slocombe, and John Hayes who kept me out of trouble in the park by bringing me to Togher to train as a teenager, or even the strict discipline of the Presentation Brothers in school, but something, maybe a combination of all of these good influences, left me in no doubt that doping was wrong, that there was no way I was going near it and if I wanted to win medals I'd have to do it the hard way.

At that stage of my career, doping hadn't really affected me yet, although I knew others, some of my competitors, were doing it. Ilya had told me the reason that he had left the Russian system and moved to Poland was because he 'didn't like what the coaches were doing to young athletes in Russia' so I was aware that others were doped, but I wasn't yet at the level where I was good enough to be fighting for medals or contesting for victories against them.

Most of my previous races had seen something go wrong in the lead-up to the event, whether it was not being able to afford to go to training camp, getting injured or simply letting life outside of sport affect my mentality in those competitions, so I knew there was still a lot I could do to improve my training, improve my technique, improve my diet, improve my focus and improve my rest and recovery. In order to remain sane and stay motivated I couldn't focus on the fact that others were obviously tempted to dope. I had to convince myself there was more I could do to get better and in Morocco I simply got up the next morning and tried to keep doing that.

Having trained hard twice a day at altitude in Morocco, after a couple of weeks or so of recovery at home in Cork, I went to the European Cup in Leamington Spa in May. I began the race well and stayed near the front for a long time. With just one lap of the 2km circuit to go and the first two walkers, Frenchman Yohann Diniz and Italian Ivano Brugnetti, well clear, I was sitting in the middle of a group of three fighting for the bronze medal.

Alongside me were Igor Yerokhin, a Russian, and the Belarusian Ivan Trotski. I was still feeling good so when I looked around at the lads with 1km to go, I was almost smiling to myself. I remember thinking, 'There's not a fucking hope either of these will beat me over a kilometre.' I was about to win my first medal in international competition.

They both kicked shortly after that and I finished fifth in a time of 80' 15", a minute and seventeen seconds behind winner Diniz. Fifth place in a European Cup was a huge performance for me. I had broken the Irish 20km record again and Korzeniowski was very happy with me afterwards, but I was distraught at missing out on a medal.

When I got home to Cork, one of the first things I did was watch a recording of the race in an effort to see why I hadn't finished third. I wanted to find out what I had done wrong, whether nerves had got the better of me, if I had lost concentration, or what had happened. When I timed the Russian's last 200m, though, I knew. Under normal circumstances I might have been able to do a fast 200m in around forty-three or forty-four seconds but Yerokhin did his last 200m in under forty seconds. He took six seconds out of me in the last kilometre. I realised I hadn't bottled it, that it was impossible to do that naturally at the end of a 20km race. In the last 200m of a 20km race, he had finished on 5' 20" a mile pace. Walking. It was phenomenal. Trotski wasn't far behind him either and instead of getting tired, both of them looked to be getting faster. That was the first time a doper had stopped me winning a medal. (Yerokhin was banned for EPO use in 2008 and subsequently given a lifetime ban in 2013.)

After the European Cup I raced in La Coruña, Spain, but having emptied myself in Leamington, only to be comprehensively beaten, I had no motivation to even start the race. I was completely flat and had no interest in being there, let alone competing. Paco won but I only managed a time of 82' 30", which was still enough to see me finish sixth. I thought I had done enough to get by but, knowing that I'd just gone through the motions, Korzeniowski lit on me as soon as I crossed the line.

'You were in good shape but you had no concentration. This is a disgrace!'

Robert told me I was too emotional about stuff and that I didn't deal with things clinically and practically but with my Olympic and World Championship qualification already gained earlier in the year, I thought his comments were harsh and I was happy enough with having won a few bob for sixth on the day.

That summer, Marian and Cathal came out to altitude in Guadix with me and the other Irish walkers. Having taken a year or two out of athletics to help me train at home, Marian was now back running again and after trying the 100m and 200m sprints, had found her niche in the 400m. With Marian, athletics was important and she trained every week but it was always secondary to the rest of her life. She was very good but had no idea of what she could achieve.

She ran 56 seconds for 400m before she had Cathal and a couple of months after giving birth did the same again but if she had work on the same day as a race, she'd go to work. She didn't take herself seriously as an athlete and thought that international athletics was out of her reach until she started to come away on camps with me and realised that everyone there was just a normal person who trained really hard and tried to do everything right. In Guadix, she looked after me in the morning and then did her own training in the evening and was edging closer to national team selection all the time.

With Ilya and Paco the main attractions, I was still very much seen as the scrubber of Korzeniowski's group, which also contained the Polish squad and peripheral Spanish walkers, all of whom would have been at top ten in the world standard. When I trained with them, most of them would be sneering and laughing at me. This drove me bananas. I got respect from none of them but I had to keep my mouth shut if I wanted to train with the best in the world. The only way to get a little bit of credibility was to beat them in a race and, even then, the race was never big enough to count in their eyes.

'Ah, you Irish, you can be good in the small races but you'll never be good in the major championships.'

Paco, though, did his best to make Marian, Cathal and me feel at home and it was great to have them around every day. I was no longer homesick and training went really well. In Guadix, Paco was very good to us, arranging for the three of us to stay for free in a granny flat annexed to his coach Montsé's house and giving us a loan of his sponsored car for the duration of our stay.

An Olympic silver medallist and the star of the Spanish race-walking scene, Paco was the hot favourite for the Beijing Olympics the following year and was earning very good money from appearances, prizes and sponsorship deals. He kept himself to himself when we weren't training but he knew I was on the opposite end of the spectrum financially, so when I had no money for new runners he gave me some of his sponsored runners and he even gave me some clothes at one point.

At the end of June, Alberto Armas got me a few hundred euro in start money to compete in a 5km Grand Prix race in Gava. After a training session in Guadix that morning I flew into Barcelona in the afternoon for the race. Coming in the middle of my training camp, the race was just another session for me but even without tapering for it (easing off on training to allow myself to recover and gain the benefit of training), I finished second to Juan Manuel Molina in a time of 18' 59", knocking seven seconds off the Irish record I had set six years earlier.

I flew back to Guadix the next day and continued to train alongside Ilya, Paco and the rest of the group before flying home in July and beating Colin Griffin to win the National 10km Championships in a time of 39' 11".

Before the World Championships in Osaka in August, the Irish team went to a holding camp in Matsui, Japan. With athletes such as Paul Hession, David Gillick and Derval O'Rourke all there, there was a brilliant energy throughout the camp, the food was great and you couldn't meet nicer people than our Japanese hosts. It was the best Irish team and the best holding camp I'd ever been on.

Down at the track one day, I met Paul Hession's sprint coach, Stuart Hogg, and I started chatting to him about Marian. I told him her 400m times and what she was able to do while looking after me, two kids, a house and putting work and everything else before her own racing. I saw the female athletes out there and although Marian thought the chance of her making it as an international athlete was pie in the sky, I firmly believed that with a bit of coaching, she would be as good as any of them.

The Irish squad flew into Osaka the week before the championships and the night before the 20km walk, I looked back at all the great times I had done when I was younger and realised that I had never done them when it came to a big race. A lot of that was down to my mental strength as much as my physical fitness. It was about confidence, maturity, and I began to ask myself questions. 'Can you be a man and deliver on the big day? Can you follow through on the plan and be in the right shape at the right time instead of just doing it off a notion and getting a personal best in March? Who gives a fuck about that? Go out and do it in a championship.'

Although the scorching temperatures that had seen seven die of heatstroke in Tokyo a few weeks earlier had dropped by the time the racing got under way, a stifling thirty-four degrees and 90 per cent humidity in Osaka on the morning of the championship prompted the IAAF to display heatstroke warnings in the warm-up area. Despite the steamy conditions, I started well and went through the 5km mark in fifth place in 21' 42". I managed to stay with the leaders for the opening 15km and was still in contention for a medal with 5km to go. After 18km I was still in fifth position, with fourth-placed Eder Sánchez of Mexico dangling just a few seconds ahead of me. I had picked up two red cards for lifting earlier though, so I couldn't challenge him and got passed by an Italian before the line.

Ecuador's Jefferson Pérez took his third straight World Championship gold in Osaka with a time of 82' 20", with Paco closing a 15m gap to Hatem Ghoula of Tunisia to get past him for silver, while I took sixth place in a time of 83' 42".

While I'd had some good results in big races previously, Osaka was my first big performance at a World Championship level and as soon as I crossed the line, Irish team manager Patsy McGonagle came over to me and gave me a big hug.

'You did it!' he said, shaking me as he spoke. 'You've showed you can stay with the best in the world now. Next year we'll bring home an Olympic medal."

13

Beijing Bound

After finishing sixth in Osaka, Kevin Sievewright, an accountant who ran with the Eagle Athletics Club in Cork, contacted me and said he knew some business people in Cork who would like to help with sponsorship for the year ahead. The Viaduct Bar in Cork came on board and told me to give them all the receipts from my camps and that they would look after them. Seanie McCarthy from the Soho Bar gave me money on the agreement that I'd have my first medal presentation outside the bar, Robert McCarthy from Biocell gave me money and then, out of the blue, local entrepreneur Noel Marshall contacted me.

Noel had run with Togher when he was younger and is the inventor of 'The Brickie' (a tool that allows DIYers to lay bricks and blocks like the professionals), 'The BackBaller' (an advanced new foam roller for athletes) and several other innovations. He contacted me and set up a meeting in the Little Chef near the Kinsale Road roundabout in Cork. Noel asked me how my training was going and while I was in the middle of chatting, he handed me a cheque across the table. Not wanting to seem ignorant, I finished answering his question before I glanced down at the cheque. It was for €10,000! I was blown away.

Ten grand was a huge amount for me and really got my head back out of the water. It cleared my debts, which took a load of pressure off me and with everyone else coming on board as well, I decided to invest the whole lot into my training programme for the year. All of a sudden, I was able to go away, train properly and not have to worry about money. For the first time in my career, I was able to train like a professional. My only aim for 2008 was to improve enough on my sixth place at the World Championships and to take a medal in the 20km walk at the Olympics in Beijing. The extra money also meant that Marian was able to leave her job in Dunnes and go back to college with the long-term aim of becoming a sports therapist. She also started training hard herself after having taken a couple of years off to look after me.

In the races, my long-term strategy of starting out hard and fast in every event (the idea being that, as the races and years went on, I would get stronger and be able to stay with the leaders for longer every time) was beginning to pay dividends. However, in order to improve again and be fast enough to win a medal at 20km, I needed to be faster than I was before over 3km, 5km and 10km too. I wanted to break the Irish record at every distance I walked in leading up to the Olympics.

I hit my first target in Belfast at the end of January 2008 when I won the 5km National Indoor title in the Odyssey Arena and set a new Irish record of 18' 51". To top the weekend off, Marian won the women's 400m and was selected for the Irish women's 4 x 400m relay squad shortly afterwards.

My next altitude camp under Korzeniowski was in Johannesburg that March. Jamie and I stayed in Melville again with Paco, his physio Juan Louis and a few South African walkers. The camp was a bit like being in jail. We trained very hard during the day but it wasn't safe to go out in the evenings so we spent most of our time behind security railings in our accommodation.

I came home for a few weeks to recover before heading to Spała in Poland ahead of my next race, the World Cup in Cheboksary, Russia, on 10 May. I stayed in a hotel near the training centre but I was so fixated on winning a medal in Beijing that I didn't want to use up all my motivation in a World Cup race. The nearer the race got, the more hesitant I was about going.

I've always had this problem of getting motivated for all bar the biggest events on the calendar so instead of having the high of racing in the World Cup and a big downer afterwards, I wanted to do a few smaller races and be in the hunt for the win or a podium place.

While the Olympics only has three walkers from each nation, the World Cup allows five, which meant five each from Russia, Spain and all of the other strong nations so I knew it would be very hard to get on the podium there. In Spała, I did an 8 x 2km session with Paco eight days beforehand and he was so strong that I came out of the session feeling very negative about my chances in Cheboksary and decided to pull out and go to a smaller race in Sesto San Giovanni in Milan, Italy, instead. However, Paco and Montsé persuaded me to go to the World Cup and by the time I got there I felt more relaxed about my prospects.

On race day in Cheboksary, Robert told me not to go off with Ilya, Paco and the Russians at the start. Instead, the plan was to hang back in the second group and bide my time before making a late move. But I felt brilliant on the day and went against his instructions, going into the lead early and attacking the race head on.

Paco won in 78' 15" after a long battle with a new Russian walker, Valeriy Borchin, while Ilya finished fourth. Because he openly disagreed with their systematic doping, Ilya rarely went back to race in his native land because he would usually end up getting disqualified. Fourth in the World Cup, though, meant they had to select him to represent Russia in Beijing.

I was walking in the top six until, with just the final 1km lap remaining, I was passed by Luke Adams, Juan Molina and Erik Tysse and finished ninth on the day. I was frustrated with the result but I had done a great time, setting another new Irish 20km record of 77' 22" in the process. With only 48 seconds between me and third-placed Eder Sánchez, I knew if I could repeat the performance in Beijing it would put me in the mix for an Olympic medal.

I finished third in a World Grand Prix race in Poland a few weeks later behind Ilya and Juan Molina, before heading home to Cork for a short break, during which time we moved house. Marian and I had been looking around for a place that was closer to a school, with a few more houses around it so that Cathal and Meghan would have other kids to play with when they were old enough. We moved to a three-bedroom semi in a housing estate in Douglas, just south of Cork city, closer to Marian's parents and with a school just up the road. With the city just a few minutes' away, the countryside out the back and a big green area out front for the kids to play on, it was a great location for us.

At the end of June I returned to racing at the Dublin International Grand Prix in the Phoenix Park. Even though I wasn't 100 per cent fit after a couple of weeks' recovery training, after doing such a good time in Cheboksary I firmly believed that I had to be better than the rest of the field and I had to win the race.

After a few kilometres though, my heart rate was pretty high and I wasn't feeling great. Rather than read into the negatives and worry about it, instead I threw my watch and my heart rate monitor off mid-race. The level in Dublin wasn't as high as some of the other races and the time wasn't going to be as fast but it was an opportunity for me to get back to basics, stop worrying about numbers and just try and beat the athletes that were around me at the time. I wasn't flying, by any stretch of the imagination, but I managed to hang on to the front group for the whole race before finally going clear with just 500m to go.

After Dublin it was time for more altitude training: this time we went back to another of Korzeniowski's favourite training haunts, the National Centre for Altitude Training at Font-Romeu in the Pyrenees. While Cathal and I made our way over to France, Marian was en route to the European Cup in Portugal with the Irish women's 4 x 400m team. A substitute for the relay quartet, Marian got a slot in the individual event and finished third in a personal best and a time faster than three of the relay girls had done.

Improving with every outing, the squad were ranked seventeenth in the world. With two races left to move into the top sixteen required for qualification, Marian was suddenly in with a great chance of racing in Beijing herself.

Because Paco and Ilya were the kingpins of Korzeniowski's group,

I didn't stay with them in the training centre but rented an apartment beside it. I now had some sponsorship money and was able to bring Liam O'Reilly over to do my physio every day and Ray Flynn to look after my video analyses, drinks and logistics. I felt that Robert was more there for Paco and Ilya than me so part of this was to make myself feel more important, to show the other lads that I had my own backup team with me. Having Liam and Ray there, constantly encouraging me, saw me start to believe in myself a bit more. Marian came to Font-Romeu the day after her race and, after helping me each morning, continued her own training in the evenings. Having her and Cathal around all the time was lovely.

In training, Paco was flying and was way stronger than me but I was starting to be able to match and beat Ilya. Having seen him as a hero growing up, I soon began to think of him as competition, while in his eyes I had gone from the scrubber of the group to a legitimate threat. Because of this, we were constantly chafing off each other in Font-Romeu and he began trying to wind me up in every session. I knew I was never going to get respect arguing back so I just had to keep my mouth shut, stay focused and beat him in Beijing.

Marian was improving all the time too and had begun to dream of making her own Olympic debut, until Gareth Devlin called her towards the end of our three weeks in Font-Romeu to tell her that as Joanne Cuddihy was injured he didn't think it was worthwhile trying to get the women's relay team into the next qualification races in Turin. In one phone call, Marian's Olympic dream was shattered and she broke down crying on hearing the news.

Marian was very upset, but I was so focused on what I had to do that year that I gave it very little thought. In my head, I'd been to two Olympics already and was now going to a third with a chance of winning a medal whereas Marian had never even harboured dreams of going to the Olympics until just a few months earlier, so I dismissed it and had no empathy for her at all. That night I was training on the track with Jamie when he pulled me aside.

'Rob you need to relax a bit,' he said. 'This is a big thing for Marian.'

I'd been so focused on doing my own thing, living in my own bubble, that I hadn't even thought about how Marian felt and, to be honest, I don't know if I ever apologised for that. The camp in Font-Romeu was very tough but being better than Ilya there meant that I was hugely motivated for the National 10km Championships at home afterwards. I beat Jamie by a minute and a half to win the title in a cracking time of 38' 27". It was the seventh- or eighth-fastest time in history over 10km back then, so I went into the pre-Beijing holding camp in Matsui happy that I was on track for a good performance.

We stayed in the same place as the year before but while our Japanese hosts were absolutely brilliant again, there wasn't as good a vibe about the camp as there had been ahead of Osaka. While I personally found it fine, you could see people beginning to get stressed about the Olympics on our second visit to Matsui and there was a lot of giving out about flights and travel arrangements among other things.

After the experience of Sydney and Athens, I was way more professional going into Beijing and I'd also grown up a bit and was more confident in myself. At the previous two Olympics I'd felt like I was treated with no respect and I had very little self-worth. Even though we were the ones that had to compete, I felt some of the officials treated the athletes poorly and, unfortunately, it still goes on now. While all of our physical needs were well looked after, the younger athletes, the up-and-coming ones, are ignored. It's like you don't exist. All of the younger athletes are still treated like kids. In my eyes, anyone representing their country at the Olympics is at the top of their game and it's not about the officials.

In Beijing though, I valued myself enough to make sure I got some respect.

One day I came into the communal area where the team was based and for some reason Pat Ryan, who was part of the coaching staff, called me 'Robbie'. Apart from Korzeniowski, who was the king of race walking and could have called me anything he liked, I hated anyone calling me Robbie, and took umbrage at this. 'Pat,' I said, 'my name is Rob or Robert. Don't call me Robbie because then the people that don't know me hear you calling me Robbie and the next thing they're calling me Robbie and everyone's calling me Robbie. I don't want it to stick. I hate the name.'

Patsy McGonagle, the team manager, was listening in.

'Sure that's how I ended up being called Patsy,' he said.

Chef de Mission Dermot Henehan heard the chatter and jumped out of his office. Nicknamed 'The Bull', Dermot stuck his oar in straight away and put his hand up to his mouth to shush me as if I was a child.

'Dermot,' I said. 'Fuck off back into your office now, boy. Don't you be coming out here, giving out to me because you've fuck all else to be doing.'

The lads put their heads down as Dermot went red but I stood my ground. There was huge tension for a minute until Pat took me off and calmed me down and I went back into the communal area and told Dermot he needed to go away and get a massage and calm down, which broke the ice.

Marian flew out to Beijing on her own four days before the race and stayed in a hostel near the Olympic village.

On race day, the Chinese shot stuff into the air to clear the smog and for the first time since we arrived there was a blue sky overhead as we went to the line. In the opening kilometres of my race, a Kazakh took the early lead but I stayed with the chase group of main contenders. I was feeling good and, after 12km, I made a move and led the race for a couple of kilometres. Even out in front, I felt very comfortable. I thought, 'This is too easy. I'm definitely going to win a medal here.'

Genuinely, in my head, I thought, 'This is it. I'm going to win the Olympics.' It was like the scene in *Father Ted* when he's giving the speech with the trophy. I knew the big move was yet to come, though, so I eased off and went back to fifth place to relax a little bit in anticipation of that.

At the 15km mark the field was split by a move from four-time world champion Jefferson Pérez of Ecuador. Then the new Russian, Borchin, who had been second in Cheboksary, took off.

From the small village of Povadimovo outside Saransk, Borchin had been a distance runner until he met Russian race-walk coach Viktor Chegin fours year earlier and started race walking. He was second in the 10km walk at the Russian Junior Championships the year after but was subsequently banned from June 2005 to 2006 for the use of the banned drug ephedrine.

A week before Beijing, Chegin admitted that Borchin was among a number of Russian walkers who had failed a test for EPO that April but despite this, for some unknown reason, he was still allowed to compete in the Olympics.

Borchin took off with such power in Beijing that he breezed past Pérez, a legend of the sport, and watching him do it just crippled me mentally. I knew the Russians were on the gear but it was something else to actually witness the results of that up close and personal.

For anyone who runs, imagine we're walking at 80-minute pace, which is around four minutes a kilometre, or 6' 23" a mile. The next thing, this 21-year-old Russian takes off with a 3' 40" kilometre, a sub six-minute mile. Walking! I hadn't slowed down, but this guy is opening up a gap so I started to panic and fellas started closing in on me from behind.

I got really tense and my shoulders got really high and I got a red card from the Australian judge just before Aussie Jared Tallent passed me. In Guadix, Font-Romeu and Spała I had seen how strong Paco had been but he was going through absolute hell in Beijing and crossed the line just a few metres ahead of me in seventh.

I'd just finished in eighth position in the Olympic Games in a time of 80' 20" but as the Irish crowd gathered around me after crossing the line, I remember looking across at Borchin, who was standing on his own like a lost child. He had just become Olympic champion, yet nobody was congratulating him. He had no family or friends there to pat him on the back or say well done. He was just another product of the Russian system, another one off the conveyor belt, and on a human level I couldn't help feeling a little bit sorry for him.

When I met Marian afterwards we got a taxi to where she was

staying and she suddenly broke down crying. She'd really believed I was going to win a medal in Beijing and that it was probably my last shot at an Olympics. I then got upset that she was upset and I was down for a while after it, but just three weeks after Beijing I was back in Guadix, with Marian and Cathal coming out for the first fortnight of another training camp.

The reason I was still training was that the World Race-Walking Challenge final, the last race in the year-long series, was on in Murcia in Spain on 21 September and I was in sixth place overall with a chance of some prize money in the series if I finished well up there.

We stayed in the granny flat beside Montsé's house again but while I was training six days a week, the camp was nowhere near as intense as my pre-Olympic ones. I was in good shape and just wanted to hold onto that, try and perform in Murcia and finish the year on a good note.

On another blazing hot day Japanese walker Yuki Yamazaki went into the lead first, opening a 50m gap by the end of the first 2km lap. After 10km, Yamazaki was joined by Jefferson Pérez, Paco and Jared Tallent. It was Pérez's last race and there must have been 20,000 Ecuadorian fans on the side of the road that day. The support he had was phenomenal. There were busloads of them in Murcia and the organisers were panicking because they hadn't enough security to handle them if they got out of control.

Paco won the event in 83' 14" with double Olympic medallist Tallent second and Pérez finished third after vomiting his way through the last 50m. Upon crossing the line Pérez was mobbed by hundreds of his compatriots who jumped the barriers to get nearer to Ecuador's biggest ever sporting hero. There were so many of them that they blocked the road and some of the stragglers weren't able to finish the race.

Afterwards I found myself being dope tested alongside Pérez and a few others and I remember joking with him that he was like Michael Jackson with all the fans screaming at him along the course. Most of them were crying when he was awarded the bronze medal for third. It was mayhem.

Finishing fifth on the day meant I ended my season with sixth in the overall World Challenge series. I went home with a few thousand euro prize money in my pocket to tide me over for the winter, delighted with myself.

14

Panic in Tijuana

Murcia had kept my mind occupied after Beijing but with the season over and the realisation that I hadn't achieved my goal of winning a medal in the Olympics setting in, I was dejected for a long time afterwards. Seeing Borchin turn on the power and leave me for dead was really demoralising and it was hard to motivate myself for another winter.

Even looking back now, I know I had done everything right that year. I'd broken three Irish records – at 5km, 10km and 20km – on the way to Beijing and was in savage shape going into the Olympic race itself.

I was leading the Olympics with 6km to go, but when Borchin put his Russian hammer down it was mind-blowing. The whole dynamics of the race changed because Borchin was doped up to his eyeballs. I'd thrown my cards on the table a kilometre or so earlier but it was like hitting a fella seven or eight stone heavier than me with a feather. I could sense the arrogance, the power and the speed that he had left. He was almost laughing in my face, like 'is that all you have?'

A week before the Olympics, the infamous Russian walking team coach Viktor Chegin had admitted that Borchin had failed the second dope test of his career yet somehow he was still allowed to compete, not only at the Beijing Olympics but for the next six years, until he was eventually banned for eight years in 2015.

At first I used Borchin's performance as an excuse. I'd been beaten by a doper and that was all there was to it. But as the winter weeks wore on, I began to realise that I shouldn't have let external factors affect my brain: I hadn't done all I could do and I should have been strong enough mentally to carry out my own race plan.

Okay, Borchin was on drugs and there was nothing I could have done about him. But I could have still achieved what Australian walker Jared Tallent achieved in Beijing. Jared finished third and got himself a bronze medal. Why couldn't I have finished third? If I'd kept my focus, kept my head, there was something I could have done about Jared, or maybe fourth-placed Chinese walker Wang Hao, fifth-placed Ivano Brugnetti or Luke Adams who was sixth. I still firmly believe I was better than Luke on the day but I finished two places behind him in eighth.

By focusing on the one negative for a long time afterwards, I ignored the fact that I let my emotions get the better of me on the day and that I could have and should have done better. For the early part of the 2009 season, though, that trend continued and although I kept training and racing, I was sick of it and was merely going through the motions.

The new season soon saw our training group under Korzeniowski gradually fall apart. Ilya Markov had retired after the Olympics, Paco was still a huge star in Spain but he seemed to have less energy after failing to win the Olympics and Korzeniowski himself had separated from his wife and had a new girlfriend. Normally laser focused and ultra professional, he suddenly seemed distracted and not as interested any more.

Up until Beijing I had been quite happy to be seen as the scrubber in this group of stars. Now I had overtaken Ilya, finished only a couple of seconds behind Paco in the Olympics and I wasn't happy with just making up the numbers any more.

Having taken a month's break from training after Murcia, my first competitive walk of the 2009 season was a local 5km race in Guadix. With the rest of the field made up of local club athletes, I was the biggest name on the start line and was fully expected to win it but after the high of an Olympics and with nothing at stake, and little training done, I found it very hard to get motivated for it. I switched off mentally and finished sixth. The pace wasn't anywhere near world record pace yet I was on my hands and knees afterwards, absolutely wiped.

At the end of February, Paco entered a 50km race in Spain and I agreed to walk the first 30km with him to help pace him through it. It was my thirty-first birthday the same weekend and later that evening in my hotel room I began to think about what I had achieved in my career and where I was heading in life in general. I started getting really anxious and I had the first of what I later realised were panic attacks. Suddenly, I found myself crying at the end of my bed. I was in bits, but I couldn't tell Marian what was wrong with me because I didn't know what was wrong. I had a complete meltdown but at the same time, part of my brain knew that what I was doing was irrational. That was the first time it happened but it carried on throughout the year.

In March, Alberto Armas got me into a world Grand Prix race in Chihuahua, Mexico. As Paco wasn't competing, Robert Korzeniowski did not come over so I spent ten days there training alone beforehand. After having Marian and Cathal alongside me all of the previous year, I found it very difficult to cope. I missed Marian and the kids and remember feeling very lonely and isolated in Mexico.

With nothing to distract me, I had too much time to think over there and began to get very anxious again about where my career was going and what the point of everything was. I'd been to the European Championships, World Championships and three Olympic Games. I was thirty-one, still hadn't won a medal in a major international competition and here I was back starting the same old cycle again, back meeting the same old athletes on the track who were asking the same old questions: 'How's training going?' 'Are the legs strong?'

Suddenly, I felt really down. Everything was bad. I was short of breath, had pains in my chest and actually thought for a while that I was going to die. The feeling of helplessness was horrible. There was nobody in Mexico to talk to and I was terrified. It was one of the worst feelings in my life. It eventually passed but I lined up for the race a couple of days later with no motivation to be there and my morale at an all-time low.

I was rubbish in the race and finished outside the top ten, which set me off again. After doing well in the Olympics and Worlds I was back down again and I began to think about what the hell I was going to do after sport. It was very scary. In my mind, if sport was gone, my whole life was gone. My thought process at the time was completely irrational and it was very hard to talk to anyone about it, even Marian, because I knew she didn't understand what I was going through. Instead, I researched my symptoms online and started trying different ways of coping with stuff.

For me, I saw being depressed or having anxiety as a sign of weakness. I was meant to be a sportsman, meant to be so strong, meant to be winning medals for my country, but suddenly, out of the blue, everything in my mind was negative and even though I was still training and ticked all the boxes in that regard, the panic attacks kept coming and I didn't enjoy 2009 at all. It was horrible.

Eventually I rang Bill Cuddihy, the Irish team doctor, for help. I was embarrassed talking to him about it but he just asked me if I was suicidal, which I wasn't. In fact, I was the complete opposite. I was afraid of dying and wanted to live forever. The only one who really understood me was my older sister, Rhonda. She'd had post-natal depression after her first child and understood a lot of the stuff I was going through, which was reassuring.

In the end, the way I dealt with it was by hitting the panic attacks head on. By the end of the season, I'd gone through it a few times and come out the other side so for the next few times it came on, I had to tell myself that nothing was going to happen. When I got the feelings of panic, the pains in my chest, I was still afraid but really tried to just let it come and embraced it. Even though I was terrified, it was like, 'Bring it on, do your worst. Let's get this over with.' When I went through that a couple of times, then I realised I was going to be fine.

After Chihuahua, Robert wanted me to do a small race in Poland but I refused, saw no point in it. I'd already been sixth in a World

Championship, ninth in a World Cup, eighth in a European Championship and eighth in an Olympics by then and found it very hard to get motivated for any other event, apart from maybe the Irish title race.

I had spent most of my career chasing records and small wins and now I wasn't going to do it any more. For me, only two races counted in 2009: the European Cup in May and the World Championships in August. I wanted to prove to myself and everybody else that I could win a medal in one of those big international championship races. Nothing else mattered.

I spent April training hard at altitude in South Africa with Paco and some of the Irish lads and, having made another big decision before I left, I spent most of my spare time there wandering around jewellery shops looking for the perfect engagement ring. By the time I was ready to purchase at the end of the three weeks, I knew everything there was to know about engagement rings. I knew about the cut and the clarity and I was determined to get it right. It was the biggest investment of my life.

For the previous few weeks I'd been distracted a bit by the thoughts of getting married to the woman of my dreams. I spent a lot of time chatting to other athletes who had just got engaged or married, although I never mentioned anything to Marian, to see whether she might be agreeable to the idea. I finally settled on a diamond ring just before I left. I was fierce excited about it and couldn't wait to get back to Cork. I flew home on 16 April, Marian's birthday, and we began her twenty-seventh year celebrations by going ice-skating in Supernova in Ballincollig.

As we drove home afterwards, Marian started talking about how old she was after getting and how her life seemed to be flashing past before her eyes. When she made a half-hearted joke about wasting her time with me I started getting a bit nervous about my plans for popping the question later on that evening. When we got home, I told Marian that I'd arranged for her mam to look after Cathal as we were going out for a meal for her birthday. I left her to get ready and drove over to her parents' house and told them my real plans for the night.

'Oh right, Bob,' said her dad, Mick. 'Best of luck with that!'

I'd already told the manager of Fota Island Resort, who were sponsoring me that year, of my plans and he organised the penthouse suite for us for the night. I had a gourmet meal arranged in a quiet part of the restaurant and when we walked in that evening everyone in the hotel knew what was going to happen, apart from Marian. The staff had arranged a table for us in a nice private area of the restaurant and had a bottle of champagne ready and waiting for after the meal, when I was due to propose. But with the rest of the room empty, Marian made a beeline for another table when we arrived and plonked herself down next to a table containing a very loud English business-man who spent most of his time on the phone.

My nerves were already gone by this stage and, not wanting to ask her to marry me in front of this English fella, I ate as slowly as possible in the hope that he'd leave before it came around to me popping the question.

Marian tucked into her dinner and then, not knowing anything about the champagne waiting for her, ordered a pint of Budweiser. In my mind it was all going pear-shaped until the businessman upped and left. With the eyes of the entire hotel staff burning into me, I took out the ring and asked her to marry me. She thought I was messing at first but when she realised I wasn't, she was delighted and thankfully said yes. The champagne arrived and the phone calls were made to spread the good news, with my mam first on the list. She was thrilled for us.

When I told Marian that the hotel had arranged the penthouse suite for us to stay the night, however, her reaction wasn't exactly what I'd hoped it would be.

'Why didn't you tell me we were staying?' she said. 'I've no clothes with me, no makeup, nothing!'

The thought that she might need pyjamas or a change of clothes had completely slipped my mind but the following morning, the shiny ring took a bit of the attention away from the fact that she had to wear the same clothes as she had been in for dinner, and we spent the day going around our families and showing off the ring. It was a lovely time.

Having plucked up the courage to ask Marian to marry me, I didn't want us to be one of those couples who took another ten years to get married so we booked the wedding for that October, shortly after the World Championships in Berlin.

I did the 10km walk at the Munster championships the following Sunday, thinking there wouldn't be too much attention or a very big crowd there. But Rhonda and her husband Aidan turned up at the track with my nieces, and instantly I was motivated to show my former neighbour and sporting idol what I could do. I won the race in 38' 48", the fastest time in the world so far that year.

After doing such a good time, I was motivated again for the European Cup in Metz in north-eastern France, where Jamie, Colin and I made up the Irish team for the 20km walk that May. Having made my international debut at the same race as a first-year senior, I was now returning with one goal in mind: I wanted to win my first international medal.

It was a scorching hot day in France but home favourite Yohann Diniz got the race off to an even hotter start when he uncharacteristically blasted to the front from the gun. Within seconds he was gone clear. I took the bull by the horns and chased him down but, when I caught him after 3km, Diniz blew up, leaving me out in front on my own – with a full 17km still to race.

I seized the opportunity and kept going, hitting the race hard in the hope that I'd be able to hold off anyone behind who had kept their powder dry for a late charge. As the laps counted down from ten, I was still alone in the lead when the bell rang to signal the final 2km circuit. After that though, things began to fall apart. Maybe I wanted the medal too much, maybe I doubted myself a bit, maybe I just ran out of steam, but on that final lap 2004 Olympic champion Ivano Brugnetti passed me with just a kilometre and a half to go.

Immediately I started to doubt myself. Who was I fooling, thinking I was going to win a medal? Brugnetti was followed soon after by his compatriot Giorgio Rubinho and I got more and more stressed as the finish line approached.

I was still in bronze-medal position in the final kilometre or so but when I turned around, I saw African-born Jean-Jacques Nkouloukidi, who was also walking for Italy, closing in on me and I went into a panic. With about 600m to go, Nkouloukidi snatched my medal dream away from me, giving the Italians a one-two-three on the day.

Being caught and passed so close to the line was heart-breaking. It completely destroyed me. I was in a state of grief after the finish line and had a lump in my throat so big that I actually found it hard to breathe. I'd been obsessed with winning a medal in Metz and after leading the race for 18.5km only to lose out again I was absolutely convinced that I was never going to win one.

I can remember Mick Lane coming over and going on about the Italians being dirty but, as far as I could tell, I had choked again, tied up and folded in the last 2km. I'd missed out on the bronze medal by fourteen seconds and if I'd walked a little bit quicker I could have actually won the race. Afterwards I was very self-critical and it took a while for me to acknowledge the fact that my performance was still very good, brave even. I was getting closer all the time and was no longer in awe of anybody on the international scene. I hadn't got a medal but fourth place in the European Cup was a very good result.

I went back to Guadix for the month of July before coming home to win the National 10km Championships at the beginning of August in a time of 39' 11". Marian took her second women's 400m title on the day too and was now one of the strongest members of the Irish women's relay team. Before the World Championships in Berlin, I went to Spała with Korzeniowski, Paco and Olive Loughnane, who was now being coached by Montsé. In Poland, Paco didn't seem as focused as before and complained a lot about the way Korzeniowski was behaving and how his new girlfriend seemed to be taking all of his attention.

Having failed to get a medal in Metz earlier in the year, the pressure to win a medal in Berlin was immense. The pressure wasn't all coming from myself: it was coming at me from all angles during the year, whether it was Marian or Ray Flynn saying it to me, one of the Irish squad saying it to me, or other walkers saying it to me: 'You have to win a medal. You have to win a medal.' The whole year was consumed with 'just having to win a medal' in the World Championships. By the time the Worlds arrived, I was desperate for a medal.

A few days out from Berlin, after a tough 8 x 2km session, I went to a Polish massage therapist who strained my hamstring. It was so close to the Championship, though, that I didn't mention it to anyone as it would have sounded like an excuse. Rather than take the race on from the start, we devised a new plan for Berlin, where I would sit in the lead group for the opening 10km and then open up in the second half of the race and go on to win my medal.

I stayed with the leaders for the first half of the race and everything was going to plan until Olympic champion Borchin made a kick that was out of this world. Suddenly, all my medal hopes were gone. I hung onto the chasers for as long as I could. I was still in the top eight with a couple of kilometres to go but it was like I had been there already. I couldn't fathom how this guy, who started doping at eighteen to win the Russian Junior Championships, had failed two tests − that we knew of − in his career and was still winning championships. He was so strong it was superhuman and I actually felt depressed in the race, like I was being beaten up. I had no drive, no desire to fight. It was a very negative experience for me and with my head down and my morale at another all-time low, I got passed by seven more walkers in the final kilometre of the race and finished in fifteenth place.

Instantly, I blamed myself for listening to Ray, listening to Marian. Ray had been on the drinks table with Marian and his hands were shaking, giving me the drinks. Even though they were probably only advising me like they normally would have, I read negatively into everything they did, persuaded myself that they didn't understand how hard it was. Marian had always preached that I needed to win a medal in Berlin and when it didn't work out I was annoyed with her too.

I'd messed up in Metz and now I'd gone to Berlin and it had gone pear-shaped too. I told myself I should have done my usual race, been more aggressive from the start. I was never the kind of walker to hold back until the end of the race because I'd never had that massive burst of power over the last 5km. Any of the races I got good results in had been very hard from gun to tape. That was my style. All my eggs had been in two baskets in 2009 and I didn't enjoy the year at all.

I was no longer happy with the set-up with Robert either and when he texted me to meet him in the hotel later that evening, I planned to drop him as my coach. In fact, my intention was to quit the sport altogether. Korzeniowski was still on a pedestal to me and was still the boss. I was terrified of him and even though I brought Ray along for moral support, I still needed a couple of drinks before I met him.

At the bar, I met Paco who told me that he'd earlier gone to drop Korzeniowski as his coach too, but before he could get to dump Robert, Robert dumped him. Although we'd be doing our own thing from then on, Paco said before he left that I'd always be welcome to train in Guadix. When I plucked up the courage to meet Korzeniowski, he began to tell me how unhappy he had been with some of the year and that he was no longer going to be Paco's coach any more.

'You know, Robbie, you are good boy. I am like a big brother to you. I will continue to help you.'

Robert had won four Olympic gold medals, was world record holder, world champion and now here I was going to leave him without ever having won anything. I didn't know what to say but I eventually managed to blurt out, 'Look, Robert, this isn't working out.'

As soon as he gathered what I was actually trying to say, his reaction was surprisingly calm. Korzeniowski just said 'okay' and left. It didn't bother him. He was already onto the next project.

Later that night, I met Ivonne Cassin and her husband, Irish international race walker Jeff Cassin, in the hotel. Ivonne had walked for Mexico before marrying Jeff and moving to Cork. We got chatting and, having been around various teams and camps when I was younger, Ivonne began to remind me of where I came from and started going on about me not reaching my potential.

'I remember you, Rob, when you were a skinny little kid with a shaved head and a fringe. You were so talented even then,' she began.

'I've trained with all of the best Mexican walkers and I've seen you from a young age . . . You have more talent than any of those guys and I really believe you can win medals.'

It was lovely hearing it, but at that point in time, she was wasting her breath. I didn't give a shit about walking. I was retiring.

15

Tarred with the Same Brush

I love traditional Irish music. Luke Kelly, The Dubliners and Christy Moore are among my favourites and if I'm ever called upon to sing a song, it's usually one of theirs I choose. I was in the front row at a Christy Moore concert in Millstreet, Cork, in 1997 and was so excited to see him in the flesh that when he sang the line from 'Delirium Tremens' – 'as I tied barbed wire around me underpants and flagellated myself on the floor' – I let a roar of appreciation out of me and Christy began to engage with me from the stage. Afterwards, he threw me his facecloth and I still have it framed on the wall at home.

With this in mind, all I wanted for my stag do was somewhere I could have a few pints, a bit of a chat and hear some traditional music, so I rounded up thirty-five friends from all walks of life and we headed to Dingle in Kerry for the weekend.

Jamie Costin's dad, Jimmy, was sixty at the time, so the joke for the weekend was that it was Jimmy's stag. Although most of the people had never met each other before they got on brilliantly well and I remember thinking that was a good reflection on me and the friends I'd made over the years.

After spending the night in Dingle we went out to the legendary Kerry footballer Páidí Ó Sé's bar in Ventry the following day and we had great craic there. We had three or four Olympians on the stag and

I remember asking the late Páidí how he felt being the fifth most famous person in his own pub. I have a photograph at home of him shaking hands with me with a look on his face as if he was thinking 'who the fuck is this fella?'

On a beautiful sunny day in October 2009, I checked Cathal and myself into the Rochestown Park Hotel the day before the wedding while Meghan stayed with my sister Rhonda, and Marian stayed with her parents. A group of walkers from Australia and Spain came over for the weekend and with their flash suits and expensive shades they gave the whole thing an international feel. Grabbing the groom the night before a wedding is a big Spanish tradition, though, so when they all came back from the pub in the early hours of the morning they spent the next hour or so banging on my bedroom door.

With Cathal snoring soundly beside me, I spent half the night lying awake, terrified they'd get in, which probably explains the pasty and tired look on my face in some of my wedding photos. After breakfast the next morning, I went to the Turkish barber in Douglas for a shave. Even though Cathal was only four at the time, they sat him up on the chair, put loads of foam on his face and pretended to shave him too. We both got haircuts and went back for a swim in the hotel pool before getting dressed for the wedding, which was in Glounthaune church – coincidentally, the only church in Cork that decades earlier would marry people who had kids before marriage. Elton was my best man, with Ray Flynn and my two 6 foot 4 inch brothers-in-law, Shazer and Michael Andrews, as groomsmen. I looked tiny compared to the two lads in the photos.

After Elton and Shazer gave their speeches, Ray started his, which lasted fifteen minutes and turned into an election campaign for his candidacy as high-performance chairman of Athletics Ireland, even though most of the people at the wedding had no interest in athletics at all. In the last minute of his waffle he remembered to mention Marian and the whole place erupted, before I eventually had to shut him up. To this day we still slag him over it.

After honeymooning in Miami we went on a Caribbean cruise and slowly I began to contemplate the 2010 season and walking again. With all of the emotion of the World Championships gone from my system by the time we came home, I sat down with a clear head and began to evaluate everything I'd ever done since taking up the sport.

The decision to leave my coach was such a big one to make that I really only had two options left: I either quit the sport for good as I had originally intended or I had to take everything I'd learned over the previous ten years and create my own training system. After taking a stance like that against Robert Korzeniowski, who was such a great walker and is someone for whom I still have the height of respect, I knew I needed to make things work if I decided to continue walking.

I began corresponding with Ivonne Cassin and it wasn't long before I realised she knew what she was talking about. Ivonne is a maths whizz and went off and analysed everything I'd done over the years. She began to Skype me and send me stuff and when I read over it, I realised that it all made complete sense.

My endurance was always brilliant but I'd never had the top end speed needed to challenge at the end of the 20km walk. With Ivonne's help it began to dawn on me that I was better suited to a longer distance. I decided to continue walking, but with a new objective: I would have a go at the 50km walk in the future with the aim of qualifying at the distance for the London Olympics in 2012.

Ivonne started helping me with my programmes and we decided to try a first 50km race in March 2010. I planned out my year in much the same way as I had with Robert but I was now no longer part of the group: I was the one in charge and if things went pear-shaped then I'd have nobody to blame but myself.

I passed on all of my previous training diaries to Ivonne with my plan for the year and she made recommendations on my pacing and heart rates. She is a brilliant statistician and is completely mathematically minded about things. The thing that I liked about her was that anything she said was black and white. All stats and figures, she made no emotional decisions.

Ivonne is softly spoken, firm but mild-mannered, and if I wanted to do something other than whatever she had planned, she would say

'No, Rob, this is why you're doing this' and it all made sense, which soon gave me fierce confidence in what we were doing.

Although we were no longer training under the same coach, I was still good friends with Paco and planned to go back out to Guadix and train with him in the new year and stay in contact with him but towards the end of November all of that was thrown up in the air when news broke in Spain that he had been implicated in a doping scandal.

I was on a plane to Dublin at the time to meet with Ray and the Sports Council to give them my plans for the year. I was in the air for about an hour but as soon as I landed and switched my phone back on, there were missed calls from Jamie, Pierce and Luke Adams telling me about it. I was in a complete state of shock.

I had become very good friends with Paco over the years and not only had he trained with me, he had given me somewhere to stay in Guadix when I first went out there, he had given Marian and me the loan of a sponsored car to get around in and he'd even given me runners and items of clothing when I was too broke to buy my own.

When the lads rang, I couldn't believe what they were saying. I didn't want to jump to any conclusions until I found out what the story was, so I looked it up online.

According to reports from the Spanish news agency Efe at the time, Spain's police force, the Guardia Civil, had raided pharmacies and clinics linked to a Peruvian doctor, Walter Virú.

As part of a sting, called Operación Grail, the police also discovered EPO and growth hormones when they raided the homes of various Spanish athletes in Valencia, Barcelona, Murcia and Granada. A package had been intercepted on its way to Paco's house. Although Paco was never arrested and issued a statement saying that he had 'never worked with this doctor and never had anything to do with doping', it wasn't looking good for my Spanish training partner.

For me, reading the report felt like reading about the death of a friend or relative. I'd literally just got my act together, was back training with a new goal to aim for and, out of the blue, somebody I regarded as a buddy had been implicated with doping. He might as well have murdered somebody. I'd read about athletes doping before and my view was always the same: hang them out to dry, strip them of whatever they won and ban them. Maybe if I hadn't known Paco personally I might have wanted him hanged, drawn and quartered too. But I *did* know him, and he had been very good to me over the years, so I couldn't just stab him in the back and drop him as a friend, even if he had decided to go down the wrong road.

When I got over the initial shock, I wondered what he must be going through. One of the best-regarded athletes in Spain, Paco's life was about to be turned upside down, destroyed, and I was genuinely concerned for him, genuinely afraid for his mental state at the time. I was worried he might think about committing suicide and tried to contact him to talk to him, to tell him he could talk to me if he needed to. I couldn't just abandon him.

I had done the same for Cathal Lombard when he tested positive for EPO back in 2004. I'd known Cathal from the domestic athletics scene and being away on Irish teams. He was so polite and timid that he'd never even use bad language and my gut instinct at the time was, 'I know this guy is a really good person and I reckon it's the only part of his life in which he's ever crossed the line.'

I personally believe Cathal is so smart that there was never a grey area for him when he was competing internationally. I think he just knew the guys he was racing against were on it and made a clinical decision himself that this is what he had to do to get to the next level.

Because I knew Cathal and Paco, I tried to look at it that doping was just the one area of their life where they made a mistake, albeit a huge one, and crossed the line. I didn't condone any of it, but it was hard not to have some sort of empathy for the person when it was somebody I knew.

However, because Paco was somebody I knew and had trained with, people soon began to jump to conclusions about our connection and I was tarred with the same brush. If Paco had doped (and I genuinely didn't know whether he had or not), then yes, he had screwed up. But what he did or didn't do was nothing to do with me and I couldn't see the connection at all. If he had been doping

I'd have never known anything about it anyway. He had been a phenomenal athlete from an early age – winning silver was like a bad day at the office for him. Besides, why would he tell me? I was his competition.

The immediate reaction from the Irish Sports Council and Athletics Ireland was that they didn't want me to go back to Guadix, because Paco was from Guadix and they didn't want me to be seen with him. I told them that not going back there, where race walking was the number one sport and where some of the best facilities and technical coaches in the world were based, made no sense. I told them there was a really nice community out there and that they had all been very good to us over the years, whether it was me, Olive Loughnane, Jamie Costin, Colin Griffin – any of us. They'd bent over backwards for us.

'Cathal Lombard is from Cork,' I said. 'Does that mean I can't train on the track when Leevale are there? What the fuck are ye on about? There are twenty-six thousand people in Guadix and Paco is living an Almeria now anyway.'

They said they were worried about the paparazzi taking a photo of me and Paco together and that it would cause a national scandal to be seen with a doper, as if anybody cared about me in the first place. The ordinary Joe Soap wouldn't have even known who I was back then. I stayed at home in the winter and won the 5km National Indoors at the beginning of February before heading straight to Johannesburg in South Africa for an altitude camp with the Irish team. By then, Ray's election campaign had paid dividends and he was the new high-performance chairman of Athletics Ireland, which meant that, for the first time, our early season training camp was paid for and fully supported.

My 50km training went brilliantly in South Africa. Instead of a longest session of maybe 25km, I now did the odd 40km walk. Instead of 8 x 2km interval sessions, I'd do 10 x 2km or 8 x 3km, which meant my specific sessions were just lengthened slightly but the bones of my training were the same. In spite of adjusting my training to suit the 50km event, I still raced the 20km walk at the Memorial Mario Albisetti in Lugano, Switzerland. Here, Italian Alex Schwazer broke

the long-standing Italian record over the distance with a time of 78' 24"
and although I finished 2 minutes 21 seconds back – in second place –
it was a really strong time off what had been mainly 50km training.

My first 50km race came in a Grand Prix race in Dudince,
Slovakia, in March 2010. As usual, I started hard and soon found
myself out front, this time alongside Trond Nymark. The Norwegian
had taken silver behind Russian Sergey Kirdyapkin in the 50km walk
at the World Championships in Berlin the year before. We went at it
from the gun. Until Nymark stopped to relieve himself after 18km.

Seizing the opportunity, I kicked for home – with a full 32km to
go. Marian was at the side of the course and, knowing I'd never raced
this distance before, immediately shouted at me to watch my heart
rate. I turned to her and shouted back 'Fuck the heart rate. This is it.
I'm gone!'

I remembered the 30km and 35km races I had done when I was
younger and how I had been on world-record pace for 50km in the
Phoenix Park back in 2000 before the Sydney Olympics but was
made to stop by my coach. Now, in Dudince, I had found the first
18km easy compared to the pace of the 20km event and simply went
for it.

After 38km I led the rest of the field by a whopping eight
minutes. I was flying and on world-record pace again. But I was still
raw, inexperienced in the longer event and soon the wheels started
coming off. At 42km it got really tough. After another 2km I was
really struggling to keep moving forward at any sort of pace and the
last 6km were like a crucifixion.

By then, I had lapped a little Swedish competitor about four times
and, with 4km to go, I caught up with him again. He was a half an
hour behind me in the race but I ended up doing the last 4km with
him at his pace. The second and third placed walkers, who were eight
minutes back at one point, were now closing in on me but I was in
so much pain that I was crying. Marian and Ray were running next
to me now, trying to encourage me but I was blubbing to them like
the horse in the Sminky Shorts cartoons: 'I can't do it. I can't do it.
It's too hard. I'm not able to fucking move.'

My stride was breaking and I almost broke into a jog to make the pain go away. Ray and Marian had to roar at me to keep me walking.

'Rob, stop! What are you doing? You're going to get disqualified!'

The tears were rolling down my face.

'I'm not able to walk!' I sobbed.

Alongside me, the little Swedish guy was getting a front-row seat as all this drama unfolded. After going at a steady pace from start to finish, he didn't look tired at all.

Getting to the finish line that day was the toughest thing I ever went through in a race in my life. It was complete torture. What kept me going was the fact that the Irish record was 3 hours 51 minutes and I still had a chance to beat it.

I had a lead of 1' 20" on my nearest challengers with just one 2km lap remaining but after leading the race for 49.7km, I got passed by a Polish walker, Rafal Augustin, with just 300m to go. To rub salt into my wounds, his teammate Artur Brzozowski caught me right on the line and took second place in a photo finish. I walked 3 hours 50 minutes, setting a new Irish record, but earlier I had been on for a sub 3-hour–40-minute time.

Marian was now running really well and I went to Monte Gordo, Portugal, with her and the Irish sprinters to train before competing in the 20km walk in Sesto San Giovanni in May. Again, I went off hard from the gun but this time I soon got disqualified. I hadn't recovered from the 50km in Dudince and knew that my technique wasn't good, so I took it on the chin and learned another lesson.

Back home in Cork, I was self-sufficient and either trained on my own or with Colin or Jamie, if they were around. I wanted to go back to Guadix for the summer leading up to the European Championships. Athletics Ireland, though, told me I still wasn't allowed to train there. They had wanted me to have a meeting with one of their psychologists, but I'd had a bad experience with one previously. After that, I never let my guard down to any of them again.

Instead of sticking up for me, the newly elected high-performance chairman Ray, who had come away on camps and races with me, was now on the side of Athletics Ireland and told me that I wasn't going to get the rest of my funding if I went back to Guadix.

Faced with the prospect of having no money at all for the rest of the season if I trained in Guadix, I contacted Colin Griffin and asked him where he trained and what it was like. He told me he'd based himself in Livigno, in the Swiss Alps, so reluctantly, I found myself out there for my next altitude camp. Ray came out to the camp with Ivonne but then went back to Ireland after a few days. I was livid with him and told him that, as somebody who had been around me for years, he should know where I stood on doping and should have been fighting my corner instead of getting caught up in politics about where I was allowed to train.

The weather in Switzerland was terrible; there was snow, hail and freezing rain and every time we had to go through the dark tunnels carved into the mountain roads I was terrified I would be knocked down. The cold also exacerbated the problem with my hamstring but there was nobody there to treat it so, as the days passed, I was getting more and more frustrated with the set up in Livigno and just wanted to leave.

My physio Liam O'Reilly arrived out after a week or so and began to work on my leg but, shortly after he arrived, I got a phone call to tell me that my aunt Catherine had suffered a heart attack and had been rushed to hospital in Cork. Catherine was my godmother and I'd been very close to her growing up. I couldn't sleep the whole night.

At breakfast the next morning I got the news that she had died. I rang my mam, who was utterly heartbroken at the loss of her sister, but with the Europeans approaching I was torn between going back to Cork for the funeral and staying in Livigno and continuing to train. I had Marian and a family at home that I was missing too, but I knew that whatever chance I had of a medal at the European Championships would be gone if I came home for the funeral.

I'm sure I upset my cousins when I sent them messages of condolence and my apologies for not attending the funeral but I couldn't break my training if I was to have any hope of finishing in the top three at the Europeans. Shattered after a sleepless night, I went back to bed and got up at 5 p.m. and did the 30km session that I was supposed to do that morning. No matter what the circumstances, I'll always get out and train. Training for me has always been a means to an end: without training, you achieve nothing. However, the noise of the cars reverberating around the tunnels as I walked through them that evening was the last straw.

Liam had seen the state of mind I was in when he arrived, so it probably didn't come as a surprise to him when I knocked on his room door that night.

'I can't train here, Liam. I'm not happy. We'll go back to Guadix tomorrow.'

Knowing that my funding was going to be cut and that we'd have very little money, Liam simply said, 'All right, Heff. We'll go'.

We changed flights, flew into Malaga the next morning and Paco came to collect us at the airport. It was over six months since I'd seen him last and when my former training partner stepped out of his car he looked like a broken man. I gave him a hug and, as we drove, I asked him to tell me his side of the story.

I suppose it would have been easier for both of us if he'd admitted that everything in the media was true but all he said was that the doctor was to blame and that he never doped. The doctor was under investigation for supplying banned products to athletes and when he sent a parcel to Paco in the post it was intercepted and he was implicated in the scandal.

I don't know anyone who doesn't have a friend or relative who has done something wrong in their life. You mightn't agree with it, you might have a row about it, not talk to each other for a while even, but sooner or later you make a personal decision either to walk away or stick by them. Sometimes, you have to stick by your friends. If you walked away every time somebody did something wrong, nobody would have any friends. I told Paco that if he had doped, or even attempted to dope, he'd made a serious mistake but he was adamant that he had done nothing illegal. After a few minutes of uncomfortable silence I reminded him that he had been a good friend to me over the years and that while I didn't condone doping, whether he had or hadn't, I would be there for him if he needed me. Visibly relieved, Paco thanked me and we changed the subject.

To this day, Paco maintains he doesn't know what was in the package and that he never doped, but he got a one-year ban from competition and wasn't allowed to compete in the European Championships in Barcelona that year.

He drove Liam and me up the mountain and when we pulled into Guadix it felt like being back at home. Although I had come down from a higher altitude in Livigno, I was far happier to be in familiar surroundings, the weather was much better and I got straight back into training, doing 10 x 1km intervals that evening on the local track.

When Athletics Ireland found out I'd gone back, though, there was uproar. Ray Flynn phoned me the next day.

'Where are you?' he asked.

'I'm in Guadix.'

'You better fucking not be,' was his reply.

It was then that I lost the plot. I needed to train in a good environment and my career wasn't going to be dictated by rumours or gossip that had nothing to do with me.

'Who the fuck do you think you are, even asking me where I am?' I raged. 'I'll train where I want, when I want. If I go into a nightclub and there are people in the cubicles doing drugs, that doesn't mean I'm doing drugs. Nobody is going to make me do anything I don't want to do. I'm not going to be dictated to by you or Athletics Ireland. I'm out here to train, to get ready to compete in the European Championships next month and if I don't perform in Barcelona, there's going to be nobody there to hold my hand afterwards. None of you will give a shit if I don't get a good result, if I don't get funding for next year and my career is ended.'

Athletics Ireland and the Sports Council then withheld the last €10,000 instalment of my grant, half of which was due that week. That money had been earmarked for my stay in Guadix. As on all other training camps, I also had to pay for Liam's food and accommodation. Now, though, I had nothing to pay for it with. Any cash we had brought with us was soon gone.

The next morning we got up and went down to the front of the hotel lobby. The two of us were standing outside in the sunshine when, after being in foul humour the night before, I suddenly burst out laughing.

'What the fuck are you laughing at?' asked Liam.

'I'm just thinking of the boys back home. They're on about doping and here I am . . . I don't even have money for my breakfast this morning.'

There was nothing to do but laugh. A couple of minutes later, the hotel manager walked past, and I explained the situation to him.

'Look,' I said. 'I've no money to pay for the hotel at the minute. No money for me, no money for Liam, but I'll pay you as soon as I can.'

The manager, fair play to him, took me at my word, so I rang my mam in Cork and told her the story. Like any mother, she went absolutely ballistic, wanted to ring up Athletics Ireland and give out to them and it took me a good while to convince her not to.

'Mam, stop!' I pleaded. 'I'm out here training. I'm going to keep training. Just give me the money if you can and I'll have it back to you in a few weeks.'

As she had done on numerous occasions over the years, Mam went down to the credit union and applied for a loan of a couple of grand to bail out her international-athlete son.

While the Portuguese, the Germans and other squads were all in Guadix at the time with their backup squads of coaches, nutritionists, physios and video analyses, Liam was my one-man backup team. He did absolutely everything for me over the next few weeks. He had my breakfast ready when I got up each morning, my drinks ready and lined up for training. He'd loosen out my legs before training. While I walked, he had clocks, water bottles and video cameras hanging out of him as he cycled beside me. The other teams were laughing at us but I didn't care. I was getting my work done.

After training, Liam did my massage and he was always in good form. He was good fun and great to have around for morale. I wouldn't have got through that summer without him. By the end of the month, Mam had got me the money, sent it over and I was able to pay our hotel bills and book our flights back home for the National 10km Championships.

I won the championships in a really good time again, beating Jamie by thirty-six seconds, with Brendan Boyce from Donegal third. Having pulled clear of the rest of the field, I walked down the finishing straight with my index finger on my lips in a shushing motion as I looked over at all the heads of Athletics Ireland, telling them to shut up.

After the race, I approached Athletics Ireland CEO John Foley and high-performance manager Ray at the trackside.

'John, it's an absolute disgrace that you can treat a potential medallist at the European Championship in this way,' I started.

'What do you mean?' Foley asked, but I was in no mood to explain what he already knew.

'John, this isn't open to debate. This is black and white. I've lived it the last month. I've had absolutely no support, you've withheld my grant. I'm one of your biggest chances of winning a medal in Barcelona and you're not even giving me what I'm entitled to from last year. It's a disgrace!'

Before the European Championships in Barcelona a month later, the Irish team went to a holding camp in Torrevieja, a seaside town in Alicante. This time, Athletics Ireland paid for Liam to come away with me, which was great because I was still skint from bringing him to Guadix. While he was allowed to stay in the holding camp before the championships, however, he was suddenly cut loose from the team when we arrived in Barcelona and was left with no money and nowhere to stay. Embarrassed by the whole scenario, team manager Patsy McGonagle handed Liam €50 to pay for a room somewhere for the night.

While I had begun to train towards my new challenge of becoming a 50km walker, I still wanted to win a medal in the 20km race in Barcelona so I was really nervous beforehand.

There was massive Irish support over there. A big crew from Cork had travelled to spectate and I fed off that energy. I felt that the heat of the day suited me and that it would help me burn fellas off, so I decided to go and take the race by the scruff of the neck.

Immediately after the start, though, this new young Russian appeared near the front. He had really good technique, was really strong and as I was wondering who this fella was, he immediately went into the lead with Schwazer and Casandro from Romania.

Although Casandro was dropped soon after, the Russian stayed out front with Schwazer until I led a six-man chase group up to them after 8km. But here, the Russian broke away for a second time.

There were three Italians in my group, so one section of the crowd went wild every time we went past, roaring on Schwazer and Brugnetti while the Irish contingent were just as loud when we reached them each lap.

The Russian held a steady eighteen seconds on our chase group, which had now dwindled to five (Brugnetti dropped off after 11km). Schwazer put the boot down with 6km to go and got away while I was left with just João Vieira from Portugal for company. I tried to chase, only for Vieira to kick away soon after and join up with Schwazer. With four 1km laps to go, the duo were five seconds ahead of me as the Russian opened his lead.

I tried to hold the gap as tight as I could and dreamt of catching one of them at the end but while I didn't die off in the last laps, I just didn't have the legs to bring third-placed Vieira back and he crossed the line eleven seconds before me, with silver medal winner Schwazer taking another eleven seconds out of him in the run-in to the line.

A full fifty seconds before I crossed the line, however, Stanislav Emelyanov, a nineteen-year-old Russian straight off the conveyor belt from their Saransk race-walking headquarters, had proved he was the strongest in the race. In his first year as a senior, when he wouldn't even have been fully developed, he had beaten all of us easily. Like Borchin before him, I knew it just didn't add up. It had taken me ten years to get strong enough to even challenge for a medal and yet here was this teenager blowing us all away on his first attempt.

Although I was disappointed afterwards to have come so close to my first-ever championship medal, I knew I'd had a very good walk and had attacked the race all the way. Behind me were guys who went on to win World Championships and World Cups, some really strong competitors, and I felt I had done everything right in the race. Fourth in the European Championships wasn't bad and I knew that if I'd been just one per cent off, I could have finished tenth. On the other hand, if I'd been just half a per cent better, maybe I could have held on for second and taken home the silver medal.

Vieira had beaten me before and I had beaten him in other races so, as far as I was concerned, he'd just had a better walk than me on the day. Schwazer and the Russian, though, I had no respect for. Schwazer later failed a test for EPO just before the London Olympics in 2012 and was barred from competing in the Games and banned for three and a half years. It would be 2014 before Emelyanov's biological passport — a long-term blood profile built up over a series of anti-doping tests — revealed signs that he was doped in Barcelona. His results from that period were eventually disqualified and I was bumped up to third and awarded the bronze medal. When my first-ever European Championship medal arrived in the post, they had spelled my name Hefferman instead of Heffernan.

Because Marian was running in the relay two days later in Barcelona, I didn't want to go out celebrating or commiserating so I simply had a massage and tried to recover. While I hadn't initially planned on entering the 50km race in Barcelona, my time from Dudince had qualified me for the event. I had the training done and figured I'd have to do a big 50km championship race eventually, so three days later I lined up for my second European Championship of the week.

Ivonne came to the hotel for a meeting the night before the race. She pulled out all of her stats and figures and laid them on the table. 'I think it's possible for you to medal here,' she said. 'But you need to be very smart and you need to be very calculated about everything you're going to do.'

Ivonne had calculated everything from pace and heart rate to what and when I should drink. She had all of my drinks strategy made out and was on the table that day with Pat Ryan. Liam was out on the course and my physio, Mary Gleasure, had also travelled over. All the lads from the club in Togher were there again too and such good support along the course really buoyed me up.

Because of the pace of the 20km, the start of the 50km just felt so easy to me. My heart rates were really good but even so, I took it easy and followed Ivonne's plan. She knew the pace would be slower and told me that I had to take on as much fluid and fuel as possible for when it got harder towards the end – the complete opposite of what I did in my only other 50km race, in Dudince. I'd learned as many lessons in that single 50km event as I had in ten years of 20km walking: because I was older and more experienced, I was able to take them on board.

I let everyone go at the start and just concentrated on fuelling, taking in a lot of carbohydrates and isotonic drinks in the first 10km. At 12km I took on a drink that was made up of 90 per cent complex carbohydrate for energy, I took on gel for sugars at 14km and another isotonic drink after that, repeating the cycle all the way to the finish and I was relaxed even though I had been lapped by the main group containing Schwazer, Polish walker Grzegorz Sudol and a few others.

After 15km, I started opening up a little and coming through the field. I got into a rhythm and kept getting faster. Because I'd taken on so many drinks at the start though, I soon needed to go for a piss. This had never happened to me before in a race and I wasn't sure what to do. At three different points around the course I told Ivonne.

'I need to go to the toilet! What will I do?'

'I'll get back to you,' she replied. With my bladder near bursting point, I asked Liam and then Pat the same question before getting a response on the next lap.

At the sponging station, I snatched a couple of sponges as I walked past, squeezed them dry and stuffed them down my shorts and, in the hope that they would absorb whatever fluids came next, I just peed. It was a very weird feeling. In my mind it was comparable to a woman's waters breaking as I walked. It felt as if the whole crowd was watching me pissing my pants and as it ran down my legs into the sponges I remember thinking, 'Fucking hell, is this ever going to stop?'

With the sponges full, and dripping onto my legs, I threw them out and grabbed water at the next water station to wash my legs down to stop the urine stinging and chafing them afterwards. The next time I came around, the piss–soaked sponges were back in the bucket and people were using them to pour water over their heads. The lesson I took out of that was never to drink out of the sponges in a race. Later on, I wondered if that was maybe why people began to die off and I started to cut through the field.

The relief gave me another lift and I made my way past the main group and un-lapped myself from all of them bar the leaders. At one stage I was walking alongside Grzegorz Sudol, who was a lap ahead of me and in second place on the road. The Pole didn't look at me as a threat because I was still a lap behind him so he begged me, 'Robert, please help me! Help me keep it going.'

Sudol was in a heap, like I had been in Dudince, but this time I was only getting going and I soon pulled away from him. Shortly afterwards, I was in fifth place, hunting down Marco de Luca of Italy. We eyeballed each other as we passed on opposite sides of the cones and I started smiling at him, letting him know I was coming. As I edged closer he started giving out to me in Italian but I just nodded my head as if to say, 'I have you, boy.'

I passed de Luca and finished fourth behind Yohann Diniz of France, Sudol and Sergey Bakulin of Russia, who was later given two bans for doping. If I'd had another couple of laps I'd have caught Bakulin as he was dying in front of me and crossed the line only 400m ahead of me.

Afterwards, I went over to shake de Luca's hand and told him he was a big hero of mine and that the smirking had just been racing bravado and there was no disrespect intended, but he never forgave me afterwards.

Fourth place in my second-ever 50km was huge for me. The Irish supporters were buzzing after seeing me coming through the field and it was a huge performance, probably my best ever. I'd only had two days between events and had walked my last 35km faster than anybody else in the field after starting off so easy.

I'd done no 50km walks since before Dudince, as I hadn't planned doing the 50km in Barcelona so to finish fourth in a European Championship was unexpected and confirmed that the longer distance suited me better. It was the performance of the meeting, apart from Mo Farah, who won both the 10,000m and 5,000m in Barcelona. Even though I had left him the previous year, my old coach Robert Korzeniowski came over and hugged me at the finish.

I had proven to him that my decision was right, that I could do it on my own steam. I was stronger and more mature and he respected that. Afterwards, he chatted to the Irish media and told them that I could win a medal in London 2012.

Finbarr Kirwan, the Irish Sports Council's director of high performance, met me afterwards and stretched out his hand.

'You're probably calling me a bollix . . .' he began.

'I am, Finbarr,' I said.

'. . . but well done today, Rob, these results are great for us.'

'It's too late now,' I said. 'The disruption in my training was frustrating and it definitely cost me a medal in the 20km this week.'

I landed in Cork Airport to a big reception and when I got home, the whole park was out and we had a bit of a party. Derval O'Rourke had won a medal in the 100m hurdles and she was brought home privately to a big reception in Dublin. I felt I had been deprived of all that because of the drug cheats who finished in front of me. Winning a medal would have made such a huge difference to my life at the time.

Because I had just missed medals in both races, when it came to dealing with the Sports Council and Athletics Ireland afterwards, I felt the ball was back in my court. I now had a family to look after and told them that €20,000 a year wasn't going to allow me to do that. I told them that I was still very bitter about everything that happened in the summer and that I couldn't survive any more. I called their bluff and told them I was going to retire.

16

The Biggest Loss

With their backs against the wall, Athletics Ireland and the Sports Council upped my grant to the maximum of €40,000 for the 2011 season. I was delighted with the increase but even then I told them it made no sense, that their carding system was all wrong. Why hadn't they put me on maximum funding when I was younger and first showed my potential?

With that type of funding, I would have been able to afford to pay my bills, go on proper training camps, get physio and coaching more often and would probably have improved to medal standard years earlier. I couldn't understand why they hadn't put me on the top rate when I finished sixth at the World Championships in Osaka in 2007, or eighth in the Olympics in Beijing the year after.

I knew that Derval O'Rourke, who'd won a medal in the hurdles, and David Gillick, who had finished sixth in the 400m, had just been put on €40,000 contracts all the way to London. Olive Loughnane had been second in Berlin the year before and was also on €40,000 a year to London, too. They were all on contracts, while I still had no security.

In the meantime, a friend of mine from Togher, Dermot McDermott, had been telling me about this sports agent, Derry McVeigh, who worked with athletes Paul Hession, David Gillick and Ciarán Ó Lionáird, badminton player Scott Evans, swimmer Melanie Nocher and others. Dermot raved about him and told me that Derry

164

would be great for Marian and me and would be able to get us a few gigs and some extra money in the lead-up to London 2012.

I wasn't too sure about it, but figured I had nothing to lose so Dermot gave him a call and set up a meeting. The first time we spoke I was really nervous. I didn't know Derry from Adam and I wasn't good at playing the game of politics.

The only reason I was talking to him was to be nice so that he could make me money. Derry, though, was really good and began to build the Rob and Marian Heffernan brand and got us sponsors and gigs that tied in with our family profile. With the little bits of extra money that Derry brought in and with my grant increasing after Barcelona I was able to pay my bills and invest more into my training and camps. Since that first meeting we have become really good friends.

Around the same time, a new sport documentary was being filmed for RTÉ. The brainchild of Darragh Bambrick and Dhruba Banerjee, the series, entitled *London Calling,* followed various Irish athletes in their run-up to the 2012 Olympic Games. When the lads initially came down to interview me, I kind of fobbed them off. I told them they could come and follow me around when I was training but that I had no intentions of changing my routine just for them. In fairness, they just shadowed me for the rest of the year and, while there wasn't a huge effort made on my part, we got on very well together. They'd come down and do interviews and when I told them that Marian was hoping to qualify for London, too, they decided to film her efforts as well. *London Calling* turned out to be a great story and became a really popular programme.

The first race the crew came to film was in Lugano in March 2011, where I was joined on the Irish team by Michael Doyle of Tara and Brendan Boyce of Letterkenny for the 20km Memorial Mario Albisetti again. Three Chinese walkers strolled away with the medals that day but I finished fifth in 80' 54" and got my qualification time for the 20km walk at the London Olympics.

Afterwards, Athletics Ireland held a two-week high-performance training camp in Monte Gordo, Portugal, before a World Grand Prix race in Rio Maior on 9 April. With the European Championships also in Portugal that May, the race attracted a star-studded field.

This early in the year I hoped to be able to sit in the second group for the first 10 or 12km and be ready to battle hard in the last quarter of the race but it didn't quite turn out that way. From the gun, Slovakian Matej Tóth and a lead group of three went away and my group of about twenty chasers caught them after 5km. Four kilometres later, Borchin upped the pace again and walked off into the sunset, followed by his compatriot and newly crowned European champion, Emelyanov.

With the field splitting under the pressure, my instinct told me to go with the move but another part of me knew that it was only April, that I was nowhere near my best and there was a long way to go in the season.

With Borchin easing to victory, Eder Sanchez of Mexico, Tóth and Tunisian Hassanine Sebei also got clear. I ended up in the chasing group and won the battle for sixth place. I was annoyed with myself afterwards for not making a bigger effort but it was early in the year, it wasn't a big championship race and I just didn't have the motivation on the day.

I went to Guadix with a few other Irish walkers ahead of the European Cup and training went really well up to ten days before the race. Spending a month at altitude I rented a cave house dug into the mountains of the Sierra Nevada. Marian, Cathal and Meghan spent the first ten days with me. When they went home, my strength and conditioning coach Robbie Williams came out and looked after me, and I was joined by Michael Doyle in training. All in all, the camp worked out really well until I took a break in the training cycle and went home for Meghan's first Holy Communion the week before the race.

As I was flying home early on the Friday morning, I left Guadix on the Thursday evening to stay overnight in Malaga. However, I arrived into Malaga late and the only restaurant I could find was a Chinese restaurant. Not being used to the oils and fats used in the cooking process, I felt sick afterwards and got a terrible night's sleep.

I was still tired when I arrived back in Cork the next day but with Meghan running in the Cork schools championships I spent the day cheering her on trackside in Páirc Uí Chaoimh.

On the Saturday, we had her communion and on Sunday we had a party for her, inviting family and friends. It was a very enjoyable few days at the time but afterwards I was totally drained. When the hubbub was over, Marian and I trained on Sunday night but both of us were feeling terrible and I wasn't able to finish my session. I had to leave for Monte Gordo and the European Cup at five the next morning so I missed out on another night's sleep and arrived in Portugal shattered.

The added stress of the weekend meant that I just never felt right in the lead-up to the race and it took its toll in the event itself. For the first 10km I positioned myself well and, while I didn't feel fantastic, I felt that when the time came to change gears and fight for a medal I would come around. Instead though, when the battle started after 12km I just felt dead flat and the continuing niggle in my hamstring meant I had no power or fight left in me and for the first time in my life, the hot and humid conditions got to me. I drifted out the back of the lead group and finished tenth in 85' 34".

Once again the Russians were extremely strong with a couple of their team having just returned to competition from bans. This time it was Emelyanov who walked away with the gold after his second sub-80-minute 20km of the year.

After six weeks at home, I went back out to Guadix to train for the World Championships, which were to be held in Daegu, South Korea later in the year. An injury meant I was running up to 20km a day out there instead of race walking and even though Liam was treating me every day I was forced to come home for a scan, which showed a disc impinging on my sciatic nerve. Athletics Ireland got me into Cappagh Hospital in Dublin where I got a nerve root injection into my lower back, which settled things down.

I flew back out to Guadix the day after the injection and within a couple of days I was able to get back walking. I was still fit from running and got a couple of weeks' good training in before coming home for the National 10km Championships, which I used as a fitness test.

Although my flights had been booked home for the championships, my injury meant that I wasn't certain of racing until the morning of the event when I was out training and decided to start. In the race, I sat on Colin Griffin for the first 5km before opening up and winning the race towards the end. I was delighted with the win as I hadn't been able to walk three weeks earlier.

Because my training was a little bit behind due to my hamstring injury, I had to do some of the training in Cork that I should have done at altitude so I did a 40km a few days later, then took a few days off before doing more specific work in the lead-up to the World Championships.

Having packed my bags for Korea, I phoned my mam as usual the day before flying out.

'Hey Mam, how are you?'

'How are ye, boy? What are you up to?'

'I'm going to Korea in the morning.'

'What are you going to Korea for?' she asked.

'I've the World Championships, Mam,' I laughed.

'Oh yeah, I forgot about that, what are you doing?'

'I'm doing the 20k and the 50k.'

'Ah Jesus, boy,' she said. 'What are you doing that 50k for? You're only torturing yourself.'

While I might have had disagreements with my parents when I was younger, like any other teenager, I was now in a much better relationship with both of them and could see where they had come from and how they were who they were. I could see their point of view about stuff I'd been doing when I was growing up and I was now at an age where I was spending more time with them. As they had never been ones for holidays, I planned to bring them down the country for a few days after Daegu as a sort of thank-you for always being around when I needed them.

'Mam, I know we don't get to do much when I'm training and racing but after this I'll be having a break so when we get home from

Korea, myself and Marian are going to bring yourself and Dad and her mam and dad down to Killarney for a few days.'

'That's great,' she said. 'Mind yourself now.'

Now firmly part of the women's 4 x 400m relay team, Marian was also part of the Irish team for the World Championships and we flew to Korea together. Ivonne also came with us while Liam was forced to stay at home as he wasn't given accreditation by Athletics Ireland.

In Korea, as with every camp, I was so meticulous about everything that I was like a briar when I was training, but once I was finished in the evenings I'd always switch off and have a laugh.

With my last hard sessions behind me and the race just a few days away, I was laughing and joking with the team at the dinner table one night when the newly appointed high-performance director, American Kevin Ankrom, suddenly snapped and berated me, telling me to shut up in front of the whole squad.

'You're not here for a holiday!' he said.

'Who the fuck do you think you're talking to?' I asked him. 'A holiday? Kevin, my training's finished. Nothing else can be done. This week is for me to recover and relax so I'm going to enjoy myself this week and I'm going to enjoy myself when I race.'

After that, I was no longer on Ankrom's Christmas card list.

Four days before the 20km race, I did my last session on the track and was delighted with my form. I was ready to race and was also looking forward to seeing what I could do in the 50km walk. When I got back to the apartment blocks afterwards, though, there was a cluster of people hovering around and something seemed to be going on.

When I got closer, things suddenly went quiet and team manager Patsy McGonagle pulled me aside. He was very sombre looking and spoke quietly.

'I've bad news for you, Rob,' he said.

'What is it?' I asked.

'Your mother is after dying . . .'

I went into shock immediately. My brain couldn't work fast enough to catch up with what he had just said.

169

'No,' I said instinctively. 'You're wrong. Do you mean my grandmother?'

'No, Rob,' Patsy reiterated, 'your mother.'

At first, I couldn't take the news in. In total disbelief, I went up to the room to ring home straight away. Marian and Ivonne were there and when I got through to my mam's house, they were all crying at home. Within seconds I was in tears too. I couldn't stop crying. I was inconsolable.

Even now, I can still remember the exact spot where I was on the road when I last heard her voice as I phoned her before flying out to Korea. I simply couldn't take it in that she was gone.

Patsy McGonagle got my flights changed instantly and handed me a wad of money as I left the Irish camp to make sure I didn't have to worry about paying for anything on the way home. Marian and I got a taxi to the train station, where we had to buy tickets to the airport. The train journey must have been very hard on Marian because there was literally nothing she could say or do that would have stopped me crying. My whole world had just stopped.

I couldn't wait to get home to Cork, but we had to fly via Istanbul and then Dublin. It took over twenty hours to get home and I cried the whole way. It was the longest, toughest journey I've ever had to make in my life.

Upon hearing the news, Liam took it upon himself to drive up from Cork to Dublin Airport to collect us and take us home. On the way, I'd talk for a while then break down crying again. I was in bits all the way. When I finally got home and saw my mam in the coffin it hit me even harder. She'd gone up to my granny's house for a few drinks and my dad had found her at the bottom of the stairs the next morning. At first they thought she had fallen down the stairs but we subsequently found out that she'd had a heart attack, like her sister Catherine the year before. Mam was only sixty-three.

When we retraced her steps later on, we found out that her last conversation with anyone was with the taxi driver on her way home. She was talking to him about me, telling him how proud she was of me.

Over the funeral period Marian was with me all the time, but looking back now, it must have been extremely hard on her because my instinct at the time was that I wanted to be surrounded by my dad, my brother and sisters, because I didn't think anybody else understood. I didn't bring Meghan to the funeral and I spent no time with Cathal over the next few days.

Marian stayed in my mam's house with me. My brother and sisters and I stayed up all night and retold stories about Mam from when we were young. As we had often done as kids, we all slept together down in the sitting room, the night before the funeral.

While my World Championship was over before it had begun, Marian's race was later in the week. She had put in such a huge effort since Beijing and we had even put off having more children so that she could chase her dream of going to the Olympics. She had been number two on the relay team all year and was very strong but I reckoned that if she didn't go back to Korea, they mightn't even qualify for London. We were trying to get in contact with Kevin Ankrom while I was at home to get her back out to run the relay.

In the end, Marian had to go straight from the burial to the airport for the flight back to Korea. She had to pay her own way over and when she landed was forced to run a time trial to see if she would make the relay quartet. Her time was so fast that she made the team easily and a few days later she ran in the World Championship and the Irish women's 4 x 400m relay team set a new Irish record and qualified for the 2012 London Olympics.

With Marian gone, Jamie Costin stayed with me after the funeral and we ended up top-to-tail in my mam's bed that night and he stayed with me the next morning, too. The day after, I got my brother-in-law Gavin's camper van and brought Cathal away for a few days. We drove down to Youghal and parked up on the beach. I don't know if it was instinct or memories from my childhood that brought me to Youghal but we had a lovely time over the next three days.

One night, we lit a fire on the beach and had a barbecue. My brother, Elton, came down with his kids and, as we reminisced about the time we used to spend our summer holidays with Mam on the same beach, Cathal ran around with his cousins. That night was freezing but we wrapped up well in sleeping bags and we had great craic together. It was a very nice time.

A few days later I walked the beach with Cathal and I can remember being on the phone to a friend for about a half an hour as we strolled along the sand.

When I finally put the phone down, Cathal turned to me and said, 'Dad, you're on the phone all the time.'

I said, 'Cathal, I'm still very upset, boy. Nan's only after dying. It's very hard.'

He looked up at me as we walked. 'Dad. Come on now, like, she's dead four days!'

I looked down at him and realised that while he didn't know what he was saying, in a way he was right. She was always going to be dead and I had to get over it sooner or later. My mam wouldn't want me to be wallowing around Cork going drinking or feeling sorry for myself.

Cathal and I visited Jamie and his family in Dungarvan the next day and I trained with him for a little bit. I still hadn't qualified for the 50km walk in London and knew that if I didn't do it soon, my whole year was gone. There was a 50km walk on in Naumburg, Germany, five weeks later and I decided to do it. I drew out a plan, with Olympic qualification in Naumburg the objective, and gave Liam a call and told him. He came down and spent every day with me doing my physio and coming training with me.

Within minutes of arriving home from Korea Marian was back into her normal mammy routine of looking after everything – school runs, cooking dinners, helping with homework – while I just got up and trained in the morning and cried in the afternoons. It must have been very hard for her because I didn't believe she understood what I was going through.

I had absolutely no emotion for race walking after Mam's death. It made me realise that it wasn't life or death. It was only sport. You wrote down your plan, you did your training, you finished it and went home.

A week before Naumburg, I raced in the World Challenge final in La Coruña. The flight to Spain brought back the memories of the flight home from Korea and I went into a depression again. I can remember walking around before the race and everything just felt numb. All of the top walkers were there, it was a big race, but I didn't care.

Again, Borchin dominated proceedings, winning the 10km race in 38' 42" ahead of Chinese duo Zhen Wang and Yafei Chu. I finished thirteen seconds behind Chu in sixth place. I had set another new Irish record of 39' 19" and won myself some prize money but I remember being drug tested after the race and spending the whole time looking out the window so that nobody could see the tears rolling down my face. I was on my own, had nobody to talk to and it was a really tough time.

I was upset when I should have felt happy. But I wasn't supposed to be happy. My mam was dead and walking was still only sport. No matter how tough things got after that, how bad my training or racing went, whether I got injured or had no money, I realised it wasn't a life-or-death situation. It was going to pass.

In Germany the following week I started the race with a black ribbon on my arm in memory of my mam. I finished second behind Spaniard Jesús García in a time of 3:49:30, ten and a half minutes inside the Olympic qualification time for the 50km walk in London, after training only once a day. That time would have finished me in the top eight or nine in the worlds. I had a massive sense of satisfaction when I qualified and felt my mam was with me that day.

Letterkenny walker Brendan Boyce achieved a personal best when he finished sixth, two seconds inside the qualification time and he would also represent Ireland at his first Olympic Games in London.

After getting the qualification time for the 50km in Naumburg I took a few weeks off but when the time came to start back training I still felt like I wanted to get out of Cork, out of Ireland, and go away for a while. So in December 2011, Marian, Cathal and I went to Australia to live near Marian's brother Michael in Albury-Wodonga, four hours from Melbourne.

Michael is married to a lovely Australian girl. He met Kyley on the first night she arrived in Cork as a student in 2004. They hit it off, got married a year and a half later and set up house together in Australia in 2006.

I was only in Australia two days when I met up with Jamie, who had been training there and was still trying to qualify for London. He had entered a 50km race in Faulkner Park, Melbourne and although I was still exhausted from all the travelling, I paced him for the first 30km. Jamie dropped out shortly after, though, and didn't get his qualification time.

Dermot McDermott, from my club in Togher, came out to Australia with us while another walker, Timmy Healy, moved into our house with his girlfriend for the couple of months that we were away. From a working-class background in Sligo, Dermot was a real character and a maths genius. He was on the Irish Maths Olympic team after his Junior Cert.

Dermot stayed with us in our rented house in Albury and took over Liam's role, cycling or running with me while I trained, and looked after Marian during her evening sessions. Scott Hargreaves, a very good local physio, treated me for free four days a week. Marian and I got involved with the local athletics club and they gave me keys to the stadium so that I could train whenever I wanted.

The only problem I had out there was that it was plover season and for some reason these local birds saw me as a threat and would swoop down from the trees nearby and attack me every time I neared the 300m mark. At first I thought I was imagining it. But when Dermot came with me one day they didn't go near him and just attacked me as he rolled around the place laughing. I read up about the birds and found out that they could recognise their previous victims and would only attack if you were looking away from them. Because of this, any time I trained on the track afterwards I wore a white hat with eyes drawn onto it in Marian's eyeliner to keep them away, which did the trick.

On another training session, a 10 x 1km session, I was doing my intervals along the river with Dermot when we came upon two teenage girls, whose dinghy had capsized, hanging onto a branch in mid-stream, screaming. I can't swim so Dermott told me to keep going and he'd sort it out. He jumped in, saved the two girls and, soaking wet, rejoined me towards the end of my session.

Because we had both qualified for the London Olympics, Marian and I soon had a little bit of a celebrity status in Albury. The local media latched onto us and we got plenty of news coverage. As Cathal was in the middle of his school year at the time, we got him into a local school to keep him mixing with kids his own age and it was a great experience for him. He ran with his school and won a few children's races out there.

We stayed in Australia until the end of January 2012, training hard in preparation for London, my fourth Olympic Games and Marian's first.

17

London Calling

Having returned from Australia in January, my fourth Olympic year began with a fifteenth National 5km Indoor Championships in Athlone shortly after.

I trained in Cork from then until my next race in Lugano in March. Liam would come over in the morning and stretch me before training. Afterwards I slept in an altitude tent at home. I put a double mattress into the spare room, put the tent around the mattress on the floor and slept in there on my own.

The first time I used the tent it felt really stuffy and claustrophobic. Fed by a hose connected to a hypoxic air generator which pumps low oxygen air into the tent akin to the air at altitude, there was an alarm in the tent in case the electricity went off. If you didn't hear that, you would suffocate. I was so worried about that happening that I didn't get a good night's sleep for the first few nights.

I needed to spend as much time as possible in there to get the benefit of it, so I'd watch films in there, have wrestling matches with Cathal in it, anything to pass the time. Sometimes Marian would sneak in. It got really hot and clammy inside but you only really noticed it when you got up in the morning or had to go to the loo in the middle of the night.

The tent was a new stimulus and kept me motivated. It also kept me at home. I'd been away long enough.

In March, I went to Lugano again, where I finished sixth in the

20km in a good time of 80' 39" but Schwazer won the race, smashing the Italian record in 77' 30", with Frenchman Yohann Diniz just thirteen seconds behind him in second place.

Most of my early season training was still based around the 20km race but I covered the odd long walk of 35km or so to keep in touch with my 50km ambitions and by the time I got to altitude in April I did my first 40km session on a camp in Guadix.

I went to Portugal on 14 April for the third round of the IAAF Race Walking Challenge, the Rio Maior International Grand Prix. In howling wind and rain, Matej Tóth won the 20km race in a time of 80' 25", with the Mexicans Eder Sánchez and Isaac Palma in second and third. I was fourth in 81' 28", fourteen seconds off a medal, with two more Mexicans, Horacio Nava and Ever Palma (Isaac's younger brother) just behind me.

I didn't have a great race but was happy enough with my performance as I was in the middle of a very heavy training load. Afterwards, though, I was in agony from the accumulation of training and the race itself and the pains in my stomach on the flight home were so bad that the Aer Lingus flight attendants gave me the whole back row to lie down on.

At the time, former BLE chief Chris Wall was involved with the Great Ireland Run and had been very supportive towards me after Barcelona, despite our pre-Sydney falling out. He told me that he thought I could win a medal in London and that he'd do whatever he could to support me. I got €1,000 start money the next day, which went towards my next training camp.

My next trip with the national team was to Saransk in Russia for the World Cup. This time, Athletics Ireland paid for everything and the support for the race was very good. With Patsy McGonagle as team manager, we also had a couple of team physios there and both Ray Flynn and Liam O'Reilly were accredited as coaches for the race. We arrived in Russia only two or three days ahead of the race and the time difference meant that I was still a bit jet-lagged by the time the race started.

Four hours from Moscow, Saransk is in the Republic of Mordovia, and is the home of Russian race walking. Its Olympic Training Centre is the biggest facility in the world devoted to race walking and under national team head coach Viktor Chegin the high-tech live-in sports centre is a conveyor belt that has consistently produced European, World and Olympic champions for well over a decade. The fact that most of Chegin's 'champions' were later banned for doping didn't stop President Putin announcing plans to erect a statue of his head coach in Saransk in 2010 and approximately €7 million was pumped into the training centre in 2015 alone.

Like most parts of Russia, if you walked a mile in either direction of Saransk you were onto dirt roads, dotted with rusting water pumps that served the shoddily built houses, with no running water or electricity nearby.

The Russians were tough boys. They didn't mix with other people and most of them saw race walking as their ticket out of poverty for them and their families. Any time I raced against the Russians, they'd be eyeballing me and other walkers in the call room as if we were a threat to their livelihood, which in a way, we probably were.

I genuinely don't think a Russian athlete who dopes has the same choices as an Irish athlete who dopes. They're not sitting down Googling stuff and ordering drugs on the Internet like some Irish athletes have done. Doping isn't tolerated in Ireland like it is in Russia, where they simply accept their ban and then come back as if nothing happened. If you make that decision in Ireland it's different. In Ireland, you have a choice.

Although the Russians often don't have much choice whether to dope or not that didn't stop Ilya Markov making his. Ilya had left the Russian system because of the systematic doping and as a result of that he was ostracised and left off numerous Russian national teams afterwards.

In 2006 he didn't make the Russian team for the European Championships, which Paco won. Ilya had won the World Race Walking Challenge that year, was the only fella to beat Paco all season and probably would have beaten him at the Europeans, too, if he'd been selected.

The only reason Ilya got onto the Russian team for the Beijing Olympics in 2008 was because he had won the World Racing Walking Cup challenge, where he had to finish in the top two Russians and in the top six overall to qualify automatically. He finished fourth and that qualified him so he bypassed all of the politics by doing it in a World Cup race.

Ilya was a tough man, a hard man, who had no interest in gossip or what other fellas were doing. I'd asked him why he worked outside the Russian system and why he moved to Poland and he'd said, 'I don't agree with what they do with young sportsmen in Russia.' That was the end of the conversation but you knew what he was on about.

If Ilya had stayed in Russia and followed their rules he would have been given a brand-new apartment, a shiny new car and treated like all the other Russian race-walking stars but instead he lived on a shoestring in Poland. He lived a very simple life and even if we rubbed each other up the wrong way while training the odd time, he was one of the nicest fellas you could ever meet. The talent he had physically was unbelievable. He won some of the world's biggest races. And he wasn't doping.

The race in Saransk was won by Chinese walker Zhen Wang in 79' 13". Two Russians, Andrey Krivov and Vladimir Kanaykin, were second and third around half a minute back. It was a hard grind of a race in very hot temperatures. I was in third place after 5km but the front group broke up early and I finished up eleventh in 81' 51". Initially, I felt I could have done a bit better but considering I'd done a lot of 50km work at altitude beforehand and was training for the 50km in London rather than the 20km, it was a solid enough result.

I went back to Guadix in the summer and a few others came with me, including Brendan Boyce, who had qualified for his first Olympics back in Naumburg. Boycey was a student at the time and he had no plan. A bit like me when I first trained with Korzeniowski in South Africa, he would mangle himself in training and die a death every single day.

In Guadix, Liam and I stayed in a cave house up on the hills and once again he was my one-man support team and was always good for my morale. Athletics Ireland had given me €10,000 towards the cost of coaching at the start of the year but Liam had now given up everything else to look after me and was going to be with me full-time whenever I trained or raced, which was more or less every day. He would have got more on the dole.

Initially, Athletics Ireland wanted to give me the money so that I could pay Liam, but I didn't want that: I wanted them to pay him directly. I was already trying to manage his flights, accommodation and everything else and I also felt that Liam needed to be recognised by Athletics Ireland for the amount of work he put in. After a meeting with John Foley and Kevin Ankrom they agreed not to put the money through my account but to keep it on a professional basis and give it directly to Liam.

Liam was my one-man coaching team for the whole year and he went way above and beyond the call of duty. We'd often have rows where we wouldn't say a word to each other before and after training but it would always be parked for the duration of whatever session I was doing. To be fair to Liam, even if we didn't speak to each other for days, he would always get the work done and he'd always make sure I trained and didn't want for anything. He was brilliant.

In Guadix, Liam would be up before me and have my breakfast ready and waiting. He'd have all of my drinks done right, mixed properly and ready to go for training. He'd have the video camera ready, the physio's bench up and he'd massage me two or three times a day. He'd stretch me before and after training and, physically, I was in great shape.

While I slept in the middle of the day for a couple of hours, Liam would burn up energy by going on little adventures. He climbed on top of one of the cave houses one day and when he saw a branch jutting out across the roof leading to another peak, he tried to jump across the divide. He missed the branch, fell and rolled all the way down the hill, arriving in the door covered in dust and looking like Indiana Jones on a bad day.

Even when we'd been briefly based in Livigno, one of the Italian runners ran by us as his coach cycled alongside him while I was

World champion! I had a big celebration planned for whenever I won my first international race but I was so tired after the 50km walk at the World Championships in Moscow in 2013 that I could just about raise my hands.

We did it! Marian is always the first person I look for after a race and to have her there in Moscow was extra special. GETTY IMAGES/FRANCK FIFE

The night before every race I put on my Irish singlet and look at myself in the mirror. When they raised the tricolour on the podium in Moscow my heart nearly burst with pride. SPORTSFILE/STEPHEN McCARTHY

Looking tache-tastic for Movember with Usain Bolt at the 2013 World Athletics Gala in Monaco.

Swapping medals with Sonia O'Sullivan at Bramley Lodge in Cork, September 2015. I am holding her gold medal from the 5,000m at the 1995 World Championships in Gothenburg.

The two Roberts: meeting four-time Olympic champion Robert Korzeniowski at the 2000 Sydney Olympics was the turning point in my career. The Polish legend took me under his wing and became a coach, mentor and good friend to me. Pictured here in London after the 2015 London Marathon.

Having abandoned the 50km at the 2014 European Championships in Zurich, I felt it appropriate as world champion to congratulate the winner Yohann Diniz afterwards. To my surprise, Diniz grabbed my hand and kissed it.
SPORTSFILE/STEPHEN McCARTHY

If it hadn't been for Marian's support, I would never have got through a nightmare 2015 season, let alone finished fifth at the World Championships in Beijing. SPORTSFILE/STEPHEN McCARTHY

FACING PAGE: A week before the 50km walk at the 2015 World Championships in Beijing, seven people died of heatstroke and athletes were warned to try and stay cool. SPORTSFILE/STEPHEN McCARTHY

Proud Dad: with my daughter Meghan after she became the Cork County Under-Fourteen 800m champion in 2016.

The rest of 'Team Heff': with Cathal, Tara, Marian and Regan, taking time out from training camp in Guadix, July 2016.

Chatting with former sprint hurdles champion Derval O'Rourke and good friend Pat Morley of Scribe of London before leaving for the Rio Olympics, 2016.

Going for Olympic gold in the 50km walk in Rio 2016. Behind me are Jared Tallent (who went on to take silver), Andrés Chocho of Ecuador (hidden), Slovakian Matej Tóth (the eventual winner) and Japan's Hirooki Arai.

INPHO/JAMES CROSBIE

Walking tall. Sixth place in my last Olympics, Rio 2016, wasn't what I had hoped for but I was happy that I had given it my all and I tried to enjoy the final 2km lap. SPORTSFILE/STEPHEN McCARTHY

training, so Liam challenged his coach to a bicycle race. He took off hell for leather around the lake in St Moritz and pipped the Italian coach on the line but was in bits afterwards. Often after training he'd run home, which could be a distance of 10km. He just couldn't stay still.

Liam was worth ten times what Athletics Ireland gave him but they didn't recognise his work rate and how much of an integral part of my daily routine he was and even with the coaching money he got he was still out of pocket, which made me feel fierce guilty all year.

Having been with me all year, I wanted Liam with me at the Olympics but I had a huge battle with Athletics Ireland to get him accreditation for the races in London.

Marian had decided to give up on her individual goals in order to compete with the women's relay team and was also racing throughout 2012, so sometimes we were like ships in the night on our way to or from training sessions.

With Kevin Ankrom having appointed himself as the women's relay team coach there was no shortage of money available to her squad and everything was paid for, from camps to competitions throughout the year, which baffled me as it had never happened to the walkers.

Marian was being coached by Stuart Hogg by then but was in a bit of a predicament as her training workload meant that she was only number five or six for the relay team for much of the early season, which, as far as we were concerned, didn't matter as long as she hit form for London in August. There is still the mentality in Ireland, however, that short-term results are what counts and, with no long-term planning for the development of athletes, word filtered back to us that she was not going to make the Olympic team. But I knew that as soon as she started tapering for races she would come good. She did and got selected for the sprint quartet.

I eventually managed to get accreditation for Liam as part of the Irish set-up for London which took huge pressure off me as we headed off to our pre-Olympic holding camp.

The Irish squad was based in the plush surrounds of The Lensbury Hotel and Country Club in Teddington. Close to the Twickenham rugby ground, the hotel is regularly used by the England rugby team and we had training facilities on site as well as in the nearby St Mary's University or Bushy Park.

With the kids being looked after at home, our entry to the Olympic holding camp with the Irish team was the first time that Marian and I had been away together on our own since we got married. With all of our hard training behind us, we had less work to do and, in between those last few sessions, our time together was spent trying to relax ahead of our races. It was a great time. We stayed in the same room and the hotel was really plush and quiet, and close to Bushy Park where we trained.

On an almost unanimous vote, I was nominated captain of the Irish athletics team for London. For me to have come from being almost a bag carrier in Sydney in 2000 to being the captain of the whole Irish athletics team was a huge honour and I was immensely proud of it.

I gave the squad a motivational talk along with the team management before the Olympics and also used my captaincy to drive myself on. I wanted to lead by example and show the younger athletes what you could achieve if you went about things in a professional manner.

Training went really well and the only thing that went wrong for the duration of that camp was during my last hard session on the local track. The conditions in London were uncharacteristically hot for that time of year, so in order to know whether I was going too hard or too easy, I asked Pat Ryan to bring my lactate machine to the track so that I could gauge my training off my blood lactate. I wanted to be able to control my session and make sure I didn't dig myself into a hole a few days before the race.

I was doing 600m efforts at a pace of around 2' 18". On a normal day, my blood lactate could have been four or five for this sort of effort but in the heat and humidity of London at the time it might have been eight or nine, so the machine would tell me whether I was overcooking my efforts and if I needed to adjust my tactics for the 20km race accordingly.

Pat, though, never brought the machine to the track, so I did those last hard efforts off feel. With the Chinese, the Aussies and the Japanese all watching me, there was an awful temptation to go too hard and I was raging that all year everything had been calculated and now, a week out from the Olympics, I didn't know whether I was overcooking myself or not training hard enough on my last session.

As usual, I began to get a bit antsy in the week leading up to my first race, the 20km event. I've always been like that. The closer a race the more self-sufficient I'd get. My training for the year was done and there was nothing more anybody could do for me. In those last few days before a big race, I didn't really care what anybody else was doing or what anyone else felt. I retreated into myself and all I thought about was the race itself.

Liam, on the other hand, was buzzing. With less training to be done, he also had less work to do and was like a ball of energy. I can remember looking out my window one morning before meeting up with some of the other walkers and triathletes to go training in Bushy Park. Down below, Liam was the first one to arrive in the car park and with nobody else around, he was so hyped up that he began to do press-ups. The more coiled-up Liam got though, the more relaxed I became and by the time race day arrived, I was almost serene.

On Olympic race day, your whole itinerary is mapped out, from breakfast to the start of the race. In London, after eating and resting and packing my kitbag, I met with all of the other walkers at a designated area outside the Olympic Village before boarding the same bus for the short trip across the city to the race circuit.

With each athlete eyeballed and assessed for any sign of weakness, this bus journey was often the first chance to wind up your opponents and some athletes would make little comments and snide remarks to try and unnerve others, or throw their focus before the race. It's like the preliminary psychological battle before the war, but after Sydney, Athens and Beijing, I was well prepared for it and was actually looking forward to it.

I sat down beside Liam as the Mexican walker Eder Sánchez stepped on board. Sánchez was in good form that year and had won two of the IAAF Race Walking Challenges before London. Maybe that's why he tried to wind me up first. He had done the same in Beijing when he asked me if I was nervous as we waited in the call room ahead of the race.

'Of course I'm nervous, Eder.' I'd answered back then. 'It's the Olympic Games, boy. Are you not nervous?' Instead of cracking me, Sánchez had begun to think about my question and cracked himself, finishing way down the field that day.

'Rob,' he said leaning over my headrest in London. 'You have no Irish teammate to help you in competition?'

'No, Eder, boy,' I laughed. 'I don't need one, sure I have you!' which threw it back at him again. Liam started laughing at the confused Mexican when his phone rang and he took the call.

Within seconds, I was back in my own world, looking out the window of the bus as Liam chatted away to Marian. I wasn't fully tuned into the conversation. I could hear him say 'okay' a lot and laugh heartily a couple of times but was so focused on the race that when he put the phone down I didn't even ask him what she wanted.

It turned out that Marian had phoned him to tell him that I had left my Irish singlet complete with my Olympic race number hanging in the wardrobe at the hotel. Liam knew that if I found this out, my race would be destroyed before it even began, so he had continued chatting as normal and threw in a few laughs as well for my benefit.

The bus journey ended at the warm-up area, where each nation had individual tents set up for their athletes. When we got to the Irish tent, Liam told me to go off and have a stroll around, which I did, completely oblivious to the pandemonium that was going on in the background to get my race kit to the start.

The Irish tent was next to the Italian one and I remember walking past and seeing Giorgio Rubinho in there. Rubinho was a really good athlete but I knew by the look on his face that morning that he was cracked. He was gone before the race even started. That gave me another little boost.

I had a glance at the warm-up area and then sauntered over for a look at the start before heading back into the tent. Kyle Alexander, a massage therapist, was telling me a funny story about his buddies being out in Australia when, abruptly, Marian arrived into the restricted area.

'What are you doing here?' I asked.

She pulled my race singlet and my number out from under her top. I couldn't believe it, but with a couple of hours still to go to the race start, there was no need for panic.

The first kilometre of the race itself was really slow but after that, it started to kick off and I went with the lead group. As it was pretty blustery that day I found myself walking behind Russian Vladimir Kanaykin for a while. Kanaykin had been banned in 2008 after testing positive for EPO and would later be given a lifetime ban for repeat offences. In London, though, he still had the neck to turn around and give out to me for using him as a wind shield during the race.

He probably didn't understand the words that came out of my mouth immediately afterwards – which were something along the lines of 'Shut the fuck up and turn around, you cheating bastard, before I hop you off the barriers,' but my body language ensured he didn't utter another word to me for the rest of the race.

The Irish support all the way along the 2km circuit was phenomenal. There were tricolours flying everywhere and there were an unbelievable amount of people cheering my name and urging me on.

I was five seconds down in second place at around the halfway mark and when I got dropped from the front group a couple of kilometres later, it was that support that saw me regain contact. With under a kilometre to go I was in eighth position but was fighting to hold off Bertrand Moulinet from France and Irfan Thodi of India. Moulinet caught me in the finishing straight and beat me by six seconds but I managed to hold off Thodi to finish ninth in a really good time of 80' 18". After crossing the line, Moulinet came over and apologised for beating me but he had done a very good walk and I told him so.

'Jaysus, no! Don't be apologising, boy. Well done. You did excellent.'

Although I'm never happy with any of my performances, I had done one of my fastest-ever times over 20km in London and finished ninth in an Olympic Games, in an event that was no longer my main event, so I went back to the team hotel afterwards pretty content with my day.

Usually after an Olympic race you're out partying and celebrating because your year is finished but with the 50km walk a week later, I went and had my lunch with the rest of the athletics team. Although their event was almost a fortnight away, Marian and the relay girls had already been sent into the village by Kevin Ankrom, so I went back to an empty room where I had an ice bath and got into bed. It was a weird experience, lying there watching the highlights on TV afterwards. We had passed Buckingham Palace ten times in the race but I hadn't even noticed it until I watched the playback.

My training for the 50km had gone really well in Guadix and I was completely fixated on winning a medal the following week, but I also knew I had to be relaxed. I'd had the experience of what the crowd was going to be like from the 20km event and I knew not to get carried away at the start and that I could use the energy of the Irish fans to my advantage when the time came.

Aussie walker Luke Adams, who I'd consider a good friend, had a pop at me on the bus this time, saying that I was going to get disqualified. I jotted his name down in the little black book stored in the back of my brain and tried to forget about it.

On the way to the start, I reminded myself that this specific day had been planned for years. I knew I had the ability to do a good 50km walk after Dudince, where I was working off sporadic 50km training. Now, with the proper groundwork done, all the 40km and 35km tempos in training, everything was riding on this one day.

I knew the dynamics of previous championships from going back and studying them. I knew that while you could start the race with fifteen people in the same shape, not all fifteen of them would be able to produce the goods on the day. If I could concentrate on my own performance and do everything right, I had a good chance of an Olympic medal.

Although the Russians – Kirdyapkin and Bakulin – and the Chinese and Aussies were all gone from the gun, I had to stick to my own plan and, as I had in my previous 50km outing, I worked off my heart rates for the first 20km, ignoring everything else. I went through the first 20km in 88 minutes, eight minutes slower than I had done in the 20km race a week earlier, and about forty-five seconds behind the leading pack, in around fifteenth place. The pace felt slow to me and I was walking within myself, taking on drinks and sticking to the plan.

My heart rates were still really good though so there was no panic just yet. I knew I could go faster over the last 30km, as I had done in Barcelona. I was also in better shape than in Barcelona. If I controlled what I was doing for the first half of the race, people were going to implode up front and start falling back.

After 25km I looked over at Ivonne on the drinks table. She asked me my heart rate and when I told her it was 155 bpm, she said 'OK, Rob, now it's time to start moving.'

From then on, I started cutting through the field and progressively got faster. I had the quickest split of the whole race from 30km to 35km and when the crunch came after that, the buzz of the Irish crowd really lifted me, and I passed Yohann Diniz and then Slovakia's Matej Tóth.

I'd always felt that if my event was showcased on the highest level on the international stage and the Irish people got to come out and watch it, that they would appreciate it and that's what happened in London. I'd never, ever experienced anything like the atmosphere in that Olympic 50km – not even in the 20km walk just a week before.

I began to pass more and more fellas and when I caught and passed Luke Adams I couldn't help but remember what he'd said on the bus and thinking karma had come back to bite him. The Kiwi Nathan Deakes, a former word champion and a legend in the sport, had been in the lead at the halfway point but was now just ahead of me on the road. I was still feeling strong, while his wheels were coming off. Fair play to Deakesy though, he actually encouraged me as I went past.

All of my family and friends were there in London. Some of them had never seen me race in Ireland before and the boost I got from their support all around the circuit was incredible. As well as Ivonne, Liam and Ray shouting encouragement to me, I could also hear my old coaches and friends from Togher roaring me on. I fed off the Cork accents all along the route calling my name. I even geed up the crowd at one point and there was a wave of support for me all the way around the course as I cut through the field.

I was up to sixth place with around 8km to go and caught the Russian duo of Sergey Bakulin and Igor Yerokhin just as we came to the drinks station. Their coach, Viktor Chegen (who was banned in 2016 after coaching over twenty-five Russian walkers who failed dope tests), made eye contact with me and, in a condescending manner, gestured for me to slow down.

Bakulin, who I'd had words with in the 20km, was the current world champion and I caught him first. We got into a bit of a race between ourselves for a while and I got a massive kick when I dropped him with 5km to go and moved up to fifth place on the road, a few metres behind Yerokhin. Ahead of me, I could see Yerokhin was suffering and the sight of his Russian singlet gave me fierce motivation to reel him in because the Russians were meant to be so strong.

Cathal and Meghan were at both races in London and every time I went down the finishing straight Cathal had been hanging over the barriers banging the hell out of them with tears rolling out of his eyes because he wanted me to do well. That was another really powerful motivation.

I caught Yerokhin with a kilometre and a half to go. He came back at me again but there was no way I was ever going to give up when my young fella was watching me race. I knew the Russians weren't on a level playing field but if I gave up, how could I face Cathal? How could I face Meghan? How could I be a dad to my kids, be someone they could look up to if I gave in to the negative emotions going on in my head?

Coming down the finishing straight, Yerokhin and I went at it hell for leather towards the line. There were maybe 200,000 people on the course that day but all I could see was Meghan on one side of the finishing straight and Cathal on the other. That spurred me on. I could see Cathal banging the barrier with tears on his face, screaming, 'Go on, Dad, you can beat him!' In the final sprint for fourth place that day, that's what got me over the line ahead of the Russian.

I could lie and say that if the race went on a bit longer I would have caught the others. The winner, Sergey Kirdyapkin, had set a new Olympic record of 3:35:59 and both he and second-placed Jared Tallent of Australia were well clear. The Chinese lad in third, Si Tianfeng, was dying, maybe half a minute in front of me, but I admired his tenacity in holding me off and not cracking under the immense pressure he must have been feeling. There had been millions invested in Chinese race walking in the lead-up to London and one of them was expected to deliver. I knew the pressure of being in a medal position and he could easily have folded and dropped back ten places.

Fourth in the Olympic Games, though, was very hard to take, even though I had smashed my previous Irish record over 50km, with a time of 3:37:56. I'd been fourth in big championships before, but I really thought that this time I was meant to get the medal. I'd heard that Jared Tallent had got five yellow cards out on the course and two reds. All it would have taken was for one other caution to come in from one of the judges and I'd have had a medal. I was praying that Kirdyapkin, who I was sure was doping, was going to be caught in the drugs test afterwards, have his gold medal taken off him and I'd be bumped up to bronze. Patsy was clearly hoping the same as me when he reached me.

'This isn't going to be the end of this,' he said. 'We could have a medal out of this yet.'

But all of this was clutching at straws and both mentally and physically I was in a heap afterwards. As soon as I crossed the line I was down on my hands and knees on the hot tarmac. By the time Liam arrived on the scene, I was sitting on the road with my head in my hands. My Olympic dream was finally over. Gone.

The medical team were trying to put me in a wheelchair but I was too embarrassed to let them. Through the mayhem, I waited for Marian. I wanted her take on the race, her approval. I still hadn't won a medal but when she ran through the crowd and reached me she gave me a big hug and told me I'd done brilliantly.

The emotion of the day finally got to me and I started crying but copped onto myself a few seconds later when Liam started bawling. I was the one after missing out on a medal in the race and I couldn't understand what Liam was crying for. In fairness, he had been with me all year and wanted a medal as much as I did but I wasn't comfortable with it at all and it made me wipe my eyes and stop my own snivelling.

Immediately after the race I went into a nearby bar, The Bag of Nails, and when word got around I was in there, the place filled up with people from Cork. Cathal and Meghan, my dad and all of my family were there and after a while Yohann Diniz came into the bar too. He congratulated me and we had a drink together.

After not having had alcohol all year, I was feeling tipsy after just one pint of Guinness when word came in that Bill O'Herlihy and the panel in RTÉ wanted to talk to me. John Foley of Athletics Ireland also had a drink with me first and about an hour later I spoke to them live on air. I was half-cut by that stage and must have said 'thank you' about seven times in a row. I was glassy-eyed and happy.

From The Bag of Nails we went to the official Irish bar where some of the boxers had arrived in with their medals. Singer-songwriter Bressie and Niall Horan from One Direction were there and it was a great night. At one point I was behind the counter dishing out Ireland T-shirts and signing them for people. We stayed there until four in the morning.

Five or six hours later, I woke up feeling absolutely wrecked. I was never so sore after a race and could barely move. Even my arms were cramping. I still couldn't walk by the time the closing ceremony came around later that night, so Marian had to give me a piggyback into the Olympic stadium.

I enjoyed the closing ceremony but was so shattered that I spent most of it sitting on the ground, unable to stand to watch the acts on stage. Marian and I tried to leave the stadium a little bit early to avoid the stampede but when we got to the gates they wouldn't open them until the closing ceremony was over. Having left the track centre, though, we weren't allowed back in either, so we were stuck in no man's land as Take That came out and sang our wedding song, 'Rule The World'.

The Olympic Council of Ireland had a bit of a party in the village afterwards but I was so tired that I lasted only about half an hour before I had to go to bed.

When we flew back home afterwards I was taken aback by the reaction from people in Ireland. Because I'd been away training when the *London Calling* documentary series was aired, I hadn't realised how many people had watched it and how much of a following I had at the time. My profile had gone up and everybody seemed to know who I was. I couldn't go anywhere without being recognised and congratulated. So many people were going on about the race and telling me they were there or watching it live that it almost felt as if I had won a medal.

When the dust settled and things quietened down, however, the realisation sank in that I didn't have a medal and I had to go back to Athletics Ireland for funding for the following year. Derry and I met with Kevin Ankrom of Athletics Ireland and Finbarr Kirwan of the Sports Council to try and secure funding for another tilt at the Olympics in Rio in 2016.

When Olive won a medal, Derval O'Rourke finished fourth and David Gillick finished sixth in the World Championships in Berlin in 2009, they'd all been contracted right up to London whereas I'd never had that security. I knew that the boxers had come back from London and were immediately given four-year contracts all the way to Rio, at the highest level of €40,000 a year.

My performance in London would have won a medal in every single Olympics prior to that and would have won gold in most of them. I was sure that the winner of my race, Kirdyapkin, was dirty and I tried to explain how close I had come to getting bronze.

I argued that while I had a good training programme set up, I needed the security of a long-term contract to be able to go one more Olympic cycle without having to worry about my family. But I was told I was too old, that they only could support me for another two years and would review things after that. Under their own rules, they had to give me two years anyway.

191

I tried to make the case that while the boxers had a full-time live-in training centre, that all of their training camps were paid for, their full-time coaches were paid for and that they still got their funding on top of that to use for whatever they wanted, I'd had to pay for all my own training camps, had to book flights and accommodation, pay for my own physio and whoever else was coming with me, all out of my funding, which left me with very little to live on. I tried to secure a full-time coach in the meeting but they told me it wasn't their job to find me a coach.

Derry was taking notes and trying to get things tied down but they gave me nothing more than I'd already had, apart from 'guaranteeing' me a job when I retired. Naively perhaps, I came home happy because of this. It gave me a sense of security and relief but it was only a verbal agreement, which, as the old saying goes, isn't worth the paper it's written on.

18

Top o' the World, Ma

After meeting with Athletics Ireland at the end of 2012, I sat down with Marian and asked her if she thought it was worth trying to get to Rio at all. Although I had funding secured for 2013, even after finishing fourth in London I still had to perform again in order to secure funding for 2014 and if I had a bad year, there would be massive pressure on me the following season.

Marian though was adamant that she'd seen things over the year that I could improve on and that I could still win medals in the run-up to Rio and in the 2016 Games itself.

Soon after, Marian, Cathal, Meghan and I went on holidays to Benalmádena in Spain as a family and, even there, other Irish holiday-makers were still coming up to me congratulating me on my performance in London.

While the altitude training and being away on camps is just part of the job, the one thing I hate about my training schedule is being away from the kids. At home we spend all of our time together as a family. When I'm not training I'm at their matches or their races and when I am training, half the time they're training with me on their bikes or doing their own training down at the track.

Although Meghan lives with me only at weekends or during holidays, I talk to her every single day and we're very close. I'm proud of the way she has grown up and she's becoming quite the athlete herself. Cathal has come away on most of my training camps and has even done my drinks on numerous occasions. He's seen me train and race so often that he knows my walking technique inside out. He's like a mini-coach and has no qualms in telling me what I'm doing wrong. 'Dad, your arm is going this way . . . your leg isn't landing right.' Most of the time he's right.

In the pool in Benalmádena, we were having a great laugh when, during a break from messing around in the water, we were chatting about the Olympics.

'You know, lads, it's very hard going away all the time,' I said. 'What if I said to you I was going to retire?'

Straight away, they both said, 'No! Dad, you can't!'

'But if I retire, we could do stuff like this all the time,' I insisted.

They were still adamant they didn't want me to retire. Cathal and Meghan loved what I was doing and that was a massive support for me because if I felt for a second that the kids thought they were missing out on me being their dad or if I was distant from them, I wouldn't have carried on.

Another major disappointment for me after London was the fact that Liam still hadn't got a full-time job with Athletics Ireland. His workload looking after me was huge and while it was grand doing it for a year, it was a completely different ball game to ask him to sign up for another four-year Olympic cycle with me without him even getting an official position, or at least some more money from Athletics Ireland to be able to continue what he was doing.

I'd always felt responsible for Liam not having a full-time job as he'd been at my beck and call for the previous year. He was buzzing from London when we came home but when he applied for a position with Athletics Ireland afterwards, he didn't even get called back for a second interview. There was no respect there and Liam was understandably under pressure from his family for spending so much time with me for no financial return. In fairness, I probably saw more of him than his wife did that year.

At the start of 2013, I planned out all of my camps as usual and asked him if he was able to come on board again. At the time, Liam was waiting on job offers from the GAA and others and wasn't sure what commitment he could give, so I waited. But when 1 November came and I was back into training, I told him that I couldn't wait any longer.

'If you're not coming that's OK,' I told him. 'I just need to know whether 1 have to get somebody else or not.'

'Look, Heff,' he said, 'I can't commit,' which was fine. Liam was upfront about everything and, even though we'd often had arguments, we never fell out and to this day he is one of the first people I phone for advice or if I have a problem. When I returned to racing without Liam, however, there were rumours that I had dumped him. Ever the athlete, I focused on my training and the upcoming 2013 season.

I had experienced the post-Olympic hangover from Sydney, Athens and Beijing and was determined not to let that happen to me after London. I wasn't going to take my finger off the pulse. I had made too many inroads and knew that if I could tidy up a little bit of my training over the year that I could improve that little bit again.

But even though I'd just finished ninth and fourth in the 2012 Olympics, I was going back to training in 2013 with absolutely no support team. Marian offered to come on board as Liam's replacement. Having gone to a European outdoor championships, a world outdoors and the Olympic Games, she figured she had achieved what she was going to achieve in her sporting career and wanted to help me reach the full potential in mine.

We talked it through, looked at the pros and cons of her having to look after the kids, the household and do my drinks, massage, video work: everything Liam had done. Marian had been offered a place on a degree course in University College Cork in 2012 but had already deferred it to run in London. Now, she was offering to put her whole life on hold again to look after me. I was hesitant to put her under such a big workload but, with no other choice available, we tentatively agreed to give it until Christmas and review things then.

Having spent the previous summer with me in Guadix, and competed in London, Brendan Boyce asked me to coach him for the 2013 season. I knew it would be a big commitment to take him on but having seen how ridiculous his training was, it was hard to say no to helping him.

Boycey had just finished university, been to an Olympic Games and his only other option was to go back to the hills of Donegal, so he left his student accommodation in Coventry, moved to Cork and suddenly, he was my responsibility. I got him somewhere to live, got him sorted out with a gym. He had me making out his training plans for the year and Marian helping with his drinks and logistics. Within days, Brendan had as good a training system as anybody in the world while I now had to balance coaching, training and family life.

I was also coaching a young Cork walker, Luke Hickey from Leevale, at the time and I put a lot of energy into both of them. The duo came training with me every day and I found that telling them how to periodise their year and what training to be doing at what time of the season reinforced what I should be doing myself. Having started like I had, with no guidance or advice, both of them were coming into a professional structure that had taken me over ten years to learn and they soon made big improvements.

Because I was coaching Brendan and Luke, Marian had the added responsibility of looking after them on every training session. Everything was balanced on a fine line between looking after the kids and training. I had to get on with my training but we still had two children to look after and we had always planned to have another one after London.

The weekends were manic. On a Saturday we'd go to the track with the kids so that I could tie in my training with theirs. They were training with Leevale on a Saturday morning so I'd start my training at the same time to kill two birds with one stone. I'd still have to sleep in the afternoons, and in the evenings Meghan or Cathal would come out on the bike with me or jog alongside me on the road. If I went to the track, they'd come and play hurling in the track centre while I trained. Everything in our house revolved around me and my training.

I don't know how she did it but Marian was brilliant. By the time December came, there was no stress and I was happy with the way things were going. I trusted Marian 100 per cent and I could just concentrate on my training. Some of Marian's workload had been eased briefly when I was given more access to Athletics Ireland's full-time physio Emma Gallivan that winter. Emma came down to Cork once a week, or if I went to Dublin she'd treat me there, which was great. But that all dried up pretty quickly when Ankrom decided to change things around as he felt it was too expensive.

He sent me an itemised bill of how much it was costing to send Emma up and down to Cork and how much it cost to send her to a training camp. I felt that that was none of my business and that it was really unprofessional of him. Emma was a great physio and was employed by Athletics Ireland to keep their athletes healthy so they could perform on the biggest stage. Anyone based in Dublin had physios available to them on a daily basis but now I was being told it cost too much to send her to Cork once a week. I had a blazing row with him over it.

'Does the groundsman in the Aviva Stadium's pay get taken out of Robbie Keane's wage bill?' I ranted, telling him that he placed no value on his athletes at all.

I began my 2013 season with the Munster Indoor Championships and then did the National Indoors in February before heading to Lugano in Switzerland once again, with Marian and Ivonne for the Memorial Mario Albisetti World Grand Prix race.

In an effort to spend more time with the family, I'd spent almost a month sleeping in the altitude tent at home before heading to Lugano where I had an absolute shocker, finishing almost three minutes off the pace in tenth place behind Chinese winner Zhen Wang.

My training had gone really well but I was depressed after such a bad race. I'd gone off with the leaders but got dropped after 10km and, in freezing rain and hail, the second half of the race was hell. I needed to go up to higher altitude for my next training camp so I headed to Morocco with my charges, Brendan and Luke. With the weather bad in Europe, Morocco was a better option for me than going to South Africa or Mexico, as the flight to Morocco was much shorter in the event that I was needed back home. It's a great environment to train in while having the Irish Sports Council carry out four or five random anti-doping tests on me over the three weeks was also a huge improvement from the lack of testing on my first time there.

With nobody else able to come out for the full three weeks, Dermot McDermott came out for the first week or so and Athletics Ireland paid for Dave Campbell, a former 800m runner who had been coached by Sonia O'Sullivan's husband, Nic Bideau, to fly out for the latter end of the camp and I paid his wages while he was there out of my coaching money.

In Morocco there was a 5km loop around the grounds of a nearby hotel, a local track not too far away and loads of quiet roads to train on. A little higher up, at just under 1,600m altitude, we had a lake with a 7.5km tarmac lap around it, which we used for specific sessions. We also went up to El Hariba, which was at 2,200m altitude, and had another tough course up there.

Having rented an apartment for the three-week camp, I paid a local woman to come in and cook for us every day. She ran the place like a hotel and while it was a really good camp, the weather was miserable. Some days we had minus temperatures during training, with wind and rain, and it was so cold some nights that we all slept in the same room with a gas heater on for warmth.

Every morning, we'd get up and have breakfast before a little bit of stretching and massage and would then grab a coffee on the way to training, just to break things up. My easiest day would consist of a 12km walk in the morning and an 8km walk in the evening. The next day would be 15km in the morning and 8km in the evening and the following day would be 25km in the morning and 8km in the evening.

As usual, the first week of altitude training was generally aerobic: nearly all of my basic winter training condensed into seven days. The next week we did more threshold stuff with a few intervals thrown in later on and I'd build my mileage gradually up to a 40km walk on the tenth day. After that 40km session, there would be three easier days of 10km, 12km, 8km and then I'd go onto 15km efforts with rhythm stuff at the end.

After that the intensity went up, with the emphasis changing to 8 x 3km race pace efforts with a kilometre of rest in between each and 10 x 2km efforts with 1km of rest in between, which is 32km covered at a pace somewhere in between my 20km and my 50km race pace.

Luke was doing his Leaving Cert that summer so any time we weren't training or sleeping, I made him study. I'd made so many mistakes myself that I tried to stop him doing the same. He didn't like it at the time but he got over 500 points in his exams and went on to study psychology in University College Cork. He also qualified for the European Juniors that year.

As always happens when people go away to training camps, it was very hard to sleep at altitude and if you missed a night's sleep you would be wrecked for the next training session. But you're just there to train, even if you're always so tired that there's never enough time between training sessions. In the afternoons, you're in bed for two hours and up again to eat and train in the evening.

Altitude can make you sick near the end and people get cranky: you start picking up on another fella's habits and if they're late or untidy or upsetting the training in any way at all, it irks you so that by the end of it you're just dying to get home.

As I was now calling the shots and in charge of everything, I felt I had to lead by example. If I was going to be coaching the boys and telling them what to do, I couldn't be weak myself, couldn't let them see my emotional side at all. Brendan was still in his sloppy student phase and I'd get annoyed with him if he was a minute late for training.

It was like the Big Brother house for walkers; for me, ringing Marian was like going to the diary room. I'd have her on the other end of the phone listening to my complaints without mentioning to me that the kids were sick or whatever was going wrong her end of the line.

With an accumulation of miles in my legs, my final week consisted of anaerobic stuff like a dozen 1km efforts followed by 400m of recovery in between each one. That last week, the week you have to get to with all of your work done, is always really hard. When you come back down from altitude you get the benefit of all of that effort by changing to more intense training, but with a lot more recovery in between efforts. After that, you're ready to race.

My 50km training went well in Morocco and I had no hiccups until I was doing a 35km tempo session one day, where the last 15km got progressively harder. Dermot had gone home so Dave Campbell ran some of the session alongside me and Brendan, with Luke driving the car after his training had ended.

After 31km, just when things were getting hard, Luke lost concentration and drove into me, knocking me to the ground. As I lay on the road, Dave checked me over. There were cuts all down my legs and arms but he stayed calm and just said, 'You're fucking grand, come on' and I got up and finished out the session.

I didn't speak a word for the last 4km and there was complete silence on the journey back in the car. It was only afterwards that the shock hit me and I nearly collapsed back in the apartment. Looking back now, I probably shouldn't have had an eighteen-year-old driving in a foreign country but that's what we had to do. I had no other support and if I wanted to get my training in I had to manage with whoever and whatever I had.

Mentally, it was tough to deal with the cold over there. There was sleet, rain and snow some days. The roads were often flooded when we left the apartment to train in the evening and we'd arrive back with frozen hands and feet. I don't like wearing a load of gear in the wet because it gets saturated and weighs me down, which means I can't feel my technique. Because of this, I'm always caught between wearing too little and being freezing and wearing too much and not being able to walk properly. In the mornings I'd brave it out with tights and a tight top but in the evenings for the non-specific, more recovery stuff, I'd add a few layers but it eventually caught up with me.

When I came back home I was flying and walked the 10km Great Ireland run in 39 minutes on a really hilly course in the Phoenix Park. I did a hard 8 x 2km session when I got home to Cork but got a chest infection after that session and was on antibiotics, which meant I missed a race in Sesto San Giovanni because I was sick.

Back home, Marian and I began to talk more about our plans for having another baby. Just like my training programme, the baby's proposed arrival was planned and scheduled to cause minimum fuss. We also wanted him, or her, to have a chance to develop properly for school and sports. As ages are taken into account from 1 January, rather than have a child go into school seven or eight months younger than their classmates or have to play sports against somebody who was in the same underage bracket but maybe eleven months older and more developed, we planned for a January baby.

Before the European Cup in May, I went out to Almeria to train in the sunshine with the whole Irish team, which also included Brendan, Luke and Colin Griffin. As it was an official Irish team camp, everything was covered. Emma was on hand for physio every day, which was great as I was struggling for a while to get back to full fitness ahead of my next race in Dudince. As the camp coincided with our family-planning schedule though, I also had other duties to fulfil, so Marian flew into camp for two days. I was in the middle of hard training and worried I mightn't be up to the challenge. It was the first time in my whole life I felt totally emasculated.

After the camp in Almeria, I travelled to Dudince, Slovakia, for the European Cup, with Boycey and Cian McManamon for team-mates. There, in a 20km race I had finished fourth and fifth in before, I was racing hard in the lead group and remember having words with a Russian before I got tripped accidentally by Norwegian walker, Erik Tysse, after 12km and fell.

I just about got my hands out in time to stop my face from smashing into the ground but managed to get straight back up and began to chase the group down. The adrenaline of falling spurred me back into the lead group but having used my kick to regain contact I had nothing left when the winning move came and I finished ninth in 83' 27" as another unheralded Russian, 23-year-old Denis Strelkov, won in 81' 41".

The field in Dudince was really strong and the best I probably could have hoped for was a top six anyway, so I was happy enough with ninth on the day. After Dudince I took the tough decision to skip the National 10km Championships at home because I felt I got too hyped up about the Irish title race. Instead, I wanted to put all of my motivation into racing the World Championships in Moscow later in the year.

I went back to altitude in Guadix again that summer, with Brendan, Luke and Marian. We stayed in Rolando's Cave Hotel in the hills. The best thing about Guadix is that the whole place shuts down for four hours in the middle of the day because it's so hot, so after being up early every morning I had a midday siesta and then went training again at eight each night.

When we were in Guadix, Paco, who was now retired, often came down to the track to keep an eye on my technique and look over my training plans for the year so on that camp I asked him what time he thought I should do my 10 x 2km x 1km sessions in. He answered that I should be doing each hard 2km interval in around 8' 10". I was stunned at his answer and told him that before I finished fourth in Barcelona, where I was in great shape, I only did 8' 10" or 8' 15" for seven 2km efforts.

I remembered doing the same session before London and it might have only been 8' 25" or 8' 20". Paco simply shrugged his shoulders and said, 'You did three hours thirty-seven for 50km in London. You were fourth in the Olympic Games. Now, you need to push on to a different level.'

What followed was the hardest training session I ever did. I was struggling with 6km to go, blew up with 2km to go and in the last 500m I was getting sick all over myself. I was whimpering like a beaten puppy at the end. But I had done the sessions in 8' 10".

Guadix was very tough but it went really well and after finishing the camp with a hard 40km effort, I flew home the next day and walked in the Cork City Sports a few days later.

Cork City Sports is one of the best-run track meets in the country and over the years has drawn some of the legends of athletics to the track at Cork Institute of Technology in Bishopstown. With my profile still huge from London there were thousands trackside that day and although I was walking in a much shorter and faster 3km event and I had a load of mileage in my legs from camp, the atmosphere and support from the crowd helped me beat the Polish walker Jakub Jelonek to win the race in 11' 11" and break Jamie's long-standing Irish record over the distance.

After a few days recharging with the kids, I went to Salzburg to taper off before the World Championships. With more specific sessions followed by longer recovery between each one, I wasn't training as hard and, as often happens at that time of year, I began to feel more energised and my mood began to lift.

It was lovely and sunny in Austria, so after some sessions Marian, Brendan and I would go down to the river to have a dip and we spent some of our spare time relaxing outside in the sun. The whole camp was very laid back, to the point that when a drug tester called to my hotel room one day and I couldn't go to the loo straight away, the two of us sat down and watched *The Sopranos* until I could go.

Even after my berating him in Morocco for being untidy, Brendan was a slob in Salzburg but at least he had his own room. It had no air conditioning, though, and he hadn't washed his gear in about a week so I couldn't help but pity the drug testers when they paid him a visit.

We spent ten days in Salzburg before flying to Russia for the World Championships, where I was due to skip the 20km race and focus all my energy on the 50km walk. When we got to Moscow and I did my first training session out there, my heart rates were really high and I felt awful. As had happened in Saransk a few years earlier, all the travelling combined with the time difference made me feel lethargic and jet-lagged.

Three days before my race, I went for a walk around the local roads and felt much better but my feet got caught up in some sort of thin wire hoop on the road and I just about managed to hold myself up from falling. If I'd hit the deck that day I could have been out of the World Championship with a stupid injury and ended the season in disaster.

The morning of the race I got up and went for breakfast in great form. As usual, Marian, who was now five months pregnant, had everything done for me the night before. She had my number on my singlet, all of my drinks ready for me. I sat down to breakfast, happy that the kids were being minded at home, Marian was with me and I had nothing else to do only walk.

Although I had done a couple of 40km sessions in training, Moscow was my first 50km walk since London the year before. When I began to warm up, the realisation hit me of what was in front of me: I was here to win a medal at the World Championships, my whole year had been built around this race and if I didn't win a medal I'd have nothing to show for my season at all.

The nerves began to churn my stomach and within minutes I was retching and puked my guts up. The same thing had happened to me before some of my big races and in a strange way the puking made me realise that I was ready for the race. Recently, if I didn't get sick before a big race, it made me worried that I wasn't up for it – I wasn't sick because I wasn't nervous – so I'd be nervous that I wasn't nervous enough.

When I get sick, it's so loud that you can hear me retching for miles. Often Cathal would be around when it would start and he'd be bursting out laughing and turn to Marian. 'The bear is out again, Mam!'

In Moscow, I told myself that I was fine. The puking meant I was ready to go. I had carbo-loaded for the race, my muscles were full of glycogen and I tried not to worry about it. I remembered my 50km walks in London and Barcelona and the pace of both of those races. I knew that if I could control myself, hold back at the start like I had then, that I would cut through the field later on and would be in contention at the end.

By default, though, I found myself in the lead straight after the start and had to hold back and let myself be overtaken as we left the stadium and went out onto the road. Although I got one card off a Polish judge early on, my technique was very solid in Moscow and the whole race went perfectly from there on. I'd worked with a Spanish sports psychologist in the summer who had given me five different cues to work on throughout the race. I'd work on a different one every kilometre and that was all I was focused on for the whole 50km.

The first kilometres were all about my legs: 'My legs are very strong. My legs feel great,' I told myself. The next kilometre was 'my hips are very strong.' I told myself that my arms were moving well and everything was good in kilometre three. The fourth kilometre was 'I'm flowing. I'm strong. I deserve to be here. I'm the best. This is my day.'

For the fifth kilometre I drew on motivation from home: Cathal, Meghan, Marian, our new baby that she was now carrying and all of the people in Ireland who had supported me after the Olympics. Then I'd go back to my legs, my hips, my arms . . . and kept working with that all the way through the race, which meant I never looked too far ahead or got carried away, even when I found myself out in front towards the end.

Marian and I often had massive rows in training about stuff, but when it came to the races there was a connection between us and she never got excited or did anything impulsive. Ray was on the table, too, and if he was nervous, he didn't look it.

When I moved into third and then caught up with the two Russian leaders after two and a half hours, I grew in confidence. When it was only me and Mikhail Ryzhov left with 15km to go, I remember thinking, 'This lad's only a young fella. I'm after walking three hours thirty-seven minutes, boy. You might be from Russia but I'm tougher than you.' I enjoyed the challenge and when I got away from him I tried not to get too excited and kept on working in the moment.

I called on all of my previous experience, like when I thought I was going to win a medal in Beijing, or when I thought I was going to clear all my bills in Copenhagen, and I never lost concentration once. I took every kilometre one at a time and never thought about a medal until just as I arrived at the entrance to the stadium, alone and in the lead. Suddenly I started getting anxious about it. I passed Peter Marlow, a judge, and asked him how I was. He said, 'You're fine, you're away, relax.'

I walked into the stadium and looked up at the big screen to see a close-up of myself on the track. I ran my hand across my chest where the word Ireland was written. I wanted the rest of the world to know that we could do it too. We were as good as any other country and I always believed I could do it, that Irish people could do it. No matter how often I pull on an Irish singlet, I always get a buzz out of it. I got a shamrock tattooed on my leg with 'Éire' underneath it when I was nineteen. I love being Irish, being from Cork, and it made me fierce proud coming into the stadium in the lead with an Irish singlet on.

With 300m to go, my nerves got the better of me and my stomach turned so badly that I actually thought I would collapse. For the next hundred metres I was worried about what would happen if I did collapse and didn't make it home.

With 200m to go I looked at my time on the screen – 3:36:10 – and remember thinking 'Oh my fucking God!' and although I was stiff and sore, I tried to kick for home to break my own Irish record of 3:37:54, but was just three seconds short at the line.

I've always had visions in my head of how I would celebrate if I ever won a medal at a major championships, how I would throw my arms into the air and look so majestic as I crossed the line. Now, I had a minute to spare on second-placed Rhyzov and was going to win the World Championship but I was so tight and bent over as I came down the finishing straight that I couldn't even straighten my arms when I got to the tape.

The minute I crossed the line I scanned the stadium for Marian. She jumped over the barrier and came running towards me and we hugged and kissed each other on the track.

'You did it,' she said as the tears started flowing. 'You did it! I knew you could do it!'

I have a framed photograph of that moment in my house now and it sums up everything about our relationship. We did everything together and if it hadn't been for Marian I would never have been world champion, maybe wouldn't even have been at those World Championships. Two years earlier I had been in the worst possible scenario at the previous World Championships and throughout the race in Moscow I had been thinking of my mam. The chain she had given me before she died bounced around my neck in a constant reminder of how proud she was of me.

After Mam passed away, I knew nothing was ever going to be as bad again as it was in Daego. 'Suck it up, Rob,' I told myself any time it got hard, any time I had an injury or something didn't go to plan. 'Enjoy the misery, boy. It's not as bad as things can get.'

Now twenty-four months later, here I was on top of the world and I felt my mam was with me that day, looking down on me, smiling.

I'd never won a major championship before so I didn't know what I was supposed to do next. Patsy McGonagle and Emma Gallivan were in the stadium but Ray was still out on the drinks table waiting for Boycey. Somebody threw me an Irish flag and, awkwardly, I started doing a lap of honour but I didn't know if I should even be on the track. I got around to the 200m mark and an official moved me over because other walkers were finishing and I felt like a young fella again, like I was in the way and shouldn't have been here.

After the race Marian and I rang the kids at home but, while they were absolutely delighted, it wasn't the same as having them there and I couldn't wait to get home to see them.

In a show of support for how they thought I was going to get on in the race, Athletics Ireland had booked my flight home for the following morning – before the medal ceremony – which meant they had to buy new tickets for Marian and me so that I could stand on the podium and collect my first-ever gold medal.

The CEO of Athletics Ireland John Foley and the President Liam Hennessy had been in Moscow when I went down to watch the lads in the 20km race a few days earlier, but they had flown home before the 50km started. These were meant to be the people who knew the sport, loved the sport and supported their athletes but they were gone before I even lined up to race. How could you ever have any trust or faith in them after that?

The night of my victory, we went to an Irish bar, where I pulled a few pints and sang a few songs. It was a brilliant night but Marian and I left early because we were due to be interviewed on the BBC the next morning by Jonathan Edwards, Michael Johnson and Colin Jackson.

Everything seemed to happen so fast in Moscow and in contrast to my 50km walk in London, I couldn't sleep with excitement and the elation of winning. To be in the BBC studio the next morning chatting about race walking was brilliant and I had a good craic with the presenters. I had watched all three win their respective European, Olympic, Commonwealth and World titles over the years and to be interviewed by them felt a bit surreal and dreamlike. But the lads were lovely and very down to earth. However, as a fellow 400m runner, Marian was in a bit of awe of four-time Olympic champion Johnson when she was called into shot. It was the first time I ever saw her stuck for words.

Before the medal ceremony that evening, I had to attend a press conference with Jared Tallent and Rhyzov. All of the Irish journalists were there and most of the questions were aimed at me. When one of the British journalists asked me if winning the World Championships would make me bigger than Roy Keane in Cork, I said 'What are you on about? I already was bigger than Roy Keane in Cork.' The whole pace erupted in laughter and I really enjoyed my fifteen minutes of fame.

Immediately before the medal ceremony, Ryzhov, Jared and I were brought into a little room where we were to wait before being brought out onto the track. It was pretty quiet as we sat waiting to go out onto the track centre and it felt a bit weird to be sitting in a little room with my competitors. I didn't know how I would feel on the podium but I felt very uneasy with the attention at the start. It was strange to have all the cameras pointing at me, the world champion.

When the tricolour was raised to the sounds of '*Amhrán na bhFiann*' I really had to fight to hold myself together. I can remember my lip quivering and having to concentrate to stop myself from bursting out crying. It was such a powerful feeling. I felt so proud to be Irish.

I remembered watching Sonia O'Sullivan, Marcus O'Sullivan, Derval O'Rourke, Roy Keane, Denis Irwin, Mark Carroll, Eamonn

Coughlan and Ronnie Delany winning their various medals on the world stage and now here I was – world champion. I could hardly believe it!

After being presented with my medal, I had to go outside the stadium for a photo shoot. Because race walking is huge in Russia the photographers were actually fighting with each other to get the best photo of me. They were pushing each other and dragging each other out of the way as I looked on, dumbstruck at my new found popularity. I was in the middle of this photographer scrum and maybe if I was twenty-two I might have got carried away with it but I just said, 'This is crazy, boys. Will ye relax? I'll stay here a while, like.'

The photographers drew more attention to me and as soon as they were finished I was mobbed by the huge crowd that had now gathered around us. Suddenly I was being dragged all over the pace. There were women of all ages coming up hugging me, kissing me, grabbing me. I might as well have been in One Direction. In the end I had to run to get away, with big lipstick marks all over my face. It was bananas.

When I went back to the hotel for dinner after the medal ceremony, everyone there knew that I'd won – all of the security, the reception, the staff – everyone, and as we were going into the dining hall my name was called out alongside the other medallists of that day.

'Congratulations, Yelena Isinbayeva, world champion. Congratulations, Usain Bolt, world champion. Congratulations, Robert Heffernan, world champion.'

Marian went over to Usain Bolt and told him that her husband had just won the 50km walk and he came over and got a picture taken with us and had a bit of a chat. He was really good craic and was spotted race walking down the hall afterwards.

Back in the hotel room afterwards I was obsessed with the medal and spent the next while looking at it and running it through my fingers while Marian went through the hundreds of messages of congratulations on my phone from supporters back home.

To celebrate, we got changed and headed out that night. I brought my medal with me to the local Irish pub where I sang 'Ordinary

Man' and 'Streets of New York' to a packed house. It was a great night.

At Dublin Airport the next day it was manic. The place was thronged with cameras, supporters, friends and family, as well as the usual representatives from Athletics Ireland but the two people I really wanted to see were Meghan and Cathal. After a big hug from both of them, it was very surreal to be greeted by all these other people, most of whom I'd never seen before in my life. Although I'd barely slept since winning the race, I was still going on adrenaline. I was floating on air.

After doing a few media interviews in the arrivals hall, I went home to Cork on the coach that my family and friends had organised for the trip, which was great fun and took me out of the whirlwind of the media attention and back to basics again. But even when we stopped in a garage on the way for tea and coffee, I was recognised straight away. But I didn't have a clue what was lying ahead at all.

We arrived into Cork at around eight that evening and we were all transferred – Marian, Meghan, Cathal and my family and friends from Togher and me – onto an open-top double-decker bus for the drive into the city.

I remember looking around and feeling like I was in a dream. The bus would pass the odd person I knew and they'd shout up but I felt a bit awkward and by then the tiredness was kicking in. I couldn't really take it in. As we came up into Patrick Street, I began to realise the whole city was thronged and they had all come out to see me.

The bus dropped us off at the Grand Parade in the city centre, which was jammers. There were maybe 40,000 people there. It was crazy. A stage had been erected outside the Soho Bar, which meant I was able to keep my promise to Seanie to hold my first medal celebration there in thanks for all the support he had given me when I wasn't winning. As I got off the bus I was mobbed. Fellas were slapping me on the back, grabbing me, shaking me. I felt like a rag doll being pulled from Billy to Jack.

When I got up onto the stage it was an unbelievable feeling to look out and see how many people had come to support me. It was like getting a medal again. I had very little sleep from travelling and I remember wishing I was fresher for this. The celebrations carried on inside afterwards but I couldn't relax at all, as I was being dragged from pillar to post, shaking hands, meeting people, signing autographs, posing for photos. It was nonstop.

My club in Togher organised a homecoming night for me the next night with Trevor Welch from 96FM and TV3 as MC. The club had arranged for a convertible to drive me through the streets of Togher before arriving at the clubhouse where I'd spent most of my formative years training and socialising with friends and club mates.

As we drove through Togher, I sat on the boot of the car with my feet on the back seat and with Cathal and Meghan each side of me and Marian in the front, I found myself waving to people I'd grown up with, gone to school with, run with, played football with. People were handing me babies to kiss and everything.

After twenty years of trying, I'd become an overnight sensation.

19

McLovin

A few days after my 'welcome home' reception in the city, I went into a cafe in Douglas where I sat down to drink my coffee before noticing Irish rugby international Donncha O'Callaghan at a table opposite me and former Manchester United legend Denis Irwin at another.

Dennis and Donncha are big heroes of mine and when Martin McCarthy, an Irish international runner from Leevale, walked in behind me, within minutes we were all sitting together at the same table chatting as other customers nodded and pointed towards our group.

When Cork faced Clare in the All-Ireland Hurling final in Croke Park that September, myself, Marian and the kids were invited to the game, where I was to be introduced to the crowd at half-time. Having stood on the terraces and watched Cork play over the years it was a whole new experience for me to be wined and dined in the VIP section before the game.

When I walked out onto the pitch at half-time, the reception absolutely blew me away. The whole stadium erupted and the hairs stood up on the back of my neck as I waved my medal in the air in the centre of the pitch.

Television and radio presenter Hector Ó hEochagáin had started a walking campaign over the airwaves encouraging everyone to 'do the Heff' in honour of my win and he then challenged me to a little race walk along the touchline before I went back to watch the second half.

After the game ended in a draw, trying to get back to my car afterwards was crazy. It seemed as if the whole 80,000 capacity crowd wanted autographs and photographs and I felt embarrassed because I didn't feel any different than I had a few months before when I'd brought Cathal to see a Cork hurling match and sat in the stands like everybody else. I couldn't take in the fact that everybody recognised me.

After becoming world champion in 2013 I had so many invitations to parties and gigs that I could have gone away and led a celebrity lifestyle. I was aware that my new-found fame wasn't going to last long and after spending so many years on the breadline, I knew I had to make the most of those invitations and opportunities to make some money for my family. I had to capitalise on my title. If there was ever a time to try and make money, this was it.

But after winning the World Championships, I was determined not to rest on my laurels and wanted to win another gold medal at the European Championships in Zurich in 2014.

I also realised that I had a chance to use my new-found celebrity to get more people interested in race walking. I wanted to try and build on the enthusiasm of kids who suddenly wanted to try the sport. I wanted to get them into clubs, give them a bit of coaching and try to develop the sport here. I'd seen it happen in other countries, where athletes did well at the top level and their national federation used that to attract more participants and build a foundation for the future.

There had been talk that Athletics Ireland was going to get involved with an academic institution in Cork after London and set up a race-walking academy in the area but even though the dogs on the street knew it was all talk, I was gullible enough to believe them. I'd come home from Moscow full of hope and positivity about everything. I had really huge intentions of trying to develop walking so when I was invited onto Ireland's biggest TV chat show, *The Late Late Show*, Derry and I met with Athletics Ireland Chief Executive John

Foley beforehand and asked him if we could announce that there was going to be a race-walking academy set up in Cork.

John assured me that there was and I announced it to the whole nation on live television. Looking back now though, it seems that this assurance was just a way of making sure I didn't say anything controversial about the lack of support I had got from the federation over the years. The announcement just papered over the cracks of a system that was run haphazardly with no long-term planning for anybody, unless they did it themselves.

In the end, I set up a sort of walking academy myself in Cork and left it open to everybody who wanted to take part. Cork County Athletics board covered the cost of hiring the track every Monday night. Soon I had people travelling from Waterford, Kerry, Kilkenny and all over Munster to come and train. It was manic but I enjoyed giving people advice and it reinforced my belief that my plan to build a foundation of new walkers could be done. An Irish athlete winning the World Championships had suddenly made the sport popular and glamorous and it was great to see so many kids, teenagers and even adults trying it.

As well as going to the track to help coach these newcomers, I was visiting schools, encouraging kids to take up the sport, trying to look after Marian – who was now very heavily pregnant – and trying to do my own training for the 2014 season. But there was no follow-through from Athletics Ireland. They should have seized the moment but they didn't. They completely missed the window and it frustrated the hell out of me.

Around then, race walker Alex Wright moved over to Ireland from London and asked me to coach him. Alex had walked for Great Britain in Moscow but his great-grandfather was Irish and he wanted to walk for Ireland. He decided to just up and leave London with his girlfriend and got the boat over to Cork.

Alex had trained with me a couple of years before and I knew he was very talented, very professional in his attitude and also a nice person. I remembered back to when I was younger and how many people had helped me, so I decided to try and pass on that knowledge and do my best to help him.

I got him put up in the house where Boycey lived. Although it was almost ready to fall down, Brendan, Alex and his girlfriend Lauren lived in that house for the year. I got them sorted out with a gym and massage, and made out their programmes, while they also had Marian at their beck and call every day.

Marian insisted that I was taking on too much but I was adamant that I wasn't. Realistically, while I had all these great ideas and never slowed down, it was Marian who was left with all of the workload.

About a month later I was ambassador for Cork Rebel Week and had to walk through the city with the gold medal around my neck. I was dreading doing it because I knew what I'd be thinking if I was standing on the side of the road: 'All right, you're after winning. Would you put the medal away now, boy, and get on with yourself? Do you want more pats on the back?'

I remember feeling so awkward leading the band through St Patrick's Street. The reception was brilliant and everybody was great but because I was living it every second I thought people would be fed up with me by now.

After that there was a party on the quays with all of the dignitaries. I stayed there and shook a few hands before shooting off to meet Marian and the kids for a pre-planned trip to Tayto Park in County Meath.

I had to go to Dublin the next day for the *Irish Independent* Sports Star of the Year Awards so Marian and the kids got a lift back to Cork with friends while I stayed in the Croke Park Hotel, where the awards would take place. When I got to the hotel's underground car park I just took the stuff that I needed for the night out of the car and left my suit and everything else in it.

I was so exhausted that I didn't want to talk to anyone or see anyone so I went and got a takeaway, brought it back to my room where I had a cup of tea, watched telly and went to sleep. In the early hours of the next morning I was woken by my phone ringing and without checking to see what time it was, I picked it up to hear Derry's voice on the other end of the line.

'Rob, do you have your medal with you?'

'I do, yeah. It's down in the car.'

'Somebody just tried to sell it to a taxi driver in Dublin a couple of hours ago. Go down and check will you?'

I told Derry I would but I was so tired that I just went back to sleep before getting up three or four hours later at half past seven and going down for my breakfast. Ahead of me, a busy day had been all planned out. I had to go to the Irish Sports Institute to get physio for my hip. I would then train afterwards, before coming back to grab a shower and pull on my suit for the awards at lunchtime.

After breakfast though, I went out to the car park, where I discovered the car had been broken into and everything robbed out of it. My suit was gone. The chain that my mam had given me – the one I wore in Moscow – was gone. My phone – with all of my pictures of me and my mam on it and all of my photos from the London Olympics – was gone. And my gold medal was gone.

I went back to my room and rang Derry to tell him he was right, that my car had been broken into. He told me to ring the Gardaí but even with all of this going on I was still on autopilot. I still had to go to physio, still had to go to training.

On the way to the Institute of Sport in Blanchardstown I rang Marian and told her the news. She went berserk.

'Mar, what can I do, like? It's gone!'

'Rob,' she said. 'It's not just gone.'

'It's gone! The medal is gone. I won it. I know I won it. Big deal.'

It hadn't really hit me that my medal, the medal it had taken me years to win, had been stolen.

I continued my trip to physio and while I was there Derry arrived in with two detectives. They had tracked down the taxi driver and he told them that a Roma gypsy had tried to sell the medal to him for €200. The taxi man saw that my name was on the back of it and told the thief that he'd get back onto him. He then Googled to see who my manager was and rang Derry to tell him he had been offered it.

The next thing I knew, I was in the middle of a sting operation. The Gardaí were able to track the taxi driver's phone and when he rang the thief they were able to track his phone too. The plan was to get the taxi driver to meet up with the Roma gypsy and buy the medal back off him. I hopped into the detective's car with Derry and as they monitored everything that was going on I sat in the back seat, behind them. I felt like McLovin from *Superbad* as they carried out their sting.

They knew when the taxi was going through the Port Tunnel. They knew where the Roma guy was. They were watching everything. Eventually, the taxi driver bought my medal back from the thief, Derry met the taxi driver on St Stephen's Green and handed it in to me in the car. The detectives threw the siren on in the unmarked car and we scorched from St Stephen's Green through the city to the hotel where they got me to the door in time for the awards.

Here, RTÉ got a sniff of the story and Derry and I ended up on the six o'clock news.

When things quietened down I went out training with Derry that afternoon from his house and we were laughing at everything that happened as we did our 10km together. It was only when I sat down in Cork to have a glass of wine with Marian that night and the nine o'clock news came on that I realised how much the medal meant to me. When it was robbed, I wasn't that bothered initially. I knew I had won it and reckoned I could get a replacement if I really wanted to but then, the more I thought about it, I realised that gold medal was a symbol of what my life had been all about up until then.

On 25 January 2014, I was out on a training session, doing 7 x 2km intervals up and down a kilometre-long straight road when, suddenly, in the middle of my fourth interval, Alex's girlfriend Lauren ran up to me shouting, 'Marian's water are after breaking!'

I turned on my heels and ran back to the car where Marian, cool as a cucumber, told me to relax, that it was going to take ages. I jumped into the driver's seat, drove home, ran into the house and up the stairs, grabbed the bag she had pre-packed for the birth and drove her straight to Cork University Hospital.

After checking Marian over, the nurse reiterated Marian's thoughts on how long it would take and turned to me.

'She could be here for a good few hours. Why don't you go on out and finish your training?'

Although I already had two kids, this was my first time at a birth and even though we'd just arrived a few minutes earlier, I was already up the walls. Marian agreed with the nurse that I should go back and finish my session but I was confused and in complete turmoil. The athlete in me wanted to go back and finish my training but the husband and father in me wanted to stay with Marian.

In the end, the husband and father won and I stayed. The labour went on all day and well into the early hours of the next morning. Much of that time was spent with me linking arms with Marian as we walked up and down the corridor or up and down the steps outside in the hope that it would help her along.

At around ten o'clock that night, the nurse came over and told me that I'd have to go home but there was no way I was leaving Marian on her own. Instead, I went out to the hall for another walk with her and when she went back to the ward afterwards, I hid in the corridor for an hour before sneaking back in beside her.

Shattered from training and having missed my usual midday sleep, I remember falling asleep in Marian's bed in the early hours and refusing to go for another walk with her because I was too tired.

To be able to witness the birth the next day was unbelievable for me but I don't think any man can be prepared for that first time. Even a normal run-of-the-mill birth is a big experience but the baby was turned around slightly, with the cord briefly wrapped around her neck.

Marian was in agony and when they called in another doctor, I was really worried. I felt helpless but I knew that all I could do was stay there and support Marian and keep my mouth shut. I had to stand there and try to be calm. Whatever way the baby was positioned, they couldn't believe that Marian would be able to push her out without a section. After a bit of commotion in the delivery suite, my second daughter, Regan, was born and both she and Marian were fine.

I've always been obsessed with medals. I've been chasing them my whole life, but knowing that Marian was okay and the baby was okay, the feeling that came over me there and then, was better than winning any medal. Holding my newborn child in my arms for the first time was better than winning the World Championships a few months earlier. Instead of a fleeting moment, maybe a day or two of joy, I knew it would last forever.

Immediately, I was very protective of Regan. I don't know if it's the athlete or the father in me but when people came in to visit her I was paranoid about them touching her with germs on their hands. I didn't want to let them hold her in case they dropped her.

When we brought Regan home, I couldn't stop looking at her. I was completely besotted. I'd wake up umpteen times in the middle of the night and immediately check to see if she was OK. I'd look into her pram in the middle of the day to see if she was breathing. I was like that for months and probably put a few people out, including Marian's mam, with my overprotectiveness.

Now with three kids, we needed more financial security. I still had no security with my grant so Derry began to get me gigs with corporate businesses and associations. In front of 300 or 400 people each night, I answered questions about time management and how I fitted my training in with family, how I was able to survive on so little money and what my goals were for each year. It was great to be able to do it but driving up and down the country after training some days meant I was wrecked after it.

Having continued to train hard in the middle of all this, I began my 2014 season with a race in America in February when I got invited over to New York for five days to race the mile in the Millrose Games. The world's longest-running and most prestigious indoor athletics meet, the event is held every year in Madison Square Gardens where Eamonn Coughlan famously earned his nickname 'chairman of the boards' on his way to winning seven Wanamaker Miles.

With Ronnie Delany, Mark Carroll, Niall Bruton and Marcus O'Sullivan also having won there, there is a great Irish link to the games and in the lead-up to the race, I appeared on TV and had to give a talk to the Irish business community in the Irish Consulate.

Because of this Irish link and the fact that I was reigning world champion, albeit at 50km rather than the mile, I wanted to add my name to the roll of honour.

The race was due to be held on Valentine's Day, and Marian stayed at home with three-week-old Regan while her mam, her brother Stephen and Les Tomkins, a buddy of mine, came over, all of them probably more for the sightseeing and the shopping than the race walking. With Ray Flynn and Emma Gallivan also there, I had loads of support.

In front of a packed crowd though, I got beaten into second by Swedish walker Andreas Gustafsson, whose best result prior to that was twenty-first place at the World Championships in Berlin in 2009 and was a guy who would never ever beat me on a normal day.

Although I'd walked 5' 39" for the mile, a really good time, I hadn't just been beaten but had been blown away by five seconds, which is a lot over a mile. Gustafsson's time was so good that he just missed the world record. By the end of the season he would fail a dope test for EPO and be banned for two years.

Having missed Regan terribly in New York, I stayed at home until March when I went to Lugano again over St Patrick's weekend with Alex and Boycey and did the 20km race there.

Lugano was my first time back in the international athletics community since winning the World Championships and I couldn't believe the difference in the way I was treated. Ron Weigel, a former 50km world champion from Germany, who used to call me a frog in the green Irish singlet and generally tried to wind me up every time I raced, was the first one over to congratulate me. He was nearly genuflecting in front of me. But if my competitors seemed to have more respect for me, Athletics Ireland, it appeared, had none and didn't even send a physio with the team.

Whether it was from driving to and from corporate talks or from lifting Regan around the house, I don't know, but I had a niggle in my back at the time and with no Irish team physio around, I found myself knocking on the Guatemalan physio's door, asking him for treatment. He could hardly believe it but was pleased to be giving the world champion a rub. The treatment didn't help, however, and my back continued to give me trouble for a long time afterwards.

Although I hadn't expected to be in the hunt for medals over the 20km distance, I was really surprised when Ruslan Dmytrenko from the Ukraine won the race with a massive jump in performance from finishing thirtieth in London a couple of years previously. He blew the field away but instinctively, I felt something wasn't quite right. There's hard and then there's that different rocket gear that you just don't get naturally. I had a good race and finished fifth in 80' 57".

After Lugano, I went to altitude camp in South Africa with Boycey, Luke, Alex and Ray for three weeks. Training went well over there but mentally I found it very hard being away from Regan again, this time for a whole three weeks. My back injury was also getting worse and I spent a lot of those training sessions in agony. Initially, we thought Athletics Ireland would support the camp with a physio but they didn't, so I had to make do with a Chinese massage place down the end of the road for the first ten days until I found a decent sports physio.

Although I kept training, the Chinese massage hadn't done anything for me and I wasn't right. To add to my problems, Boycey had begun the camp over enthusiastically and broke down. He got sick and I had to bring him to hospital. Although the camp wasn't covered by Athletics Ireland, we rang the Irish team doctor for advice. He told Brendan to fly home. But having invested his own money, like the rest of us, to come to South Africa to train, he wanted to know what the plan was for when he got home: there wasn't one, so he decided to stay.

Boycey was kept in hospital for a while and I had to go back and forward to visit him, which also interrupted my training. Shortly after coming home from South Africa, I had an after-dinner talk in University College Cork. During the question-and-answer session afterwards I was asked whether the walking team had a good chance in the World Cup in Taicang, China, a few weeks later. I answered that I thought the money it would cost Athletics Ireland to send them to China would be better off spent going to smaller Grand Prix races around Europe. I felt that the World Cup was too big a competition for Brendan Boyce, Luke Hickey and Cian McManamon to go to. As I was looking after these lads and coaching them, I had no agenda and was just being honest. I said that I'd prefer if Athletics Ireland paid for them to go to two races in Europe, where they'd get more experience, instead of flying them to China. I thought no more about it until I got a letter from Kevin Ankrom telling me that I had brought the sport into disrepute and that they were going to withhold my grant. I was fuming.

'Kevin, I was asked a question and I answered it,' I told him. 'That's my opinion and I'm entitled to my opinion. Instead of telling me you're going to cut my funding, how about Athletics Ireland taking my opinion on board and actually listening to me and doing the right thing to try and develop the sport?'

By then I had no time for Ankrom. In Moscow he had promised me the sun, moon and stars. I knew it probably cost €20,000 to send a team to China whereas they could have used that money to send support on training camps during the year instead, send teams to a couple of races in Europe. That way the money would go a lot further than sending fellas out to China on a holiday for eight days when they knew they weren't going to do anything in the race anyway.

On the first week in May, I raced the World Cup in China but didn't have a great race. Once again, Dmytrenko showed a clean pair of heels to everyone else to record what the IAAF's own website reported as a 'miraculous victory for Ukraine' and the 'most surprising of the weekend'. While I only managed to finish twenty-third, my time of 81 minutes dead was solid enough but I just didn't feel good in the race at all. On a rain-lashed day in Taicang, the pain in my back had shifted to my hip, and my knee was bothering me, too, even though I'd been getting treatment from Emma three times a day in the holding camp. It was grand to a point until the real pressure came on and then it got really sore and stopped me from trying to walk faster.

After spending three weeks in South Africa and another in China for the World Cup, I didn't want to spend any more time away from

Marian and the kids so at the end of May I raced a smaller 20km Grand Prix in Naumburg, Germany. The start was a five-hour drive from Frankfurt Airport so we hired a car and drove to the race with Regan in the back. When the race began, Marian did my drinks with one hand and rocked Regan in her buggy with the other.

As I only seem to be able to get psyched up for certain races – the World Championships, the Olympics, the Europeans – I often have to find ways to get excited about walking in other events and when 'The Irish Rover' came on over the loudspeakers at the start in Naumburg I used that as motivation. I was the Irish fella taking on the Germans in Germany.

After a decent performance, I got €1,000 prize money for winning the race, reversed into a bollard on the way out of the car park and had to hand my winnings over to the car rental company to pay for the damage.

Winning the race reinvigorated my training and even though I was still sore, I really got stuck into some quality training and broke an Irish record for 20km on the track one day doing an 8 x 2km x 400m session, which involved eight flat out 2km efforts interspersed with 400m of recovery each time.

In July, a month before the European Championships in Zurich, I walked in the Cork City Sports again. This time it was my first race in Ireland as world champion and a huge crowd turned out to roar me on. Even though I broke the Irish record again for the 3km walk, Australia's Dane Bird-Smith spoiled the party when he won, with Kevin Campion of France and Alex Wright both finishing ahead of me, too.

Although she was only six months old, Regan came with us again to Zurich for the European Championships. I was still very wary of who I'd let look after her but in an effort to get some sleep the night before the race, Ray Flynn's daughter Zola came over with us to babysit. With Regan in a different room, though, that's where my head was the night before the race. I spent half the night tossing and turning, thinking about her and worrying if she was OK.

On the morning of the race my groin was really sore and when I

223

compared it to the feeling I had before Moscow, things were worlds apart. Kevin Ankrom was hanging around the call room and his presence was really annoying me. In my head he was just jumping on the bandwagon as he normally had no time for walking.

Like it had been in China, the weather was terrible, with the rain lashing down. Neither my groin, the rain, nor Ankrom were stuff I would have noticed normally.

From the gun, Yohann Diniz went off like the clappers but I knew from experience how a fast start could end up coming back to haunt you after 50km and was happy enough walking alongside Slovakian Matej Tóth in the opening kilometres. When the Russian duo of Mikhail Ryzhov and Ivan Noskov went after the Frenchman though, it was a completely different race and my head was thrown a bit. I expected they'd go out fast, and thought they were playing into my hands again but when they weren't coming back after a while I started chasing them down.

I briefly moved up to third after 20km when Ryzhov drifted back. But I had been sucked in, deviated from my plan and went through the first 30km well over a minute faster than I had in Moscow and London. Instead of Diniz slowing down and me getting faster, Diniz started getting faster out front and I started drifting back through the field. It was then the whole race turned negative for me.

My heart rate was still low but my body just wasn't working properly. I had limited flexibility in my hip flexors but didn't want to use that as an excuse at the time so I said nothing. After 36km, I stopped at the drinks table and told Marian that I couldn't carry on. But she was having none of it and was roaring at me to keep going.

'Finish the race! This is what you've worked for all year!' she yelled. 'You get whatever result you're going to get. Get out there and keep going. Finish it!'

I went again for another 6km but nothing was happening for me. I was still in or around the top six but perhaps because I knew I was soon going to be awarded a bronze medal from the 2010 Europeans and had already won the World Championships, my mind went really negative. I couldn't understand why I wasn't challenging and even though I was probably physically OK to continue and finish in the top six, I started noticing everything negative about myself. I thought everybody was looking at me, the world champion who couldn't even keep up with the leaders at the Europeans.

After 40km, I stopped again at the table where Marian and I had a blazing row on the side of the road.

'Get back on the course and finish!' she shouted.

'I'm not able to. I'm not able to!' I said, banging the table and sending cups of water flying.

Patsy McGonagle and Ray were both there at the time but they knew well enough to stay out of it. After another minute or two of a heated argument with Marian in the middle of the road, I dropped out of a race for the first time in my whole life.

I went straight from abandoning the race to standing in front of a television camera from RTÉ and because I was so irate I said some stupid stuff on camera – that I'd stopped because I wasn't going to win. Afterwards those comments saw me lacerated on social media, with people telling me I had no right to win a medal, asking me who did I think I was, that the taxpayers' money was paying for me to be out there. All of a sudden, I'd gone from hero to zero but my main problem was that I couldn't understand what was wrong with me, why my groin was sore, why my hip was giving me trouble and why I wasn't getting results.

Even when I met Ankrom and Foley after the race I refused to blame my hip pain and told them I had gone off and deviated from my plan for the race and hadn't even carried out Plan B. I've always wanted to win, ever since I was eight years of age, but if I couldn't win then Plan B was always to beat the next fella.

Later that evening, Mikhail Ryzhov, who had finished second to me at the World Championships in Moscow the year before, and his Russian teammate Ivan Noskov, who had just won bronze in Zurich, came over to me in the hotel and bowed their heads before asking me for an autograph. I had just abandoned the race and one of them had just won a medal so I was a bit confused at first but signed the autographs for them. They then asked me to swap tops, so I went up to my room and brought them down one of my Irish tracksuit tops and an Irish singlet and, delighted, they began to ask me questions through a Ukrainian walker, Nazar Kovalenko, who spoke English.

The first thing they wanted to know was why I wore a nasal strip on my nose and why I wore sunglasses. Looking at them up close and away from competition, they looked so young and innocent and it was as if they thought they were doping devices and wondered if I got some unfair advantage out of them. We then compared training regimes and it soon became apparent that these kids didn't have much say in how they ran their lives. Russian coach Viktor Chegin – who had been banned by the Russian Anti-Doping Agency RUSADA a month before Zurich but was still on the roadside for the race – told them how and when to train, and how to race each race. They told me they were doing up to 260km a week in the mountains before coming to Zurich and, while I controlled my own environment, they had absolutely no say in theirs and were simply pawns in the Russian system.

They were young but tough kids who totally dismissed 20km walkers. They didn't do 20km and laughed at the thoughts of those that did. In their eyes the 20km event was for wimps and 50km was the man's event. Their enthusiasm for race walking was unending and even though I'd abandoned in Zurich that day, they had huge respect for me because I'd won the 50km World Championships in Moscow the year before. We chatted for a long time and eventually I had to ask them why they doped. A Russian doctor, who was on the edge of the conversation, immediately jumped to their defence and said 'No, no, no. This is all propaganda.' Ryzhov and Noskov then followed suit and denied it, very convincingly in fact, but the following summer both would be among six Russian walkers banned for doping.

After the race I had been very honest with the lads from Athletics Ireland about how I felt mentally during the race in Zurich, to the extent that I was then bombarded with paperwork from Kevin Ankrom about how I was going to sort out my psychological problems and what I was going to do if they happened again. If our relationship was fractured beforehand, it was worse after that and in the next meeting with him in Cork afterwards, I reminded him and Foley of all their empty promises.

Ankrom asked me if I was going to keep coaching Boycey and Alex but I wanted to offload them to Paco, who had retired from race walking by this time. Because he had been banned for a year though, they didn't want to touch him.

'This isn't about doping,' I said. 'This fella is after winning eight or nine medals. He's an expert. He's lived a life of high performance and has had years of experience at the top of the sport. If we can get some good out of that then it's going to help them.'

I told them it wasn't fair that Marian was left with everything, that it wasn't fair that there was no professional paid position for her. In Moscow she'd worked on the table while five months pregnant. She'd been looking after three of us and a new baby since then. She'd given up everything else in her life and did a huge amount of work for the group but got absolutely no respect.

'Kevin,' I said. 'I'm claiming five foot eight. You're over six foot, but you've no presence in a room, because you've no balls.'

By the time we got back from Zurich, Marian and I were still at war over my decision to stop racing and our homecoming was the complete opposite of the year before. I couldn't get my head around it. I was fierce depressed. I was afraid to go out because instead of congratulating me like they had after Moscow, for weeks afterwards I had grannies and mothers coming up to me hugging me and saying, 'You poor thing.'

I was still trying to figure out what was wrong with my hip so I rang a buddy of mine, Jim Cosgrove, a chiropractor, knowing he had contacts in the Elysian Medical Centre in Cork, to get scans done.

'Jim, I've a problem with my hip,' I said. 'I haven't said anything to anyone about it for the last two months but it needs to be checked.'

He got me in for a scan but nothing showed up and after my usual few weeks' winter break I went back training in November. But with the motivation of racing in a big championship now behind me, I was in agony and was coming to a halt after 8 or 10km in every session.

I then went to Steve Eustace, at the Irish Sports Institute, who did an ultrasound but saw nothing either. He decided to inject my hip with an anti-inflammatory anyway but I still got no relief. Emma Gallivan then got me an appointment with a doctor in England.

Based in Germany, Dr Ulrike Muschaweck held a clinic in the Spire Little Aston hospital in Birmingham every so often so I flew off to see her. There was an aura of competency about her as soon as I walked into the room. She told me to take my clothes off and scanned me.

'Yes, you have hernia here,' she said pointing to my right hip. 'And you also have hernia here,' pointing to my left.

'No!'

'Yes, yes,' she insisted and showed me the scan.

'Definitely?'

'Yes.'

'So this would have affected me over the season?'

'Of course. It's normal it will affect your performance. It is a big injury.'

I'd just been told that for the second time in my career I had two hernias, but for some reason I was smiling. I just remember feeling so happy to have finally found the reason why I had struggled all year.

20

Testing Times

For some reason I got the hernias done at different times again. The one on the left was more prominent so Dr Muschaweck decided she would operate on that one first, and in December 2014 I flew to Birmingham, stayed overnight in a hotel and got the operation done in a private hospital the next day.

Athletics Ireland's medical team organised everything. They paid for my flight, my hotel and also took care of Dr Muschaweck's fees, which meant I didn't have to worry about anything. The level of support was brilliant and I couldn't help wonder what it would be like to have that type of backing on a training camp.

Muschaweck did a really clean job and told me that the mesh which had been used in my previous hernia operation a decade earlier had intertwined with some of my muscle tissue and was rubbing a nerve, so she cleaned everything up, put in some really tidy stitches and, after an overnight stay in hospital, I was allowed to make my way home the next day.

Although I felt really wiped out, as though I was going to collapse on the way to the airport, the operation was a success and I was back doing my rehabilitation exercises within a few days.

With baby Regan not yet one, I hated being away from her for any length of time and had been looking for a new altitude base closer to home. In early January 2015, Marian, Regan and I went to Tenerife for ten days to check out the area around Mount Teide.

The highest of all the Spanish mountains, Teide is where a lot of the top professional cycling teams stay and train at altitude during the season, but for me, it was rubbish. There was only one road to train up and down on and it was always very blustery, so I went back down to sea level, booked into a hotel on the coast and found an industrial park to walk in and a track to do my evening sessions on.

Marian hadn't been feeling well in Tenerife and for a while afterwards was still the same, so she went to the doctor a few weeks after we got home to find that she was four and a half months pregnant and was due that May. We had always planned to have another baby but we had put it on the back burner until after the Rio Olympics, so the news left us in complete shock.

While Regan's arrival had been clinically planned almost to the day, Tara's was a bit of a surprise to all of us and I can remember standing in the kitchen with Marian and both of us wondering how the hell we were going to cope with two babies in the lead-up to the 2016 Olympics. Now heavily pregnant with our fourth child, Marian was still looking after myself, Boycey and Alex so she had her hands full.

Having failed to finish in Zurich the year before, I hadn't yet qualified for the 50km walk at the 2015 World Championships, nor the Olympics in Rio, so I had to do a 50km race in Dudince in Slovakia on 9 March 2015.

Doing two 50km events in the same year was always going to jeopardise a good result at the World Championships in Beijing later on, but even though I went into the race off lower-intensity training and with my other hernia still niggling at me, I was confident I could get the qualifying time easily enough, even if I was only at around 85 per cent.

Racing on home soil, Matej Tóth recorded the third fastest time in history that day, having gone clear straight from the gun and been on world-record pace for much of the race.

After 10km, he held a minute-and-a-half lead over Polish duo Rafał Augustyn and Łukasz Nowak. After another 20km I had made my way up through the field to that duo but Tóth was now five minutes clear of our three-man chase group.

With Augustyn setting a new personal best to finish second, I finished three minutes behind Nowak for fourth place in a time of 3:48:44, fast enough to earn automatic qualification for the World Championships in Beijing at the end of the season and Rio in 2016.

I had planned to get my second hernia operation out of the way straight after Dudince, so that I would have time to come back for the European Cup in May. When I got home, though, I found that I had to go through the whole procedure again of going to the doctor, telling him I needed a scan and explaining it all again.

Even though the tear in my hernia had opened up more after the 50km in Dudince, I didn't get the second operation until 24 April 2015, which meant I had wasted four weeks' training. This time, Dr Muschaweck was attending a private hospital in London but otherwise everything was pretty much as before: Athletics Ireland organised everything and covered everything and the second operation went well.

That afternoon, shortly after coming out of the operation, I woke up in my hospital bed. With a drip in my arm and still feeling groggy and sick from the anaesthetic, I opened my eyes to see a man with a clipboard standing at my bedside. He told me his name and that he was there to carry out an anti-doping test on behalf of the IAAF.

Anti-doping tests are carried out either in competition or out of competition. While in-competition testing is self-explanatory, out-of-competition tests can be carried out any day and anywhere in the world. In order to make the system more efficient and stop testers travelling to test athletes that aren't there, every athlete must indicate a specific one-hour time slot between six in the morning and eleven at night when they will be available and accessible for testing at a specific location. If you miss three of these tests in a twelve-month period, you are banned, regardless of whether you fail a test or not.

Normally, I specify seven to eight in the morning as I know I will be in bed then, either at home or on training camp or in winter getting ready to do the school run. Sometimes, though, life gets in the way and an urgent phone call, a trip to the doctor with one of the kids in the middle of the night or something as simple as going for a coffee after the school run and forgetting to bring your phone with you could easily cause a missed test. In almost twenty years of walking, though, I think I only ever missed two in total.

As I sat on a plane in Dublin Airport that morning, though, the tester had hopped on a plane from London to Cork to come and test me. By the time I landed in London sometime after seven in the morning and remembered to update my whereabouts to say I was having an operation in Wellington Hospital that day, he had arrived at my house and knocked on the front door. Marian told him I had gone to London for an operation, which meant that I had missed the test and would have one black mark against me – which wasn't ideal but in the grand scheme of things was only one black mark and nothing really to worry about. The fact that I was under Athletics Ireland's care in hospital on the day would probably have seen the mark rescinded if I'd argued the point anyway. Instead of giving me a black mark, though, the tester decided that as he was flying back to London and lived nearby, he would call in and test me in the hospital.

At first I didn't know if I was really awake, whether I was dreaming all of this and it took me a few seconds to realise it was actually real. We spoke for a minute or two and I explained that I'd just come out of an operation and was still feeling a bit woozy. He was really nice about it and helped me into a wheelchair and wheeled me to the bathroom, where I had to give a urine sample.

For every anti-doping urine sample, to avoid any chance of concealment or sleight of hand, the tester has to be able to see you actually urinating into the container, so you have to stand up and pull your pants down to your knees so that he can see your bits as you go. I was so dizzy from the operation though, that when I stood up to pee into the container I almost fell back into the wheelchair and the tester had to grab my arm to steady me.

After filling the container to the required level, I plonked back into the wheelchair and was wheeled back into the ward. As I eased myself back into bed, the anti-doping officer went out to reception, got a list of all the medication I'd been given during and after the operation and, with the required forms filled in and signed, headed home while I lay there sweating from the exertion for a few minutes before conking out again.

I got out of hospital the next day, flew home to Cork and started my whole rehabilitation procedure again, delighted that I was now fixed and that there would be no more interruptions in my training. I still had time to get fit enough for the World Championships in Beijing that August, where I wanted to retain my world title.

While I recovered from my operation, Marian had been nearing the end of her pregnancy and just over two weeks later the contractions began late one night. Never one to cause a fuss, Marian insisted I bring Cathal to his hurling match the following morning and that she had plenty of time before she needed to be brought to hospital.

With my sister Rhonda drafted in to look after Marian, I brought Cathal to the match in Glanmire and the plan was to ring me if things got worse and I'd drive straight to the hospital. When I got the phone call to tell me that the contractions had progressed a lot quicker than expected and Rhonda's husband Aidan was bringing her to the hospital, I was so engrossed in the match that, having arranged for Cathal to be dropped to his granny's afterwards, I walked backwards from the sideline, keeping an eye on Cathal for as long as possible, before turning and sprinting to the car at the last minute.

In order to get away with the minimum amount of hospital appointments and not to disrupt my training schedule, Marian had taken it upon herself to sign up for a natural birth, so I arrived at the hospital at 1.15 p.m. to see the nurses trying to persuade my darling wife to relax by doing a jigsaw with Meghan before having a water birth.

Although Marian was in pain and wanted the epidural, the nurses prolonged things to the point of no return and at 3.15 p.m. on 9 May, our fourth child, Tara, was born. In complete contrast to the drawn-out saga of Regan's birth the year before we were all home that night by nine o'clock.

Having two babies under one and a half was very hard on Marian. She also had two older kids and three Olympic walkers to look after.

But we had no alternative. Athletics Ireland weren't providing any full-time coaching and nobody else was going to take on that commitment. I wanted her to take some time off and just recover but Marian was having none of it.

Cathal and Meghan were brilliant, even if Cathal was now outnumbered three to one by the girls, but Marian felt under pressure to look after me. For a while neither of us was happy with the situation and we ended up arguing over who needed more rest.

The recovery from my second hernia operation was very good and a month later I was back walking, this time in a 5km outdoor race in France. Along with young sprinters Zak Irwin and Marcus Lawler, I joined SPN Vernon, the French club of Togher clubmate Tristan Druet, so that we could race over there. I went over to the meet with Dermot McDermott and Meghan.

I was so nervous about my comeback that I puked up before the race. I got into a really hard race with a French fella but came away with the win and went home happy. I planned to race a 20km walk in Lithuania a month later but a phone call from John Foley, CEO of Athletics Ireland, a few days after I returned from France brought those plans and everything else to a grinding halt.

'Rob,' he said, 'I've some bad news for you.'

'What is it, John?'

'You've failed a drugs test.'

'What are you on about?'

'I've a letter here from IAAF.' He began to read it out. 'In Wellington, London, on the 24th of April ...'

As soon as he said the date, I knew where I'd been tested. 'That's the day I was in hospital, John. I was only out of the operating theatre. It's obviously something to do with that.'

John had to read out the rest of the letter to me and told me he'd send it on by email. At first, I had thought he was joking but when I realised he was serious, I went into shock.

'That's fine,' I said. 'That's no big deal. It's just the operation. I'll get onto the doctors.'

With just six days to respond to the notice and not knowing what else to do, I sent an email to the IAAF telling them that I'd had an operation on the day and that I was just out of out theatre when I'd been tested so it was obviously something to do with that. Naively perhaps, I thought they would chase it up and sort everything out but they sent me back a really abrupt email, basically telling me tough luck, who's to say you were having an operation? Why did you need one and where's the proof of it?

I immediately phoned Alan Rankin, the Athletics Ireland doctor at the time, and told him I'd failed a test but Alan was stunned and didn't know what to do either.

I started Googling the product that had produced the positive test, hydroxyethyl starch, something I had never heard of before. I got some relief in the fact that it was used as a clotting agent for patients undergoing operations but then I also found out that it had been used as a masking agent for EPO back in the 1990s and early 2000s. Because of this, I was desperate to get proof that the operation was the cause of the adverse analytical finding. Until I had that concrete evidence, I felt that nobody would believe me.

I could see that trying to explain that it was used during the operation would have just sounded like something that people on drugs would say anyway. I've heard most of those excuses before. 'The EPO in the fridge is for my granny's leg.' 'The steroids under the bed are for my horse.' 'The dog ate my homework.' And I could hear it now. 'Your man's from Cork, how did he win a world championship? Sure we know now.'

I didn't even tell some of my family members about the test. I rang the hospital in London immediately and their answer that yes, hydroxyethyl starch was commonly used in operations put my mind at ease and I thought things were going to be easily sorted. That news got me through the bank holiday weekend until I rang Dr Muschaweck's secretary on the Tuesday, who told me that the doctor was away but she would get her husband, Dr Leonhard Muschaweck, to look into it.

Rather than put my mind at ease, his emailed response a few hours later scared the life out of me.

Dear Mr Heffernan,

Alas, the first bits and pieces of information are arriving.

Let me assemble my thoughts. Neither we as surgeons, nor the group of anaesthetists in the Wellington Hospital use hydroxyethyl starch which was found positive in your urine sample. It is very old fashioned, officially the use is not recommended any longer, and my check with the pharmacist of the Wellington Hospital revealed that it has not been in stock for eighteen months!

This clearly rules out any intentional or inadvertent (accidental) application.

Hydroxyethyl starch is no compound in any of our medication (i.e. local anaesthetic). Tomorrow morning I will receive a complete list of drugs used by the anaesthetist. The one drug containing various compounds is the narcotic Diprivan. However, if you look up section 6.1 of the information, hydroxyethyl starch is not listed.

The anaesthetist, Dr Gill, uses Baxter Healthcare's Sodium Lactate as infusion. I have also included the information of this. However, it only contains water and some electrolytes.

Tomorrow, as soon as I get the drug list, I will try to shed some light on all drugs used by the anaesthetist.

My whole world stopped. I knew he had to be wrong. There was no other explanation. It had to have been used in the operation. Tara was only a couple of weeks old but I was a complete zombie for the next few days and I don't even remember spending any time with her. I couldn't train. I couldn't eat my food. I couldn't sleep at night but couldn't get out of bed in the morning. The email had left me reeling and I couldn't function.

I can remember dropping Cathal to school one day and having to sit in the car until I stopped crying, so that I could compose myself before I went back to the house. I remember driving by Páirc Uí Chaoimh, Cork's GAA stadium, and looking over the River Lee to the pier where people had driven in to commit suicide over the years. I don't think I was suicidal at the time but I was in a very dark place and could completely empathise with someone who was. Things were so bleak I felt as though I had nothing to offer Marian, Regan, Tara, Cathal and Meghan.

I lay awake every night fearing that the story might break in the national media the next morning and that I'd be labelled a cheat. If that happened, my reputation would be in tatters. Even if I proved my innocence later on, I feared that the only thing people would remember was the failed test. For the next five weeks, chasing doctors, secretaries, receptionists, anaesthetists and gathering the proof that I hadn't doped consumed my days and nights. It was the worst time of my life. In that period I went from loving race walking, the sport that I had grown up with, the sport that I done all of my life, to absolutely despising it.

What got me through those five weeks was Marian. She lived with me and knew I didn't take drugs and she kept on telling me that I had nothing to worry about.

'Rob, you didn't do it, so we'll get to the bottom of it.'

I'd been drug tested before the race in Dudince and afterwards. I was tested again a couple of weeks later, a few days before the operation, and I was even tested again after getting home from the operation. All of my tests were clean but that didn't matter. If I couldn't prove that this drug had been put in my body by the hospital during the operation, then my life was going to be destroyed.

I spent all of my waking time on the Internet, looking up the substance to find out as much as I could about it. I got onto my agent, Derry McVeigh, who brought me to see a solicitor who had experience with toxicology reports. The solicitor began by asking me questions about whether the lab that carried out the anti-doping test was credible or not, knowing that if it wasn't they would have to nullify the test result. But I didn't care whether the lab was credible or not. I knew the substance could only have been put into my body during the operation. I'd found out since that it could only be detected in your system for a few hours after it was administered. I had been hooked up to a drip during the drug test, so I knew it had to have been either in the drip or used during the operation when I was unconscious.

Back home, I was getting Athletics Ireland's doctor, Alan Rankin, to chase it up. I was getting Dr Muschaweck's secretary in Germany to chase it up and I was trying to chase it up myself but still couldn't get any answers. Alan was trying to track the anaesthetist down while the doctor's secretary over in Germany was going through all of the medications that were given to me in the operation.

I was trying to push everything forward. I was contacting the anaesthetist, contacting the hospital, contacting Germany and getting Alan Rankin to do the same without telling him that I was doing it, just to keep the pressure on everyone.

In the end, German efficiency saved my career and I finally received an email from Dr Muschaweck's secretary with some good news.

> *Dear Robert,*
>
> *Dear Dr Rankin,*
>
> *Robert, I am so glad that, alas, I found the troubleshooter!!*
> *If you open the link below about B Braun's PARACETAMOL (PL 03551/0128) you will find in section 6.1 as one excipient 'Hydroxyethyl starch'.*
> *The administration of Paracetamol is clearly the reason for your positive HES test, where the sample has been drawn only a few hours post surgery.*
> *Please forward this email to your trainer and to the Anti-Doping agency.*
> *Your case has also demonstrated how efficient the tests are :)*
>
> *Kind regards*
> *Isabelle*

She had found that the starch was an excipient, a tiny ingredient, of the intravenous paracetamol used during the operation, which explained why it was in my system. She even sent me a picture of the bottle of paracetamol with hydroxyethyl starch clearly contained in the list of ingredients on the label.

The anaesthetist from the hospital in London then wrote to Alan Rankin with his report, apologising for the stress I had gone through and confirming that this was the definitive reason why it was in my system. Alan scanned the letter and forwarded it to me.

Re: Mr Robert Heffernan,

Dr Leonhard Muschaweck has identified one of the medications – Paracetamol (B-Braun PL03551/0128) which is routinely given intravenously for most procedures as containing HES.

Having reviewed the anaesthetic chart, as Robert's anaesthetist for the procedure, I am writing to confirm that I administered 1g of paracetamol intravenously via a drip peri-operatively starting at 13.30 and ending at 15.00.

I hope this ends the matter and any unfounded allegations.

Please send Robert my regards and apologies for the distress and any anxiety caused.

Kind regards

Dr Vip Gill MBBS FRCA
Consultant Anaesthetist

When I read the letter I broke down in tears. It was like a dam had been opened and I was in floods, shaking uncontrollably with relief that the nightmare was finally over. If they hadn't gone through every tiny detail, every ingredient of every medicine, and found that, my life would have been destroyed, Marian's life would have been destroyed and my children's lives too. Everything I'd ever worked for would have been gone forever.

I gathered all of the paperwork together from all of the investigations and sent it off to the IAAF. But they still weren't happy. They came back looking for more paperwork, including all of the blood work that had been done before the operation. I had to give more evidence of why I needed the operation, whether it was warranted or not, and whether the hospital was a reputable hospital.

When I eventually got all of the paperwork in from Germany and London and Alan Rankin in Athletics Ireland, Alan then had to fill out a retrospective Therapeutic Use Exemption form. This form allows athletes who are sick or undergoing surgery to take medication that is normally on the WADA prohibited list if a doctor can verify that it is medically required and there is no unfair advantage to be gained from taking it. This TUE form included the hydroxyethyl starch, with Alan explaining that it was an excipient of the intravenous paracetamol I had been given during the operation and he sent it off with all of the other evidence.

With the weight of the whole debacle finally beginning to lift, I started training again and was down at the track one day when I got an email from the IAAF Medical and Anti-Doping Department.

Dear Mr Heffernan,

I write to inform you that following the approval of a retroactive Therapeutic Use Exemption by the IAAF TUE Committee for the use of a prohibited substance hydroxyethyl starch on 24 April 2015, and upon consulting with the Irish Sports Council and the World Anti-Doping Agency, there will be no further disciplinary action under IAAF rules for the adverse analytical finding reported in your urine sample and the case will be closed accordingly.

Please ensure in the future that all medical or para-medical personnel advising you are made aware that you are an elite athlete subject to regular anti-doping control tests and that substances and methods identified in the WADA prohibited list should not be administered to you.

Thank you for your cooperation

Yours sincerely
Thomas Capdevielle
Anti-Doping Senior Manager / Acting Operations Manager

Everything had been sorted out and the IAAF, WADA and the Irish Sports Council had all accepted that I hadn't doped. The test result was nullifed but, to be sure, I rang the secretary in the IAAF headquarters in Monaco, told her who I was and asked her about the email.

'That's it?' I asked. 'It's all over with. I'm not banned?'

'Yes, yes, it's no problem,' she said. 'You sent in the papers. Everything is okay.'

'Just like that? Oh my God! You don't realise what my life has been like for the last five weeks.'

'Oh? I've never heard anybody be so happy after sending in a TUE form! Okay, goodbye.'

With that, the nightmare was over but I was very wary of it happening again to other Irish athletes and afterwards wrote to Athletics Ireland to try and make them put a procedure in place to ensure it wouldn't. I wanted to make certain that the next Irish athlete to have an operation would have the doctor check every substance possible and that a TUE would be issued for them all. I wouldn't wish what I had gone through on my worst enemy.

I was very disappointed at the lack of support from Athletics Ireland. After the initial phone call from John Foley, I never heard a word from him again, even after the case was resolved. Even though the operation had been organised by them and therefore I was under their duty of care, they didn't contact the IAAF to remind them that under their own guidelines I shouldn't have been tested immediately after an operation; I'd had no welfare officer or other person in the association to help me through the process of proving my innocence. Although a report undertaken on behalf of Athletics Ireland into the incident afterwards exonerated them of any wrongdoing, it recomm-ended having a confidential contact within the association for athletes facing serious difficulties of a medical or psychological nature, with backup from potential experts in these areas.

Afterwards, when I took the emotion out of it on my behalf, I realised that the IAAF had done a good job. They were very thorough with the amount of paperwork and checks they did and it would have been impossible for me to have got away with doping.

It took a while for me to come around to racing again but in the end Marian persuaded me to carry on and that the only way to get back was to jump in at the deep end again.

'Look, Rob, you've had a brilliant career and you're not going out like this. You've been world champion and you're not ending it with the way things ended in Zurich. You're going to go out on your terms.'

Just a couple of days after I got the notification in early July that I hadn't failed a test and that I was clear to race, I entered the Cork City Sports and finished a poor fourth in the 3km walk, behind South African Lebogang Shange, Alberto Amezcua of Spain and Alex Wright.

With the World Championships at the end of August, it was time for altitude camp again and this time we decided to go to Morocco. Marian and I rented an apartment in a resort where we stayed with Regan and Tara for a month while Cathal and Meghan were being looked after at home.

Although I'd been to Morocco before, it was the first time I had gone in summer during Ramadan and the place was nearly abandoned. It was like a ghost town. Once I was back training I was completely driven and focused on the World Championships in Beijing so I never stopped to think about the fact that Marian had a six-week-old baby and a one-and-a-half-year-old to look after, as well as myself, Brendan and Alex.

With no other support, she looked after all of us. As well as making our bottles for drinks during training, Marian was up making bottles for the babies during the night. Alex's girlfriend Lauren was there for a while and gave a hand with the babysitting but most days Marian had the two babies in the back of the car as she drove behind us for two or three hours. She did video analysis too. She did everything!

I get on very well with the lads I train with. They are very professional, good lads, but when I'm stuck with any group of people for a long time it drives me bananas and most people will tell you I'm a briar on training camps. Morocco was no different: I was completely fixated on my training. I'd be giving out to Marian if she handed me water instead of an energy drink or vice versa during a walk. In fairness, she was so busy, I don't know how she didn't hand me a baby's bottle by mistake.

Back home, my next race was the 10km National Championships in Santry Stadium, where Alex and I lined up as the favourites. Alex had beaten me in our previous outing at the Cork City Sports so I was fierce motivated to beat him. We were training partners and got on really well but we both wanted a hard race and a good performance before heading to the World Championships a few weeks later. I was determined to put the hammer down from the start of the race and if Alex was going to beat me then he was going to really hurt doing it.

By the halfway point, after 5km, I had dropped him and opened a gap of 100m when I got disqualified for my technique, which I had thought was very good on the day. I was absolutely hopping mad but when RTÉ came over to interview me I tried to keep it positive.

'Maybe the shorter race meant I had a different cadence,' I told them. 'I'll go home and have a look at my technique.'

Pierce O'Callaghan came over afterwards and told me I'd been kicking high on my right side. I didn't agree with him but I bit my lip and nodded. What annoyed me more was that the point when I got disqualified was when it was just starting to hurt, at the halfway mark, so I hadn't had to cope with the discomfort of fighting off Alex in the last 5km. I'd missed the hardest part of the race and with no events to compete in before Beijing would be going into the World Championships with no hard racing under my belt.

Before the World Championships Kevin Ankrom had organised an Irish team holding camp in Hong Kong, where his wife is from. I'd been to Hong Kong during the month of May and found it really hot so it seemed ridiculous to go there in the searing temperatures of August, three weeks before the competition.

For me, a training camp is about having no distractions: you train, you sleep, you eat, you get physio. But lads were going out sightseeing in Hong Kong and putting photos up on social media, then had to train around an industrial estate.

Instead of going with them, Brendan and I chose to stay at home to train together and, with all of our stamina work done at altitude, we did our specific sessions back at sea level in Cork. Afterwards, we flew out to China eight or nine days before the race, which gave me enough time to adjust to the temperature and the time zone.

When I got to China, I didn't sleep during the day so that I could adjust to the time zone and with my training load decreasing, I started recovering. Mentally I was fresher and the Chinese were great craic and very easy going. I loved it.

I went into the 50km race, which began on a very hot day at the Bird's Nest stadium, with a very different build-up than I'd had in Moscow but as I stood on the start line, I still wanted to win, to defend my title from Moscow. I knew Slovakian Matej Tóth was head and shoulders above everybody in the world after what he'd done in the 50km walk in Dudince earlier in the year so when he went off alone from the gun, the rest of us formed a group behind him and I did my own thing.

After 30km, Tóth was still sixty-nine seconds clear but I was feeling good and began to take the race on at the head of a seven-man chase group, which dwindled to five a couple of kilometres later when Andrés Chocho from Ecuador was disqualified and Erick Barrondo from Guatemala dropped off the group after receiving a warning.

With 15km still to go, Tóth's advantage was fifty-six seconds. Jared Tallent from Australia and I began to trade attacks and went ding-dong at it for a long time. Jared made a couple of breaks and I caught him. I made a couple of moves and he caught me.

This was the World Championships and I was up for it. We had broken away from the rest of the field and had a good gap on the others but when he broke me and went clear at 42km, the little doubts set in. My technique was good and I was feeling okay but I picked up a second warning. I was still in third place but the gaps in training during my year meant I wasn't confident enough to open up. Instead, I started to doubt myself. 'Do I really deserve to be here in a World Championships?'

Jared began to move clear but I was still in contention for bronze, even when I was passed by Japanese duo Takayuki Tanii and Hirooki Arai after 45km. With 3km to go they were still in my sights but then my legs started cramping up, my quads began to lock up and my arms started to seize. My technique was starting to break down and with two warnings already, I had to ease off a little and gather myself.

My hamstring started cramping so severely a kilometre later that I thought I wasn't going to get to the line but I knew that after failing to finish in Zurich the year before, not finishing the World Championships would have been catastrophic for me. I needed to consolidate my position, hold onto a top-five place in the Worlds. I told myself to relax. 'Keep going, Rob. Take it kilometre by kilometre. Fifth in the world is still very, very solid going into the Olympics.'

Looking back, if I'd had a couple of races beforehand I think I could have medalled but to finish fifth in the world after the year I'd had was a huge result. I knew if I could do everything right, if I stayed injury free, if all of my camps went well and I got to the big day in good condition I'd hopefully be in a position to challenge for an Olympic medal again in Rio.

After a disjointed season that included two operations, the whole rigmarole with the test and getting disqualified at Nationals it gave me huge confidence going forward into 2016. When I crossed the line I was actually delighted. After where I'd come from, it was one of my best performances ever.

21

Rio Grande

Although my aim for the Olympics in Rio was the 50km walk, I knew I had to do a few shorter races during the year to keep in touch with competition, stay motivated and get some fast kilometres into my legs so, having wintered in Cork, my fifth and final Olympic year began in Nenagh in County Tipperary with a hard-fought victory over Alex Wright at the Munster Indoor 5km Championships on 3 January 2016.

Two weeks later I travelled to France for a regional championship with my French club SPN Vernon. Meghan came with me to celebrate her thirteenth birthday. In front of a packed stadium, I beat Boycey to win the race, and Meghan and I had a lovely weekend in Paris.

A week after that, on 31 January, I was in Bratislava for another very tough indoor 5km race, this time finishing third behind British walker Tom Bosworth and Grzegorz Sudoł of Poland in a time of 19' 19" before returning home to continue my build-up to Rio.

The weather in Cork took a turn for the worse in mid-February so while Cathal and Meghan stayed in Cork and went to school, Marian, Regan, Tara and I went to the Canaries for a week to get away from the cold and rain. We had no TV in our apartment and no Internet but it was great to be able to spend some time together in the sun, get some good training done and, with no distractions, we were all in bed by 9.30 every night.

On 28 February, instead of competing at the Irish National Championships in Athlone, which I had won fifteen times in a row, I returned to France where one of the SPN Vernon club members picked me up in Paris for the six-hour car journey to Clermont and the French 5km National Indoor Championships, which I had qualified for by winning my previous race there. The race was televised live on TV and there was a huge crowd in the stadium but instead of getting a buzz out of that, I found myself struggling to get motivated. After 100m, I was back in eighth or ninth place and ended up having to really race hard to win it. I only got away from a young fella, Jean Blancheteau, with two laps to go. I really dug in to win the race but I didn't get any satisfaction out of it at all and didn't enjoy the weekend. Afterwards I put it down to being away on my own and having nobody to show off to, but maybe it dawned on me the huge pressure I would have to put myself under if I was to win a medal in Rio.

In the first week of March, I was away again, this time in Dudince, Slovakia, for a 20km World Grand Prix race. Previously, I wouldn't have batted an eyelid being lumped with Alex and Brendan in a small room in a pretty basic guesthouse before the race but when it happened in Dudince I suddenly began to feel as if I was getting too old to be traipsing around the world to compete.

I stayed with the leaders for 10km but had no desire for it and ended up drifting back as Tom Bosworth went through the halfway marker with a twelve-second lead. I could feel a little niggle in my hip but, worse than that, I could feel a lack of interest in the race. If it had been the World Championships or the Olympics I would have ignored the pain and got stuck in, but in Dudince I just couldn't hurt myself and didn't want to be there. Although I had drifted well back through the field, the fact that I was on target for an Olympic 'A' standard qualifying time over the shorter 20km distance kept me going to the line, where I finished about two minutes behind winner Bosworth. Getting the qualifying time for the 20km walk in Rio gave me options if I wanted to go over to Brazil early and familiarise myself with the athletes' call room or check out the course before the 50km event a week later.

This early period of the year also coincided with speculation in the media about six Russian walkers, including London 2012 winner Sergey Kirdyapkin, who had been previously banned for doping. Although Kirdyapkin had been doped before, during and after the Olympic race, the Russian anti-doping agency allowed him to keep the gold medal he won in London and other selective events before they were taken to the Court of Arbitration for Sport (CAS) in Lausanne, Switzerland, that March.

Although the Russian case had been dragged out for a long time, almost four years, it eventually came to a head on Thursday 24 March 2016, when CAS issued a statement about the outcome of the proceedings.

I was getting ready to go training that morning and had one runner laced up and the other one in my hand when I opened a generic email from CAS with the statement attached. Marian and the kids were upstairs, so I called them down before reading it out loud.

We had been expecting an announcement any day but weren't really sure what the outcome would be. The kids came down the stairs like a tonne of bricks as I nervously flicked my phone screen down to the part I wanted to read. 'The Court of Arbitration for Sport has issued its decisions in the following arbitration procedures ...' I began nervously.

The appeals concern one element of decisions issued by the disciplinary committee of the Russian Anti-Doping Agency ('RUSADA') in anti-doping cases brought against the athletes, based on irregularities observed in the athletes' biological passports. The International Association of Athletics Federations (IAAF) claimed that RUSADA had incorrectly applied the applicable anti-doping rules adopted by IAAF (the 'IAAF ADR') to implement the provisions of the World Anti-Doping Code with respect to the disqualification of competitive results (disqualification of results split in different periods). The IAAF challenged what it felt was a 'selective' disqualification of results, submitting that all results achieved by the athletes from the date of their first abnormal sample to the date they accepted a provisional suspension should be disqualified.

In each case, the appeal filed by the IAAF has been upheld and the decision issued by the Disciplinary Anti-Doping Committee of the Russian Anti-Doping Agency for each athlete has been modified, as follows . . .

There were five other names on the list but Kirdyapkin's was the only one that concerned me at the time, and there it was:

All competitive results obtained by Mr Sergey Kirdyapkin from 20 August 2009 to 15 October 2012 are disqualified.

Overruling RUSADA, saying that they had wrongly imposed selective bans which were timed in a way that meant the six athletes were allowed to keep most of their major titles, the court had retrospectively banned Kirdyapkin, which meant I was upgraded to third place in the 50km walk in London and was now due an Olympic bronze medal.

The house went mental! We were all hugging and cheering and jumping up and down. I'd previously made a pact with Marian that I'd cut out the media stuff and would go back to being an athlete again but within minutes the phone started to ring and that day every national media outlet must have contacted me about the news.

For a while I was distracted by the news and wondering how and where I would get presented with the medal. Would I get it before Rio or wait until afterwards? If I got it beforehand, would it take away from my motivation to win one over there? Again, Marian was the more level-headed of the two of us. 'Shut up, Rob,' she said. 'You need to be training. Forget about the medal, you need to be training. I'm not doing all of this if you're not doing it right.' Most of the time, I'd fight every decision with her but Marian is always right and in the end we agreed to forget about it until after Rio.

In April, a group of us went to altitude camp in Morocco for twenty days. Brendan, Alex and I were joined by young walker Cian

McManamon, marathon runner Sergio Ciobanu, Ray Flynn and his daughter Zola. I paid for a local physio out there; once again, we had no official Irish team support in Morocco but I was tested five times while out there by the Irish Sports Council, which meant they were able to fly in guys two or three times a week to take blood or urine samples but wouldn't give us any help with coaching or physio staff for the camp.

In Morocco, my hip was uncomfortable every day. I was getting all of my work done but I wasn't happy. Marian and the kids had stayed at home in Cork and I was missing them so much that I started questioning everything again, asking myself if I really wanted to be putting myself through this torture again. A few days before the end of the camp, I got a call from Spanish sports agent Alberto Armas to see if I wanted to do a 10km race in Murcia a couple of days later. If the truth be told, I was delighted to get out of Morocco and away from the drain of altitude. I jumped at the chance.

Upon arrival in Spain I was housed in a plush hotel. Even the atmosphere of the race itself was a nice change of scenery from the drab surroundings of training camp but for the first couple of kilometres I still had no interest in competing and felt really down in myself.

When I was still with the leaders halfway through the race, however, my attitude changed and I started to dig in. Alberto Amezcua from Guadix, with whom I regularly trained over there, got clear towards the end and I found myself in a battle with world 20km champion Miguel Ángel López in the final kilometres before eventually finishing third.

After twenty-two days away, I got home for only a week before I was back in Spain, this time for a short camp before the Race Walking World Cup in Rome. Although I got all of my sessions done over there and was treated by Athletics Ireland physio Emma every day, I didn't feel the sessions went well. I didn't feel good, had no energy and having had just a week at home, I wasn't feeling happy and was getting tired of the whole game.

After our last training session on the Wednesday before the World Cup, we stayed in Malaga overnight ahead of our flight to Rome the next morning. Having endured searing temperatures all week, I woke up shivering from the cold in the middle of the night. I got up in the early hours to turn off the air conditioning but my room was so cold that I couldn't get back to sleep and I felt shattered all day Thursday. I didn't know if it was because of the air conditioning or if I was coming down with something but when I got to Rome I was so worn out that I couldn't even train, which is not normal for me.

I spent Thursday evening in bed and while I still wasn't feeling great on the Friday morning, I went training with the boys, which made me believe I was better than the day before. Having been drug tested that afternoon, I went to bed early to try and get more rest as the race was on later than usual the following morning. At 6 a.m., though, I was woken by a knock on the door and another anti-doping tester. I was so annoyed and grumpy at being woken up that I couldn't get back to sleep and I remember being introduced to the crowd before the race as an Olympic medallist and former world champion but feeling so tired that it felt like a bad dream. I'd never felt like it before in a race and couldn't even warm up.

I was with the leaders for the first 5km but after that, I started drifting off the pace dramatically and had the worst race of my life, finishing sixty-eighth in a time of 86' 48", almost seven and a half minutes slower than Chinese winner Zhen Wang. I hadn't walked that slow since the Sydney Olympics in 2000 and afterwards I thought it was all over. If this was all I was capable of, there was no point in going to Rio.

When I got home the next day, Cathal asked me where I finished.

'I was sixty-eighth.'

'Ah Dad, come on, where did you finish?'

'Sixty-eighth.'

He looked at me disbelievingly, but my body language soon persuaded him I was telling the truth.

'Alex beat me . . . Boycey beat me . . .'

'Ah, come on, man! How could you let them beat you?'

'I don't know,' was all I could offer him.

Afterwards I felt terrible but didn't know if it was stress, if I had a virus or what was wrong with me. My result in Rome left me feeling very low and I wasn't looking forward to Rio at all. Things came to a head the next evening as I sat in the car watching Meghan and Cathal train down at the Mardyke. I suddenly felt dizzy and got up to call Marian, who was in the track centre, but I could barely move. I beeped the horn to let them know I wasn't well but they thought I was just beeping at them. It wasn't until I tried to get out of the car and collapsed face down on the ground that they knew something was wrong.

A trip to the doctor followed, where the bump protruding from my head was assessed before I was diagnosed with fatigue. I got bloods done the next day but when they all came back okay, I began to wonder if my poor early season performances were just a mental thing, if I simply couldn't get motivated for the smaller races.

Instead of racing in La Coruña in Spain on 8 May as previously planned, I decided to stay at home and give myself a good three to four weeks of training with no structure, no plan. If I trained, I trained once a day. If I felt tired, I didn't train. If I felt like I wanted to train hard I just turned up at the track and joined in with whatever session Alex was doing. In a way, things had come full circle and I was back training like I was when I was young, with no real plan. Sometimes though, when I'd jump in with Alex, who set a personal best in the 20km walk in La Coruña, I did some great sessions and it made me realise that I could do it if I wanted to. Pretty quickly I knew my problem was a mental one rather than physical.

When I explained to Cathal that I found it hard to get motivated in the smaller races, he looked at me and threw his hands up. A very good hurler and footballer, Cathal is big and strong for his eleven years and has plenty of skill but, sometimes, if his team is losing, his head drops and he gives up the ghost. I've always told him that no matter what the score is or what type of match it is, that he should still stay focused. 'It doesn't matter what the other lads are doing,' I tell him. 'You can still work on your tackling, work on your skills, work on your passing.'

Most of the time – especially in an important match that's going pear-shaped – he's in bad form and just shrugs the advice off as if I don't understand what he is going through. That evening he explained it in a nutshell.

'Now you know how I feel when we're losing!' he said 'It's the same thing.'

I looked at him and suddenly realised he was right. I wasn't following my own advice. I was letting my emotions get the better of me instead of focusing on the long-term goal, which was to try and improve every day and deliver a good performance in Rio. We chatted about it for a few minutes and afterwards we shook hands and made a pact that neither of us would let it happen again.

Emma Gallivan was very good to me and put me in contact with a sports psychologist in London. We discussed a lot of things, things that had been niggling me over the past few months. I went through a lot of negative stuff with the psychologist, peripheral stuff that had crept into my day-to-day routine.

When I stopped talking, she asked me one question. 'What happens if you wrestle with pigs?'

I looked at her blankly.

'You get covered in shit,' came the answer.

She told me that I was wasting energy worrying about stuff that I had no control over. 'You can't clear up everything. You can't change people's minds about things. You can't make everybody see your point of view. You have to go back and do the things you can do yourself and don't worry about anybody else.'

Essentially, that's what I did. I got back to basics, back to what was important. The Olympic Games have always been a massive feature in my life and Rio was going to be my fifth appearance at them. No other Irish athlete had ever competed at five Games before and if this was going to be my last time representing Ireland at the biggest sports event on the planet, then I was going to put everything into doing it well.

After Rome I knew I couldn't afford to let anything negative creep into my thoughts, couldn't let it drain my energy. I couldn't compare myself to others or worry too much if I wasn't going well. I needed to get back to being 100 per cent focused and from there until Rio, I had very little contact with anybody, apart from Marian, the kids, and the lads I trained with. Although I lost a lot of my old training files to a computer virus a couple of years ago I still had some of my original training programmes written down and I went back over them, setting out a new plan, one that included every single training session for every single day, right up to the Olympic race in Rio.

When I started back on my plan I wanted to get in a couple of shorter races to see where I was in terms of fitness so, having purposely done a hard 30km walk just a couple of days before, I entered a 5km race in Spain with no specific interval work done. With heavy legs, I finished third behind world champion Miguel Ángel López and his compatriot Ivan Pajuelo Paredes. My time of 19' 37" was a solid result and faster than I had done in the French Indoor Championships. All because I had a bit of hunger back.

Two days later, I raced the 3km walk at the Cork City Sports, finishing second to Alex in a really fast time of 11' 18", before flying out to Guadix with Marian, Regan and Tara for my final five weeks of altitude training before Rio. Meghan would have been completely bored over there and stayed at home with her mother. Cathal knew what to expect and came over for twelve days mid-camp with Marian's mam, Angela. If Cathal had been away on camps before and knew what it was like, it must have been very hard on Marian's mam. For me, training camp is training camp and I wanted to be isolated, with no distractions. I didn't want other things going on and between training twice a day, eating and sleeping I had no time to do anything with them.

The only day I had off during the five weeks was the day after we drove down to Malaga to collect Cathal and Angela from the airport. We booked into a hotel in Torremolinos for the night and with no training the next day I was in holiday mode for twenty-four hours. We had a meal and then went out to watch the World Cup final in one of the local bars. We had a few drinks, relaxed and had great craic between us but, wrecked the next day, I was racked with guilt and thought I'd blown my Olympic preparation.

Back in Guadix I rationalised that it was only one day and that I needed the break after training so hard and still had a lot of time before the Olympics. I followed my usual routine of training in the morning, sleeping in the afternoon and training again in the evening. With two babies in the house, a lot of our schedule is based around them. We go to bed when they need to go to bed, we get up when they get up and we have to schedule in time for their feeds and everything else associated with having toddlers so I was in bed by 10 p.m. most nights.

A couple of times I was woken by the drug testers an hour later. The worst thing about being tested just after going to bed was the fact that I'd usually gone to the toilet before bed so I'd have to get up and drink water until I could go again, which disturbed my whole sleep pattern and messed around with my training sometimes. The 11 p.m. or 6 a.m. wake-up calls for testing did more than upset my routine: more often than not, the doorbell woke either Tara or Regan, or both, which meant that they were out of sorts the next day too, which made Marian's job even harder.

I brought Tighearnach Ó Murchú and Dermot McDermott out as physios for different parts of the camp and Marian looked after the group in the mornings while Brendan and Alex's girlfriends also helped out when they were there. Even Marian's mam got stuck in, handing up bottles to me, which she did very well, even with a buggy in the other hand.

I put myself under that much pressure in Guadix that 'the bear' was out again and I was vomiting with nerves and anxiety before my key sessions. As this hadn't happened earlier in the year though, when I'd been doing badly, I took it as a good sign – a sign that my body was getting ready. I reasoned that I hadn't got sick earlier in the year because I didn't care about my training sessions or races.

After five weeks in Guadix, I came home to Cork nineteen days before the Olympics. Like Beijing the year before, I opted not to go into the Irish team holding camp before the Olympics until the last minute. Instead I stayed in one of the lodges at Fota Island Resort for a few days and continued the routine, with Boycey. By all accounts the camp was good but I still had a few hard sessions left and I felt it was too long to be in the same group before a big championship. I had all of my big mileage done with just had two or three specific sessions left to do in Cork. My fourteen 1km intervals went really well, even though I got a bad night's sleep before it. I did my last 25km session in 1:47:40, faster than any 25km I've ever done in training and faster than I'd done in the race in Rome.

Two days after that 25km effort I flew to Rio with Boycey. A nice meal, a few films and a glass of wine on the plane made for a relaxing eleven-hour flight from Frankfurt and we arrived in Rio around five o'clock in the morning where, alongside golfing sisters Leona and Lisa Maguire, we were directed to the Olympic desk to get our accreditation before hanging around for a couple of hours for the bus to take us into the Olympic Village seven days before the race.

Inside the gates of the village we were met by Ray Flynn, who was part of the race-walk coaching staff, and he brought Boycey and me to a four-bedroom apartment where we were housed with marathon runner Fionnuala McCormack and modern pentathlete Natalya Coyle. They were lovely and we had good craic with them throughout our stay. Next to the physio room there was a communal TV room with beanbags thrown on the floor. That was where we would gather any time there were Irish athletes in action. The boxers were two floors below us and had their own TV so we'd go down there and watch the boxing with them. I found the boxers to be great fun, really hard workers with great personalities. They reminded me of my own background and some of the lads I grew up with. All of the Irish squad mixed really well.

We all watched the O'Donovan brothers win silver in the men's lightweight double sculls. It boosted us all when anyone did well. There was a great camaraderie amongst the whole team.

To be honest, logistically Rio was the worst of the five Olympics I've been at, with journeys of at least an hour necessary to get to anywhere. The village was basic enough, with the food nowhere near as good as it had been in London, Beijing, Athens or Sydney. A lot of athletes had stuff stolen out of their rooms. A pair of my sunglasses went missing, while Brendan had money robbed from his room. The accommodation wasn't anything special either and Boyccy had to use our shower when his got clogged up after a couple of days.

Marian flew over two days after me and, with no babies to look after and no physio work to do, as the team had lots of physios, her workload was reduced hugely and she could relax a bit in the days leading to the race. In fairness to the Irish set-up, it was a completely different world from what we were used to normally. We were waited on hand and foot.

The weather was really bad when we arrived and was very humid. For the first few days I just tried to adjust to the time zone and the conditions. Temperatures gradually increased, building to a crescendo on the day of the 50km walk before cooling off again afterwards.

Training once a day, on my first day in Rio I had 10km to do followed by ten 100m efforts on a 2.5km lap around the inside circumference of the Olympic Village, where everybody trained. Outside the village was dodgy enough and there wasn't really anywhere to go but we found a coffee shop about a kilometre up the road that we could walk to for a change of scenery. Day two saw me walk 6km followed by ten 200m efforts. On day three I did 16km intervals with each hard kilometre followed by an easy one. Three days out from the race I walked 12km, followed by 10km the next day and a final 6km pyramid session the day before the Olympic race.

With all of her work done on the eve of the race, Marian went to see Thomas Barr run in the 400m hurdles final, where he put in a fantastic performance to finish fourth, almost snatching a medal in his first Olympics and setting a national record. While she was gone, I passed the afternoon by sorting out some of my twenty-five separate bottles, one for each lap, with different drinks for the different stages of the race. Up to 10km I used a red mix of carbohydrate and isotonic drink, 12–14km was a cloudy Isostar drink, 16km Sustain, 17km a mix of gel and water and then repeating those last three to the finish. Both Ray and Marian were very good on the day and didn't put me under extra pressure.

I decided to shave my head, borrowing a razor from one of the pentathlon coaches. I like the feeling of having no hair, the lightness of it. It makes me feel like I'm ready to race. But I hadn't shaved my head in ages so it took a long time to get that smooth bald finish. Afterwards my scalp was bone white and contrasted starkly with the dark tan I had earned on the hot walks around Guadix earlier in the year. When I went down for dinner that night, there was plenty of good-humoured slagging about my new haircut from the rest of the Irish camp.

After dinner I lay on my bed and watched an episode of *Marvel's Agents of Shield* before hanging my singlet and shorts on a hanger and packing my bag. Cathal and Meghan both sent me good luck messages from home, telling me not to worry, that I had the work done, that I could win a medal and that they were proud of me and loved me whether I won a medal or not. The messages were lovely to get and almost made me cry. I went to bed motivated to do my very best for them the following morning.

With the 50km walk starting at 8 a.m., I was up at 5 a.m. for breakfast. Marian brought me food from the canteen and we opened the physio room and used their coffee machine. Boycey came down and ate with us and we watched a few YouTube videos of Big Joe Joyce to ease the tension.

With two buses organised at 5.30 a.m. and 6 a.m. to bring the walkers to the course, we chose to take the second one for the journey of under half an hour.

Marian, Boycey and I boarded the bus with team manager Patsy McGonagle and Ray Flynn while Alex had gone on alone before us. Competing in his first Olympics, Alex was in cranky humour that morning but it wasn't until afterwards that we found out he'd been woken the night before by noise in the village and couldn't get back to sleep.

I was in my own bubble on the bus and the journey passed in a blur. It wasn't until I disembarked and walked towards the athletes' call room that it dawned on me that I would be walking in my last Olympic Games in just over an hour. This was my last shot at winning the biggest event in the world.

Within seconds I was bent double behind a bush, vomiting. The noise was so loud you could have heard it around Rio and, paranoid, I kept popping my head up to see if anybody was watching. Patsy McGonagle walked past as I puked but never even flinched and kept going. Even he knew by now that it was a normal part of my pre-race nerves and a sign that I was up for the race.

Emma Gallivan stretched me out before I went out and did my warm-up. I was late going out to warm up and after a few minutes the stewards were trying to round us up to get us back in before the start of the race but I just walked straight past them as if they weren't there. I did a minute and a half out, a minute and a half back, got my bag and walked up to the call room with Marian.

Having got my race number the day before, I was now given a chip to put on my running shoe. The large Portakabin's walls were lined with eighty chairs side by side and opposite each other. Each chair had a walker's race number with their name on the back.

My chair was to the left of French world record holder Yohann Diniz, with Australian Jared Tallent, who was now the official defending Olympic champion, almost within touching distance directly opposite me. With none of the support team allowed in the call room, that would be my spot for the next half an hour.

There was just room for my bag on the ground in between my legs, both of which were touching off the walkers either side of me. Diniz tried to engage me in conversation but I was in a good frame of mind and didn't want to talk. I walked over to the drinks machine, got a bottle of water and looked around the room.

As I did so, I felt as if everyone was looking at me. But I didn't care what was going on around me. I felt as if I owned the place, which gave me even more confidence. I knew this was where I belonged. I loved it. While some fellas were visibly nervous, I enjoyed the build-up and knew that I was ready to race. I had trained as hard as I could for the race, eaten properly, rested properly, even shaved my head. I'd done everything possible. If somebody beat me that day, they were going to get it hard. Half an hour in the call room is a long time if you're nervous but I was calm. In my head, I was the most important person in there and I just concentrated on myself and what I had to do that day. This was my last Olympics and I was determined to make the most of it.

At the start of the race it was 26 degrees with 80 per cent humidity – and that was at eight o'clock in the morning. Even though it was only going to get hotter during the race, I didn't put sun cream on my newly shaven head for fear that it might clog my pores and overheat me, or run down into my eyes and sting me as I threw water bottles over my head to keep cool during the race. Looking back now, shaving my head came back to bite me later and may even have cost me a medal as my head was burnt to a crisp after the race. I didn't wear a cap to protect me from the sun because the whole idea of shaving my head was that I felt light, ready to race, and wearing a hat would have done away with that feeling.

From the gun, Diniz went off like the clappers again, instantly opening up a lead on his own but I knew it was impossible to stay out there with the conditions, the pressure of the Olympics and the calibre of walkers behind him.

My plan for the race was to hold back as much as I could with the feeling that I could open up after 35km or so and start to challenge. For the first time ever, though, a large lead group went off together with me in it. Before, I had always come through the field from the back in the last 20km or so. In Rio, though, a big chase group of a dozen or so pulled clear after Diniz and there was nowhere else to go but with them.

On the two occasions that I intentionally dropped off the pace of the group to save my legs for the last part of the race, I got a yellow card. To most judges, dropping off the group is a sign that you're tiring and your technique is falling apart, even though mine wasn't. Walking on my own, I was easy pickings. I felt like turning around and telling the judge 'I'm fucking grand! I don't need to be with the lead group now! I don't need to be on TV! I need to be strong in the last third.' After the second caution though, I was forced to get back into the safety of the chase group.

At the halfway mark, Diniz was a minute and forty seconds clear but as Matej Tóth and Canadian Evan Dunfee led us along, everyone seemed comfortable. For much of the race, I went from phases of feeling comfortable to patches where I thought the pace was so fast that we were all going to die in the heat. On each lap I grabbed a drink from Marian at the drinks table and a bottle of water to pour over my head. It was so hot that the water I was pouring over my head felt warm so I told Marian and Ray to get more ice because there was no cooling effect. I also grabbed ice-cold water to pour over myself at a second point on each lap.

'Rob,' I told myself, 'your heart rate is good. You've the training done for it. You're able for this. Just concentrate. Your legs are really strong. Your hips are really strong. The kids are at home watching you. You've loads of support back home.' I was using the same cues as I had when I won the World Championship in Moscow but this time I was only using them every 2km, at the end of each lap.

When Diniz began to visibly fall apart and come back to us after around 30km, my chase group got a sniff of blood and the race changed. Unknown to us, he'd had stomach problems leading into the race and was forced to stop with gastric cramps after around 32km. With 18km still to race, he needed to go to the toilet. Unfortunately for him, stuffing a sponge down the rear of his shorts didn't stop the TV cameras getting a close-up of his unplanned bowel movement as he walked.

Up ahead, we could see Diniz stopping, leaning against the barriers, and then starting again as Dunfee caught him. Suddenly the Olympics were there to be won. The group got quicker and some of the other guys started falling away just before we caught Diniz, around a lap later. As the five of us that were left closed in on him, I noticed he looked disorientated and then, just as I passed him, with 14km to go, he collapsed in front of me and flaked out on his back in the middle of the line of cones marking the route.

'Come on, Yohann, get up. You can do it.' I shouted as I went past. Although he was my competition, part of me felt sorry for him. He had done the same amount of training as me and now his Olympics was gone if he didn't finish.

Soon after, Tóth and Tallent joined Dunfee at the front as we began to lap more fellas that had succumbed to the tropical temperature, some of whom would have been pre-race contenders. After Diniz collapsed things started opening up. After 40km, I was still in contention for a medal in a group of three chasers alongside Japan's Hirooki Arai and Yu Wei of China. As Dunfee faded, Jared Tallent was now twenty seconds clear in front with Matej Tóth trying to get across to him. I wasn't feeling great but I knew 10km was still a long way to go and I told myself to keep taking on drinks and hoped that one or more of the three leaders would fall back in the last few kilometres.

I started to get twinges in my hamstring and in my calves soon after. Going around the U-turn towards the finish with 8km to go I tried to push on, but a spasm in my hamstring told me that I had to ease up a little for fear it would get worse and I wouldn't be able to finish.

As I approached the drinks table, Marian shouted to me. 'You look so good, you can go, Rob. You can win this!'

'I can't,' I replied. 'I'm cramping. I've cramps.'

'Okay,' she replied. 'Just keep doing what you're doing!'

Marian knew as well as I did that if you cramp in a walking race and your knees go, your technique gets thrown out the window and unless you can hold yourself together you risk being disqualified.

I had suddenly gone from wanting to win the Olympics to wanting to get to the line. Her reply was very positive and rather than looking at things negatively I told myself to keep going. I just had to keep walking solidly and try and stay in touch, hold onto my sixth place on the road. 'Sixth in the Olympics is good,' I told myself. 'You're thirty-eight years of age. You finished sixty-eighth in the world cup. Sixth is good. You fight for what you have now. Fight for everything. Just get home!'

The crowd in Rio was very different from London and for me it was hell every time we got to the far end of the course, which was empty. Towards the end Kevin Ankrom went up there and, to be fair to him, even with all of the problems we had in the past, he gave me great support. He watched the whole race and he was roaring at me every lap. The Irish team were great support to me too and while I normally don't see anybody during a race I could hear the Irish voices towards the end and was looking for them.

Unable to walk any faster due to the spasms in my legs and shoulders, I had decided that I couldn't afford to push any further and had to walk at around 90 per cent of my maximum capacity. With 3km to go, I knew that if I could keep my form I had a big enough gap to hold onto my sixth place. Because of this, on the last lap I was able to take in the crowd a bit and I tried to enjoy those final couple of kilometres, reminding myself to 'Keep this going. This is the last time you'll be coming down a finishing straight at the Olympic Games and you're still in the mix. Enjoy it a bit.'

I knew how awkward it was to get to Rio and that the Irish contingent had gone out of their way to come out and support me, so in a show of appreciation for all of the Irish support I waved to the crowd, coming down the home straight. I had a big smile on my face as I crossed the line two and a half minutes off a medal.

Afterwards, Marian and Ray knew how close I had come but were satisfied with my performance. I was bumped up to fifth for a while when third-placed Arai was disqualified for bumping elbows with Dunfee earlier in the race, only for the decision to be overturned later on. Even though I would have moved up a place, I thought it would have been a harsh decision and felt sorry for Arai when I heard it first. Earlier in the race I had been cut up by a Guatemalan by accident. Back in Beijing I threw an elbow back and broke Erik Tysse's watch by accident. I got tripped in a European Cup and landed on my face but these things happen in walking and I didn't think the Japanese athlete deserved to be disqualified for it.

I had given a good account of myself, proven I could still match the best of them, even at thirty-eight years of age and with a family-based coaching system behind me. Apart from the tiredness, though, the biggest problem I had afterwards was whether I was going to do it all again the next year or not.

22

Future Tense

t's just over a week since I got back from Rio and I'm only starting to come around now. The trip itself was the stuff of nightmares. Up at five in the morning for the return journey, Team Ireland had a nine-hour bus trek to São Paulo before we even saw a plane. After a few hours in the airport we had a twelve-hour flight to Frankfurt, where we hung around again before flying into Dublin almost thirty-six hours after our trip began.

Obviously more worried about their chief Pat Hickey having been arrested in Rio on suspicion of ticket touting than the welfare of their athletes, the Irish Olympic Council had nothing arranged for us when we arrived into Dublin and everybody just came out the arrivals gate together to be faced with the assembled media and some diehard supporters before going their separate ways.

For my first few days at home, I was so tired that all I could do was lie around the house. In this period I had plenty of time to ponder my final appearance at the Olympic Games. I was annoyed that something as simple as shaving my head the night before might have cost me a better performance. Other than that, I was happy enough. I had done all I could on the day.

All of my life, being told I couldn't do something drove me on to do it, to prove people wrong. My journey has always been about self-development and I firmly believe that if you keep trying to better yourself and you don't stop doing that, then there are huge opportunities out there, whether in sport or in business. I never let other people set limits on what I could achieve and I was always willing to work hard to get to where I wanted to go.

After finishing twenty-eighth in the Sydney Olympics in 2000, I thought I had done everything in sport. Since then I have become the only Irish male athlete to win medals at European, World and Olympic level. I followed my heart, followed what I loved, and becoming the first person to represent Ireland at five Olympics was just a by-product of that.

Athletics in Ireland has changed a lot since I made my debut on the international scene. The Institute of Sport is getting better, the Sports Council is getting better and Athletics Ireland is getting better. Things are 100 per cent improved on even five or six years ago. But there is still a lot that could be done to give Irish athletes a better chance when they go away to represent their country. We need to have more officially supported training camps, with more focus on long-term training towards specific peaks during the season, like World or European championships. The physio and medical support if you're injured or sick is top class but it's better if you're living in Dublin. If you're down in Cork or over in Mayo you're a bit isolated. There are still no full-time professional coaches in the system and that needs to change.

Thanks to Marian, I had somebody working on me every day, doing my physio and massage. All I had to do was eat, sleep and train. If I didn't have Marian, even with top-level funding, I wouldn't be able to train at the level that I do. Not many people have that kind of support and that's not to mention all of the other day-to-day stuff she automatically does for me. But I can't expect that to go on forever. She has put her life on hold for me and it's time she had her turn to do what she wants to.

I'm proud of how race walking has become much more popular in Ireland of late. You can never ask for respect for a minority sport but you can earn it and I think that over the years people like Olive Loughnane, Gillian O'Sullivan, Pierce O'Callaghan, Jamie Costin,

Colin Griffin, Alex Wright, Brendan Boyce and I, as well as our predecessors, have helped that.

Since I first took up sport, whether it was soccer, Gaelic football, running or walking, I've always been obsessed with training, obsessed with getting the best out of myself. For the past twenty years or so I've given everything to race walking so the thought of not doing it or doing something else in the future is daunting. But equally daunting is the challenge to keep doing it at this level. There is so much sacrifice involved, so much commitment and it's so hard on your body that I'm not exactly relishing the prospect.

The World Championships are in London in 2017 and it's very tempting to keep going towards that new goal. Like the Olympics in 2012, I expect London to be really well organised, with loads of Irish support over there, so I already have one eye on the 50km race. I'd love to go out with another world title but the problem with that is that it would be very hard not to compete as world champion the following year. It's a vicious cycle, but I'm getting way ahead of myself here, and in the next few weeks and months I will sit down with Marian and the family and work out whether it's viable to chase that goal or not.

I'd love to have the opportunity to develop race walking in Ireland. I'd love to have the support system the Russians have – without the drugs. I'd love to see the talent identification they have, the coaches going into schools pulling out the talent and coaching and developing that talent over the years. I'd love a national athletics centre like they have where people can eat, drink, sleep and train, developing a culture of excellence, a mindset of excellence. There is this idea in Ireland that Irish athletes can't do it, can't compete with the best in the world, but we can. I've done it. Sonia O'Sullivan has done it. Eamonn Coghlan, John Treacy, Ronnie Delany, Marcus O'Sullivan, Thomas Barr, Derval O'Rourke, Fionnuala McCormack, Ciara Mageean and many others have all done it. The list goes on. Why not ask us how we did it? Learn from our mistakes and benefit from our knowledge.

Over the years I've adapted my own high-performance system

and I'd love to be able to use my profile to go around schools and educate children of all levels about the benefits of health and fitness in their life. I'd love to give young athletes the opportunity I had, be able to guide them through their life and share the experiences I've had. The positive implications that being active, fit and healthy have on the rest of your life are huge. There are obviously different levels of fitness, but exercise is for everyone.

Eventually, my body will tell me when it's time to stop and, while I haven't thought about it properly yet, that scares me a bit. Walking has been my life for as long as I can remember. I've been privileged to do what I've been doing and I'll be retired long enough. When I retire I intend to follow my other passion: coffee. I love coffee! I've acquired a taste for it over the years, have done a few barista courses and maybe, some time in the future, I'll have my own coffee shop.

While I may have resented it at the time, I now appreciate the upbringing that my mam and dad gave me. Now that I have kids myself I realise how hard it must have been for them and I also realise that we didn't have it all that bad. We all want to give our kids the best possible future. When I was a child, my parents' vision stretched as far as me getting a job and having a steady income – one that would allow me to buy a house, pay my bills and look after my own family.

My biggest regret is not having spent more time with my mam before she passed away. She was my biggest fan. Very strict with me when I was younger, Mam ensured I was brought up with good manners and let away with nothing. I knew what was right and what was wrong and if I did something wrong I was berated for days, until she was sure the lesson had been learned and I wasn't going to do it again.

For my parents and many others of that generation, there was no such sentiment as 'go out and follow your dreams' or 'follow your heart'. They had to put bread on the table and clothes on our backs. My dad couldn't see how race walking was going to do that for me and, in fairness, even though we fell out over it when I was younger, looking back, I can now see where he was coming from. In wanting me to learn a trade and follow him into plastering, he had my interests at heart but I strayed off the path and took a gamble. If the truth be told, I've been trying to impress him and gain his approval ever since. My dad's a lot more open to my athletic career now and after Rio he gave an interview to a local paper admitting that he'd told me I'd never make it as a walker. He also told them he was proud of me, which was lovely to hear. We get on very well now. He's not just my dad: he's my friend and a good man. He still has my interests at heart and I love him for that.

My mam taught me discipline and how to stand up for myself while my dad showed me that you have to work hard in life to survive. From a very young age, working hard became normal for me and I carried that with me into my sport. I got more opportunities than my parents ever did and was lucky enough that I actually got to follow my dreams. Nobody knows what the future holds but if I can pass those two lessons of hard work and discipline on to my own kids, I won't be doing half bad.

Acknowledgements

When Ger Cromwell first came down to Cork to interview me at the end of 2015, this book seemed a very daunting prospect. How was I going to tell a complete stranger about where I came from, my family and sporting life, all in the middle of training for a final tilt at Olympic glory?

Getting to know Ger over the following months, though, was such a positive experience and, in a lot of ways, writing this book was a bit like therapy. I found myself revealing my deepest and darkest secrets, to the extent that some of the stories in this book will surprise even my own family. Thank you, Ger, for listening and understanding and getting my story across they way I wanted it told. Thanks also to Sinead, Aoife, Jack and Katie for letting him spend so much time doing it.

Thanks to everyone at The Collins Press in Wilton, Cork, for your help, advice and belief in this book.

Like everything else in my life, this book wouldn't have been possible without the support of my family. My life changed for the better when I met Marian Andrews. From day one, Marian believed in me, even when I doubted myself. Everybody in life has doubts and a lot of the time it depends on who's around you, whether they pull you through those doubts or drag you down by reinforcing them. It's very important to have a backbone of support, somebody who genuinely believes in you and, for me, Marian was, and still is, my rock. Not only are you always there for me, but my kids have the best mother in the world and they want for nothing. Thanks for everything, Mar. I love you.

I have four amazing kids (so far) and they too have sacrificed a normal life to enable me to train and race at the highest level. Family holidays usually include watching Dad train or handing him drinks from the side of the road or out the window of a car. Thanks for being the best kids in the world.

Meghan, from the first day I set my eyes on you, I loved you. You make me so proud of everything you do. We have an incredible bond and I'm so proud you're my daughter.

To Cathal, my sidekick, assistant coach and best buddy all rolled into one. I'm so proud to be able to call you my son and look forward to watching you grow into the 6' 5" monster you are going to be. Take it easy on your little oul' man in the next few years. Thanks for the good luck messages, man. And all the words of advice, man. Love you, man.

Regan, I cried tears of joy when you arrived into my life and words can't express how happy you make me. I love you so much.

Tara, even though you arrived a few years earlier than planned, I'm glad we didn't have to wait that long to meet you. I can't imagine my life without you. Waking up to you every day feels like Christmas Day all over again.

Mam, I know you're watching over me and I know you are smiling down on me now. I miss you so much. There is not a day goes by that I don't think about you.

Dad, you've always been a hero to me. If the truth be told, I've been trying to impress you since I could walk, let alone race walk. One day soon, I might even do it.

Rhonda, you're not only my big sister but you've always been like a second mam to me. You fed me when I was hungry, listened to me when I was down and were always there for me unconditionally. Thank you.

Elton, my not-so-little brother, thanks for everything, especially for leaving the labouring job open for life.

ACKNOWLEDGEMENTS

Anthea, thanks so much for all of the support over the years and sorry for locking you in the wardrobe when we were kids.

Lyndsey, my baby sister, you've come a long way from when you used to dance to the sound of the hoover. Thanks for everything, lads. You have always been there for me and have always been protective of me. I love you all and hope I haven't embarrassed ye too much.

Good mothers-in-law are hard to come by apparently, but Angela Andrews, you're a star. Thanks for all the support over the years, with everything. The log cabin is all yours in a few years. Thanks to Mick Andrews senior, the soundest crank I know. John, Steven and Michael: not just brothers-in-law but good friends. Thanks a lot, lads.

Growing up in Togher, Ballyphehane and Turners Cross, I was lucky to have some very good influences watching out for me: Shazer, you were like my big brother as a kid and still are. I always know you have my back, boy! The late Sean Buckley kept me off the streets by driving me around the county to play underage football for Nemo Rangers. John Hayes took me under his wing in Togher Athletics Club and allowed me to develop at my own pace. Brother Sweeney and Brother Colm were brilliant to me in school and along with Kevin Cummins and Cork's own athletics guru, Brother Dooley, were passionate sportsmen and their enthusiasm rubbed off on anybody lucky enough to meet them. Thanks to all of you for keeping me on the straight and narrow.

When I was at a difficult time of my life in my early twenties and struggling to keep going, people like Noel Marshall, Seanie McCarthy, Kevin Sievewright, Robert McCarthy, Colm Lyons and Aidan Logan were some of the first to come on board and gave me the financial support to keep plugging away. Hard-working businessmen who came from a background similar to my own, they knew that sometimes you need a little help to chase your dreams. Thanks also to Nissan Ireland, Fota Island Resort and Pat Morley of Scribe of London, who has dressed me since I was a kid.

Liam O'Reilly is a one-man whirlwind. A massage therapist, video analyst, bottle maker, chef, agony aunt, crime fighter and intrepid explorer all rolled into one, Liam is one of those friends that was always there when I needed him, even if we were arguing at the time. Without your help, I wouldn't be the proud possessor of an Olympic medal from London 2012. Thank you for everything, Liam, and one day we'll go looking for those glasses you lost in Guadix.

Ray Flynn is a madman and athletics fanatic from Sligo who has kept me entertained for the past seventeen years. A great worker and a loyal friend, you've helped me through some some tough times and were a great mentor to me growing up. Thanks for everything, Ray (except the wedding speech).

Ivonne Cassin is a lovely woman and really helped me in 2009 when I doubted everything and was going to leave the sport. A mild-mannered superhero without whom I wouldn't have become world champion in 2013. Thanks for believing in me, Ivonne.

Meeting Robert Korzeniowski at the Olympics in Sydney in 2000 was a huge turning point in my career and to have the King of race walking take me under his wing and teach me everything he knew was a total game changer for me. Robert, you are a gentleman, a champion and a great friend. Thank you for everything.

Ilya Markov, a complete gentleman and a warrior on the road, thanks for being such a great mentor during the years we trained together.

Paquillo Fernández has been like a brother to me since we first met at a cold winter training camp in Poland. Since then Paco has seen it all, both good and bad. When you were on top of the world you treated me as your friend and equal and I'm glad to say that friendship remains intact. The best technical walker ever, you were always willing to help out or offer advice and for that I am very grateful. *Gracias, amigo.*

Derry McVeigh understands sport and since the first day we met in 2010 he has always had my best interests at heart. He has helped Marian and me tremendously since coming on board and even helped get my World Championship gold medal back when it was stolen. Derry, I'm proud to call you my agent, secretary, event organiser, medal chaser and very good friend. Thanks a lot from McLovin.

ACKNOWLEDGEMENTS

Pa Buckley from Lismore, you're an inspirational man and I really appreciate all of the support over the years. Dermot McDermott, thanks for being a great friend, supporter and occasional river rescuer over the years. Emma Gallivan, a great physio who has become a great friend. Mark McManus, thanks for tricking me back into training when I was injured. Thanks to Rob Williams and all the crew in Fitness Worx Gym. Thanks also to Athletics Ireland and Sport Ireland, without whom I wouldn't have had an athletics career at all and to all of Team Ireland, no matter what the sport, thanks for twenty years of friendship, support and craic.

The Cork athletics community as a whole have always been good to me, while Cork City Sports has long been known as one of the best-run sports in Europe. Thanks to the number of great people involved who love athletics and are in it for the athletes. Finally, to all the Irish fans, athletes and supporters who have cheered me on at races, sent me messages, met me on the street and shook my hand, patted my back or congratulated me on my performances, your support means so much to me and makes me as proud as punch each time I pull on that green singlet.